R. MURRAY THOMAS

HUMAN
DEVELOPMENT
THEORIES
WINDOWS ON CULTURE

Sage Publications, Inc.
International Educational and Professional Publisher
Thousand Oaks   London   New Delhi

For information:

Sage Publications, Inc.
2455 Teller Road
Thousand Oaks, California 91320
E-mail: order@sagepub.com

Sage Publications Ltd.
6 Bonhill Street
London EC2A 4PU
United Kingdom

Sage Publications India Pvt. Ltd.
M-32 Market
Greater Kailash I
New Delhi 110 048 India

Printed in the United States of America

Library of Congress Cataloging-in-Publication Data

Thomas, R. Murray (Robert Murray), 1921–
    Human development theories: Windows on culture / by R. Murray
Thomas.
        p.   c.m.
    Includes bibliographical references and index.
    ISBN 0-7619-2015-3 (alk. paper)
    1. Socialization.   2. Cognition and culture.   3. Child development.
4. Developmental psychology.   I. Title.
    HQ783 .T57   1999
    306—dc21   99-6589

This book is printed on acid-free paper.

99 00 01 02 03 04 05 7 6 5 4 3 2 1

Acquiring Editor: Jim Brace-Thompson
Editorial Assistant: Anna Howland

To
S. Lester Guinn

Contents

Tables and Figures

Tables

Figures

Preface

The contents of this book are based on the observation that the human perceptual system and a camera are both bound by the same limitation. Neither the camera nor the person can focus on everything at once. The camera, in order to portray a panoramic landscape in all its detail, must take a succession of individual snapshots, each featuring a particular center of interest. The person, in order to comprehend a culture in all its complexities, must perceive the culture from a succession of vantage points. Throughout this book, those vantage points are provided by 25 theories of human development. Each theory is intended to delineate a particular aspect of culture, thereby contributing toward a broad understanding of what cultures are all about. However, because cultures are so elaborate, the 25 models employed in these pages cannot pretend to furnish a complete account. Hundreds of additional theories would be required to even approach an encyclopedic description of cultures. Thus, the book is a demonstration of the value of diverse viewpoints toward culture rather than an exhaustive portrait of the diverse guises cultures can assume.

Finally, I wish to express my appreciation to Paul Pedersen and Jim Brace-Thompson for their advice and support. I am also indebted to the Sage staff members for the care and wisdom they dedicated to this venture.

1

Visions of Culture, Visions of Development, and Careproviders' Interventions

This book has been designed to answer three questions: (a) In what ways do different theories of human development contribute to an understanding of cultural influences on young people's growing up over the first quarter-century of their lives? (b) What differences among cultures can each theory reveal? (c) How can understanding cultural influences guide the activities of people who seek to foster the development of children and youth?

The first question is based on the assumptions that (a) each theory of development functions as a window or lens focusing attention on selected aspects of how people grow up and (b) the way culture influences development can be portrayed differently in each theory. Hence, a many-faceted understanding of the interaction between culture and development can be derived from analyzing the roles assigned to culture in diverse theories. As the question indicates, our attention throughout the book centers on cultural influences during the 25-year term extending from biological conception into early adulthood. The words *child* and *childhood* encompass the period from conception (the unborn child) through birth and infancy up to puberty at around ages 10 to 15. The word *youth* refers to life between the age of puberty up to the time of early adulthood in the mid-twenties. Thus, the book focuses on what have been called "the formative years"—that segment of time during which physical self and personality are being initially constructed.

The second question stems from the observation that the cultures in which the young are raised can differ markedly, and that these differences affect children's physical growth, aspirations, abilities, values, life chances, and personal-social adjustment. In short, theories of human development are useful for identifying how different cultures influence the destinies of children and youth.

The third question is founded on the expectation that (a) parents, teachers, counselors, psychologists, social workers, pediatricians, and other careproviders welcome guidance in how to promote the development of children and youth and

1

(b) such guidance can be discovered by interpreting development from different theoretical positions. Therefore, the book not only analyzes the role of culture as portrayed in a wide variety of theories but also describes practical activities for childrearing and for understanding youths that are implied by each theoretical perspective.

There are several ways of analyzing the role assigned to culture in human development theories. One way is to inspect a single theory in order to provide an in-depth assessment of how adequately that model can explain people's development in a wide range of cultures. A second approach involves adopting a few theories—perhaps five or six—as the lenses through which to gain a somewhat less detailed view of the likenesses and differences among cultures. A third method emphasizes the great diversity of perspectives on cultures that results from using a wide variety of theories.

The third approach is the one adopted in this book. Compared with the first two viewpoints, this third method offers greater breadth-of-theory coverage by addressing cultures through the windows of 25 theories, but it does so at the expense of the detailed analysis of any single model. Therefore, what readers can expect from each of the 25 theory descriptions is (a) a brief sketch of the model's guiding principles, (b) examples of differences among cultures that are discovered by using the theory as a window, (c) sample cross-cultural encounters as seen from the theory's perspective, and (d) illustrative practical applications of the model. Thus, the book highlights the multiple ways cultures can be understood when they are viewed through the lenses of a wide selection of human development models.

The purpose of this initial chapter is to furnish an interpretive framework for viewing the contents of the chapters that follow. The framework is described in terms of (a) a sample theory, (b) qualities of culture, (c) the nature of development theories, and (d) careproviders' interventions.

A SAMPLE THEORY

Chapters 2 through 5 summarize 24 development theories and the role assigned to culture in each theory. To prepare readers for what to expect in those chapters, the following example demonstrates the way the linkage between culture and theory is presented throughout the book. The example is Ambert's *peer-abuse model*. I chose Ambert's model because within a few pages it adequately illustrates the following six steps that are employed for analyzing each theory in subsequent chapters.

Step 1: *Title.* What name does the theory bear?
Step 2: *Key tenets.* On what foundational beliefs is the theory built?
Step 3: *Principal variables.* What are the theory's main variables and how do those variables influence development?

Step 4: *Differences among cultures.* How can differences among cultures affect development as portrayed from the theory's vantage point?

Step 5: *Cross-cultural encounters.* How does the theory contribute to an understanding of development problems that may result from cross-cultural differences?

Step 6: *Practical applications.* What sorts of culture-based experiences enhance development and what sorts impair development? This question is answered in relation to a question about problem resolution: What steps can be taken toward understanding individuals' development and resolving problems that arise from their cross-cultural encounters?

An Interpretation of Peer Abuse

Title: Peer-Abuse Theory as formulated by Anne-Marie Ambert, a professor of sociology at York University in Toronto, Canada.

Key tenets: Ambert defines peer abuse as "acts, omissions, and words that *intentionally* inflict physical, and/or psychological, and/or social injury to a peer or peers." The term *peer* designates children who are the same chronological age ("give or take one year") as the recipients of abuse. "Peer abuse is always intentional and often premeditated. It is meant to hurt and demean" (Ambert, 1995, pp. 182-183).

She identifies four types of abuse in terms of the methods abusers employ.

1. Direct physical acts—hitting, assaulting sexually, knifing, shooting
2. Verbal, expressive acts—repeatedly taunting, insulting, spreading malicious rumors, threatening, expelling from a group
3. Omissions and passive acts—purposely failing to warn peers of danger or excluding peers from a group's activities for a prolonged period
4. Acts that damage possessions—repeatedly stealing, hiding, discarding, or damaging a child's toys, school equipment, items of clothing, or pets

Methods 1 and 2 involve direct assault; 3 and 4 involve subterfuge.

Principal variables: I constructed the diagram in Figure 1-1 to display the four main variables implied in Ambert's model: (a) environmental locations in which abuse occurs (*sites*), (b) significant people in those locations at the time of the abuse (*actors*), (c) methods of abuse, and (d) consequences of abuse. Although Ambert did not directly describe causes of abuse, her presentation suggests that abuse results from interaction between attributes of sites and attributes of actors. In other words, whether abuse will occur, and the form it will assume, depends on the confluence of a particular site and particular actors. Thus, as Figure 1-1 shows, causal factors determine the methods employed for inflicting abuse, and those methods can result in five kinds of consequence for the abused child (physical pain, emotional suffering, loss of social status, anxiety, deprivation) and one kind for the child's parents (distress).

In the diagram, I have proposed subvariables (attributes) within both the site and actor categories, subvariables that contribute to the likelihood of abuse and the form it might assume. To illustrate how different permutations of sites and actors could affect the occurrence of peer abuse, consider these three incidents that might be observed in a typical American city.

Situation 1: On the school playground during recess, two teachers supervise the play of 50 second-grade pupils.

Situation 2: At dusk, a 14-year-old boy from a distant neighborhood crosses a parking lot in which six members of a teenage street gang are smoking marijuana and listening to loud music on a stolen portable radio.

Situation 3: Five 9-year-old girls are dining at an expensive restaurant as the guests of one girl's parents.

We may now ask: Which configuration of site and actor characteristics is most likely to produce peer abuse? My own estimate is that the greatest probability of abuse is in Situation 2, the least in Situation 3, and the next least in Situation 1.

Choosing Situation 2 as the one most likely to result in abuse (physical and verbal) is founded on my expectation that (a) members of street gangs are often protective (motive) of their "turf" and actively oppose (aggressivity) the intrusion of outsiders; (b) if the members are smoking marijuana and listening to a stolen radio, they do not mind breaking the law (values); (c) no adults with supervisory power are present (authority); and (d) the risk of harm to themselves is negligible. However, this estimate could be in error if the gang members—or at least the ones in greatest authority—empathize with the potential victim of abuse and thus let him pass unmolested.

In contrast, I would guess that the girls in Situation 3 are unlikely to engage in peer abuse (particularly physical abuse) because adult authorities with punitive powers are present, and cultural expectations for behavior in restaurants differ from expectations for behavior in such settings as parking lots and playgrounds.

I ranked Situation 1 between the other two because (a) authorities (teachers) were present to supervise the pupils, (b) the pupils would be aware of the rules (values) about peer interactions they were expected to follow, and (c) they knew that if they violated the rules they risked punishment. However, supervising 50 children on a playground can be a demanding task for two teachers, so that aggressive, nonempathetic pupils might chance abusive acts—particularly verbal ones—with some hope of not being caught.

However, such speculation, pursued without knowledge of the actual attributes of the individual actors in the three situations, can easily be wrong. In effect, the task of offering an accurate prediction of abuse from the perspective of Ambert's theory requires a good knowledge of the actors' personality characteristics, the power relationships among the actors, and influential features of the sites.

Differences among cultures: Because Ambert, in her sketch of her model, did not address matters of culture, I have taken the liberty of suggesting the following cultural aspects of peer abuse. Cultural components relevant to the theory concern (a) what a social organization (a cultural group) defines as *peer abuse* and (b) the methods, incidence, and consequences of abusive acts found in different social settings.

Figure 1-1

A Social-Cultural Framework for Analyzing Peer Abuse

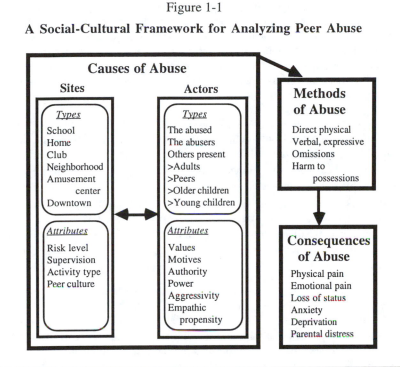

Defining peer abuse. At any given time, peer interactions viewed as normal and acceptable within one culture may be seen as abusive in another culture. For example, among the Polynesian inhabitants of the Marquesas Islands in the Southeastern Pacific, children often criticize or attack peers for making mistakes, for endangering themselves, for disturbing group consensus, or for failing to show sufficient deference toward their more dominant agemates. On occasion, children may also be attacked without provocation or become scapegoats for other children's status problems. Martini (1994, p. 79) suggests that such hazing serves the normal socializing functions of (a) teaching children that their individual plans and products are less important than those of the group, (b) punishing children for breaching social customs, (c) encouraging them to display care and competence, and (d) alerting them to heed the directions of the dominant members of their group.

Martini contrasts this Marquesan emphasis on group solidarity and collective standards with American society's emphasis on individuality and objective justice. Consequently, certain peer interactions regarded as acceptable devices of social control in the Marquesas would be deemed abusive in North America.

> Because American children believe in the sacredness of the individual and of personal plans, they react strongly and self-righteously to any attacks on their ideas, interests, or property. They have been led to believe that social life should be fair and that the individual should be allowed to pursue his interests as long as these do not impinge on the interests of others. . . . The everyday social hazing that Marquesan four-year-olds learn to handle with poise and humor would devastate most American preschoolers and would be considered emotional abuse by our [American] courts. (Martini, 1994, pp. 100-101)

Furthermore, during any given period in the history of a society, certain forms of physical and verbal interaction among peers that earlier were viewed as acceptable social behavior will now be seen as unacceptable, be labeled *abusive*, and be punished. During pioneer days in the Americas, rough treatment of peers—as in fist fights—was often viewed as a useful device for inuring the young to the vicissitudes of a hard life. But in modern times, which demand less physical prowess to survive, fighting is more often viewed as abuse.

Cultures can also differ in the sorts of interaction permitted—and perhaps even encouraged—between the sexes. A study of school life in an Okinawan village revealed that

> Girls remain on the receiving end of much teasing and horseplay. . . . Teachers, like parents, expect the boys to bully girls. . . . Hardly a day passes in school without several girls crying as a result of assertive boy tyrants. Occasionally a boy is punished, but usually he escapes with distinct pride showing on his face. Recently teachers have resorted to ridiculing those who intimidate girls, but the tradition is so strong that even if bullying on the school ground is curbed, there is a great deal on the road to and from school. (Maretzki & Maretzki, 1963, p. 530)

In many societies—perhaps all—whether an act qualifies as peer abuse depends on the particular conditions under which the act occurs. This point can be illustrated with games, initiations, self-defense, and retribution.

Every game has its own culture—aims to be pursued, a social structure (specified number of players, their assigned responsibilities, their designated interactions), operating procedures, formal rules of conduct, and unwritten customs. The rules and customs include the identification of the degree and kind of verbal and physical harm that can legitimately be done by participants (players, referees, spectators) to other participants. Whereas damage permitted by rules and customs is not considered abuse, damage beyond the harmful acts that are defined as acceptable for that game is regarded as abusive and thus subject to censure. On the football field, bone-bruising tackling and blocking are not only allowed but highly commended. Yet the same behavior on the volleyball court would be deemed brutal and qualify as peer abuse that invited punishment. However, rules are not necessarily permanent. They can be revised following a reevaluation of whether the damage they permit is "reasonable." In recent decades, serious injuries suffered by quarterbacks and kickers in American football have brought rule changes intended to reduce the incidence of such injuries, so that behavior not defined earlier as abuse is now considered abusive.

In many cultures, painful initiation rituals are imposed on young adolescents to mark their transition from childhood to adulthood. These trials of mind and body are not viewed as abuse but, rather, as necessary tests of whether the youth is worthy of adult status. In a similar way, joining a college fraternity, a social club, a new school, or a street gang often involves initiation activities in which neophytes are introduced to the organization's doctrines and practices. Such initiation rites are also frequently designed to test a novice's mettle—to determine if the initiate truly deserves the privilege of membership. The hazing activities that are part of such rites often subject candidates to humiliation, pain, and risk of harm which, under other circumstances, would be judged unduly abusive and thus not tolerated. Sometimes an initiation ritual also obligates novitiates themselves to harm people or property. A street gang may require that a candidate beat up a member of a rival gang, mug a pedestrian, or hijack an auto as evidence of the candidate's daring. Initiation rites, like rules of games, are subject to revision when the consequences of the practices are deemed abusive. For instance, college fraternities today are less likely than in the past to endorse hazing that is judged psychologically degrading or physically dangerous, a change perhaps brought about by increasingly humane attitudes in the broader society.

By pleading self-defense, a person may be exonerated of blame for harming a peer. Hence, when picked on by a "tough guy," a youth may respond by pummeling his attacker without being considered an abuser. However, whether a charge of abuse is warranted can depend on the extent of damage the defender has wrought on his or her assailant. A defender who bludgeons an antagonist senseless for having called the defender a bad name is likely to be charged with exceeding the limits of reasonable defense and therefore is judged guilty of abuse.

Retribution can be defined as deserved retaliation by a victim—or by a victim's representative—for the victim's having suffered a wrong. In its most familiar form, retribution is the application of the talionic principle (*lex talionis*), which holds that justice is done when wrongdoers are obliged to bear the same consequences that their victims were forced to bear. The principle is reflected in the biblical injunction:

If any mischief follow, then thou shalt give life for life, eye for eye, tooth for tooth, hand for hand, foot for foot, burning for burning, wound for wound, stripe for stripe. (*Holy Bible*, 1611, Exodus, chap. 21)

Therefore, by appealing to the right of retribution, a youth may seek to absolve himself of blame for destroying a bully's school supplies or for spreading rumors about an antagonist's sexual behavior.

Abuse methods, incidence, and consequences. Cultures can vary in the kind and amount of violence they sanction. This is true no matter how culture is defined, whether in terms of nationality, ethnicity, social class, religious affiliation, school, fraternal body, or family.

Mixed attitudes within a culture toward different kinds of violence can be illustrated at the national level with the case of the United States, a country that has long permitted the widespread distribution of guns, thereby leading to a high incidence of homicide and assault by firearms. At the same time, the nation has passed increasingly strict laws governing child abuse and spouse abuse in an attempt to reduce harmful acts among family members.

Within a society, violence in one type of personal relationship (parent/child) may serve as a model to be copied in another type (child/child). Consider, for example, a New Zealand anthropologist's estimate of the effect that parents' childrearing behavior exerts on children's peer relations in the Pacific Island kingdom of Tonga.

The Tongan mother has not the slightest hesitation in herself picking up a stick or coconut switch and beating her child with a thwarted fury that seems nine parts pure sadism and one-quarter part altruistic-disciplinary. To us, as we watch the scene, these child beatings seem to exceed all that is reasonable and just. . . . The repressed aggressiveness that is aroused [in children] by these adult whippings seems to find an outlet in the equally sadistic beating that goes in in the children's groups. (Beaglehole in Kapavalu, 1993, p. 313)

Cross-cultural encounters: Cross-cultural problems of peer abuse occur when, within a particular cultural setting, (a) an individual or group inappropriately applies standards of abuse imported from some other cultural context, or (b) individuals of one cultural group act on the basis of negative images they hold of people from a different group. Three types of social intercourse in which such conflicts are displayed are ones involving child/child conflicts, child/adult confrontations, and adult/adult encounters.

A typical child/child conflict can be illustrated with a series of incidents on a high school girls' volleyball team. Four players consistently criticized one of their teammates, rarely set the ball for her to hit, and avoided sitting next to her on the bus when the team traveled to play at another school. When the coach asked the four why they abused their teammate in such a manner, they feigned surprise, pretending not to understand. The coach estimated that the basis of the conflict lay in a difference in the girls' social-class status, which caused the four to be suspicious and jealous of their teammate. In effect, the ostracized girl's parents were wealthy, both were in professional occupations, and they lived on a 6-acre estate that included a paddock for three horses. The quartet of abusers had parents who were either day laborers or were on welfare and lived in small rented homes or apartments.

Child/adult confrontations often occur in school settings in which pupils and their teachers disagree over acceptable ways to settle disputes among peers. Such incidents can involve pupils who, in their family contexts, are used to settling peer disputes through violence—punching, kicking, gouging, pulling hair, and cudgeling foes with rocks, sticks, rulers, textbooks, and the like. In contrast, teachers approve of different ways to settle quarrels, such as peaceful negotiation, decision by an unbiased judge or jury, or—at most—physical or intellectual struggle that will not result in injury.

Adult/adult encounters arise when childhood peer disputes spread to adults, producing confrontations between parent and parent, school principal and parent, police and parent, coach and coach, coach and parent, and the like. Such conflicts can extend beyond individuals to involve cultural groups. For example, in France during 1995, students' taunting of Muslim girls for wearing head scarves led to education officials proscribing the wearing of scarves in school, a decision that drew strong objections from the Muslim community. When officials claimed that displaying traditional Islamic head coverings violated the state's prohibition against religion in the schools, Muslim leaders responded by pointing out that Catholic students were allowed to wear crosses (Burdin & Thomas, 1995, p. 193).

Practical applications: Theories can serve as the source of suggestions about measures that might be adopted for solving problems of human development. In regard to peer abuse, the components of the model in Figure 1-1 can function as guides to preventive and corrective methods of reducing the incidence of abuse. Preventive methods are intended to stop abuse before it can occur. Corrective methods are responses to abusive acts, responses designed to change the conditions that led to abuse and thereby decrease the likelihood of abuse in the future.

In way of illustration, consider how suggestions can be generated from the analysis of likely interactions among the components (subvariables) under *Causes of Abuse* in Figure 1-1. As a first step, the analysis can involve the creation of rules-of-thumb that guide decisions about how to prevent abuse in sites in which abuse might occur. Here is one such rule of thumb bearing on authority/power: "Peer abuse is unlikely to appear where potential abusers perceive their own power as less than the power of the potential victims of abuse or of other actors (bystanders, people in authority) who would disapprove of abusive acts." However, predictions of abuse cannot be founded on this principle alone but only in combination with other rules of thumb, such as one bearing on the motives of potential abusers: "Abuse will not occur unless potential abusers assume that doing harm to others will help fulfill one or more of their own needs (whether or not abusers actually recognize the existence of such needs)." Another rule of thumb that interacts with the foregoing two principles relates to the risk of apprehension in the particular site: "The probability that a potential abuser will commit harmful acts decreases with each increase in the abuser's estimate of the likelihood of being caught and punished."

As a second step in this process, we can combine principles derived from the model in Figure 1-1 to estimate the likelihood of peer abuse in particular sites that are inhabited by particular kinds of actors. This estimate equips us to take the third step—that of proposing measures for reducing the occurrence of such abuse. Take, for instance, the probability of abuse in the immediate vicinity of a high school located in an inner-city, high-crime-rate district. Upon analyzing the high school site in terms of our several rules of thumb, we may decide that the best way to reduce peer abuse in such a context will be to increase the number of police officers patrolling the streets and to institute an evening curfew for anyone under age 18. In contrast, to control peer abuse in the immediate vicinity of an elementary school in a middle-class suburb, we may judge it sufficient to appoint respected sixth-grade students as monitors responsible for maintaining order among pupils in the vicinity of the school—before school, during the noon hour, and after school.

To summarize, in this illustration of using theory components as guides to problem solving, we have centered attention on the interaction of selected site characteristics (risk level, supervision, peer culture) and actor attributes (motives, authority/power).

A different approach to reducing peer abuse focuses on the social values that guide actors' behavior, particularly those values bearing on which types and degrees of harm are permissible and on which conditions warrant doing harm to one's peers. The dual purpose of the approach is to encourage youngsters to adopt socially constructive values (as defined by the culture that the caregiver seeks to promote) and to encourage their empathizing with agemates. In the classroom, this method can consist of values-clarification exercises in which students discuss incidents of peer abuse, estimate the consequences that can result for both abusers and the abused, and weigh the desirability of different reactions to the incidents by various participants in the incidents. The teacher's hope is that the exercises will alter students' values in a way that improves their behavior in all sorts of situations that could lead to peer abuse.

A third application involves personal counseling aimed at reducing future instances of abuse by alerting children to the harm done to others whenever they address peers in a derogatory manner. On the playground during a softball game, a fifth-grade boy, new to the school, told his team's pitcher, "I never knew a Nigger could throw that fast." The problem in this case was that the word *Nigger,* in common use in the culture of the newcomer's family and associates, was considered abusive in the cultural climate of the school he now attended. He had made the error of inappropriately transferring a practice from one cultural setting to another. The school's solution called for a counseling psychologist to explain to the newcomer the harmful connotation of *Nigger* in the school's cultural climate, to suggest that the boy apologize to his teammate, and to propose that he speak to classmates as individuals rather than as supposed exemplars of some demeaning group label.

Conclusion

As the foregoing cases demonstrate, picturing peer abuse from the vantage point of Ambert's theory can help children's and youths' caregivers generate approaches to solving problems of peer abuse.

By means of the foregoing portrayal of peer-abuse theory, I have illustrated the framework used in this book for analyzing the role of culture in diverse theories of human development. With that framework in mind, we turn now to the conception of *culture* on which the contents of the book are founded.

QUALITIES OF CULTURE

So far in this chapter I've used the word *culture* in a rather glib fashion, as if the concept were simple and every reader would assign it the same meaning. Such, of course, is not the case. The concept *culture* is complex and therefore requires rather detailed analysis if its role in human development is to be adequately described. Thus, the examination of the role of culture in people's lives can profitably be considered from the vantage points of eight concepts: aspects of culture, a hierarchy of multiple groups, extent of commitment, monolithic versus heterogeneous cultures, transmission of culture, acculturation, cultural change, and cultural conflict.

Aspects of Culture

Few words, if any, in the social sciences have been defined in as many ways as has *culture*. Nearly half a century ago Kroeber and Kluckhohn (1952) compiled 164 definitions, and a good many more versions have appeared since then. The variety of forms that definitions assume is suggested by the following samples, beginning with the classical version offered by Sir Edward B. Tylor in 1871:

> Culture or civilization, taken in its wide ethnographic sense, is that complex whole which includes knowledge, belief, art, morals, law, custom, and any other capabilities and habits acquired by man as a member of society. (Tylor, 1958/1871, p. 1)

> [Culture consists of] the conventional understandings, manifest in act and artifact, that characterize societies. (Redfield, 1941, p. 132)

[Culture is] the collective programming of the mind which distinguishes the members of one human group from another. (Hofstede, 1980, p. 25)

Culture is the customary manner in which human groups learn to organize their behavior and thought in relation to their environment. (Howard & McKim, 1983, p. 5)

[Culture is] an historically transmitted pattern of meanings embodied in symbols, a system of inherited conceptions expressed in symbolic form by means of which [people] communicate, perpetuate, and develop their knowledge about and attitudes toward life. (Geertz, 1973, p. 89)

Culture is human-made; it includes ideas, values, and codes known to all members of the group; it is a learned system of behavior based upon symbols; it is transmitted from generation to generation. . . . Culture is the society's blueprint for behavior: what must be done, what ought to be done, what may be done, and what must not be done. (Farb, 1978, pp. 11, 352)

Culture may be defined as behaviour peculiar to *Homo sapiens*, together with material objects used as an integral part of his behaviour; specifically, culture consists of language, ideas, beliefs, customs, codes, institutions, tools, techniques, works of art, rituals, ceremonies, and so on. (White, 1994, p. 874)

As suggested by this last definition, culture can be divided into a variety of components or aspects, such as *material culture* (tools, living quarters, foods, modes of transportation), *language* (written, spoken, gesture), *beliefs about reality* (including convictions about supernatural forces), *values* (moral, artistic, economic), *processes* (patterns of thought and action), *rituals* (religious, birth, marriage), and more. No theory described in this book pictures *culture-in-its-entirety* as influencing development. Instead, each one identifies certain components of culture that affect the lives of children and youth. Thus, our analysis of the role of culture as depicted in theories will gain in precision if we define culture as a system of components or aspects, a system in the form of a culture typology. In adopting this approach, I am proposing that culture, as seen through human development theories, can be envisioned as a system of:

1. Shared social-structure affiliations in terms of:
    1.1 Types of groups to which a person belongs, mainly:
        1.1.1 Family—nuclear and extended family
        1.1.2 Age—a cohort of people born the same year
        1.1.3 Gender—male or female
        1.1.4 Ethnic—national or tribal ancestry
        1.1.5 National—citizenship or habitation in a sovereign state
        1.1.6 Religious—philosophical persuasion
        1.1.7 Socioeconomic—social class or caste
        1.1.8 Political—political party or political conviction
        1.1.9 Educational level—amount of schooling

1.2 The status (in terms of power, opportunity, and privilege) of one's own group within the hierarchy formed by the particular type of group under consideration. For instance, where in the ethnic hierarchy does a person's own ethnic group rank and why? In the age hierarchy, what rights and responsibilities are assigned to the person's own age cohort and why?

2. Shared beliefs about:

2.1 Reality—distinguishing the real from the imaginary, illusionary, and fictitious (the philosophical domain of *ontology*)

2.2 Knowing—deciding how people come to their beliefs (the philosophical domain of *epistemology*)

2.3 Abilities and skills—determining the nature and significance of human competencies

2.4 Personality structure—identifying personal traits and their relationships

2.5 Values—judging which things are more desirable than others and why—in moral, economic, aesthetic, political, and prudential matters

2.6 Motives—identifying what fuels people's actions (needs, drives, goals, interests)

2.7 Causes—deciding which factors produce which results, including which factors shape human development (how and why children and youths grow up as they do)

2.8 Enculturation agents—identifying the people and media that transmit culture to children and youths, and proposing how such transmission is effected

2.9 Emotions—determining the nature and significance of feelings, and deciding which expressions of emotion are appropriate on which occasions

2.10 Social interaction—conceiving of how and why people relate to each other, and which kinds of interaction are more desirable than other kinds

2.10.1 Interpersonal power relationships—recognizing the how and why of people's influence over each other

2.11 Physical environment—understanding Nature and how it interacts with humans

2.12 Self—identifying "who I am" in comparison with "who other people are"

3. Shared material conditions in terms of the physical things of the world, including:

3.1 Geographical location—physical-social environments

3.2 Cultural hardware—tools, machines, facilities

3.3 Cultural software—ways of using tools, machines, facilities

4. Shared customs and patterns of behavior, including kinds of:

4.1 Social interactions—language and other modes of communication

4.2 Rites and rituals

4.3 Occupations

4.4 Recreational, leisure-time pursuits

5. Shared sociocultural history—recognizing the historical backgrounds of the cultural groups to which one belongs

Throughout the following chapters I am presuming that each theory of human development serves as a window to a different combination of the foregoing aspects of culture. In way of illustration, Ambert's peer-abuse model exposes the influence on human development of (a) age groups, (b) social interaction, (c) interpersonal power relationships, (d) values, (e) motives, and (f) causes. In contrast, Howard Gardner's model of intelligence, which is described in Chapter 2, focuses on a different set of cultural elements: (a) abilities and skills, (b) enculturation agents, (c) values, and (d) causes. And Sanders' theory of grief in Chapter 4 casts light on still another combination of components: (a) social support for the bereaved, (b) stigmatic death, (c) religiosity, (d) crises concurrent with a death, and (e) the dead person's socioeconomic status.

A Hierarchy of Multiple Groups

Each person is a member of multiple cultural groups that are distributed throughout a complex, overlapping hierarchical structure. At the top of the hierarchy are cultural entities that include a great host of members. For example, one kind of broadly encompassing cultural entity contains members who are alike in their use of the same kinds of tools or technologies. Throughout the world, all users of hatchets, hoes, and shovels would be of this sort. They form a category of people who are similar in their handling of basic agricultural instruments. Likewise, in the realm of communication, users of written language would be another such broad group. Then, within each of these populous clusters are more specific subgroups, such as those whose members share the same agricultural methods (subgroups of grain farmers, orchardists, flower cultivators) or write the same language (Arabic, Russian, Italian).

As we descend into the lower reaches of the hierarchy, we find the cultural groupings becoming more complex, involving more characteristics that their members share in common, and becoming smaller in size. Terms that identify groups reflect this progressive complexity as we move down in the cultural structure. For instance, in the realm of religion, a high-level category containing 2 billion members in 260 countries is the worldwide group known as *Christians.* A subgroup of this general category is *U.S. American Christians,* numbering 230 million. Within the U. S. subgroup there are 122 million Protestants, a cluster that itself contains dozens of denominations—Baptists, Congregationalists, Methodists, Presbyterians, Unitarians, and far more. Whereas devoted Christians throughout the world could be expected to hold a certain portion of their culture in common, far more cultural beliefs and practices would be shared among Southern Baptist American Christians, who all read Bibles written in English, are bound by the rules of their denomination's governing body, and subscribe to their church's particular interpretation of religious doctrine.

Figure 1-2

A Multicultural Hierarchy

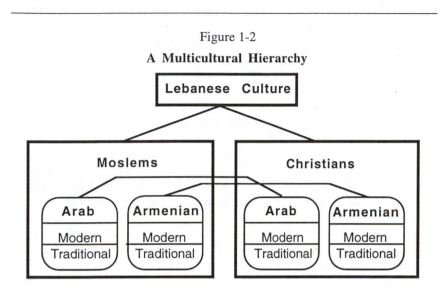

Cultural hierarchies can involve multiple dimensions, as illustrated by child-rearing customs in Lebanon (Figure 1-2). At the apex of the structure are Lebanese customs, ones common to all subgroups in the society, distinguishing inhabitants of Lebanon from those of such nations as Great Britain, France, and Italy (Prothro, 1967). Typical of mothers' attitudes throughout Lebanese society are their delight in having children, their general opposition to aggressivity in the young, and their use of corporal punishment or threats of punishment rather than rewards to cultivate obedience. Within the overall Lebanese category are subgroups that differ from each other in certain childraising practices—Christians versus Moslems, Arabs versus Armenians, and modernists versus traditionalists. Christians and Moslems obviously differ in at least part of the religious lore and rites they teach their children. Furthermore, Moslem mothers are more likely than Christian mothers to place less responsibility on a child, seldom reward good behavior, and rely heavily on empty threats as motivators. Within each of these religious groups, modern mothers (chiefly urban residents with more formal education) as compared with traditional mothers are emotionally warmer in their treatment of young children, more often withhold favors as a disciplinary method, and believe that children should learn to fight when necessary (Prothro,

1967, p. 157). As suggested by the overarching connecting lines in Figure 1-2, multiple linkages exist among cultural subgroups.

The multiple groups in which a person holds membership can be described by designations of nationality, region, locality, ethnic background, gender, religious affiliation, occupation, level of education, age, social class, fraternal association, recreational pursuit, athletic team, political preference, and more.   For example, a 21-year-old man of Danish ancestry is a native-born United States citizen, long-time resident of San Francisco, member of the Democratic Party and Methodist Church, supporter of the gay rights movement, and an enthusiastic bowler and stamp collector; he lives in an apartment with three other male university students while he is completing bachelor-degree studies in chemistry at the University of California's Berkeley campus. In contrast, a 15-year-old girl of Haitian ancestry has lived in a small Louisiana town with her parents and four younger sisters ever since her parents brought the family from Haiti 9 years ago. In the parochial high school that she attends, she is a member of the girls' chorus and the Catholic Youth Club.   At home she speaks Haitian Creole; in school she speaks English. On weekends she works as a counter girl in a fast-food restaurant.

The personality of each of these individuals—the San Franciscan and the Louisianan—is a mixture of beliefs and practices derived from those cultural groups with which each is associated, a mixture that also includes idiosyncratic features unique to the particular student.

Extent of Commitment

The phrase *extent of commitment* is used here with two meanings.   One meaning refers to the breadth of components that a person appropriates from a given cultural group. The other refers to the strength of a person's dedication to cultural components.

As for breadth, consider the culture of the Church of Latter Day Saints as found in the *Book of Mormon* and in subsequent interpretations by church leaders. A member of a Mormon congregation could subscribe to the entire body of that belief and practice or else to only selected portions.   In adopting only portions, a follower of the faith might embrace the denomination's moral principles and missionary practices but reject Joseph Smith's account of the ostensibly divine events that inspired him to found Mormonism.   In effect, people can subscribe to either a broad or narrow selection of the beliefs and practices that typify each group of which they are members.

As for depth, people's emotional investment in a belief of a cultural group can range from unshakable allegiance to shallow, ephemeral interest.   Consequently, some cultural acquisitions become permanent components of a person's world-view, highly resistant to criticism and attack, whereas other acquisitions are easily abandoned in favor of alternative beliefs or behaviors.   Throughout the history of the world there have been persons willing to die for certain of their beliefs, thereby reflecting great depth of commitment. In contrast, others have willingly changed their convictions, either because they have found new alternatives that seem more reasonable or else they have considered it prudent not to resist the people who advocate those alternatives.

Thus, the items of knowledge that make up the broad array of a person's culturally derived beliefs can vary in their levels of commitment, with some items more labile and subject to change than others.

Monolithic Versus Heterogeneous Cultures

In cultural diversity, societies can vary from the highly monolithic to the highly heterogeneous. A monolithic or homogeneous society is one in which a very restricted range of alternative beliefs and customs is approved and propagated. A heterogeneous society—sometimes referred to as a *plural society*—is one in which a diversity of cultural choices are found and, if not encouraged, are at least tolerated.

A typical monolithic culture is that of Saudi Arabia, founded on Islamic doctrine. Saudi Arabian society actively rejects cultural alternatives that are seen as contrary to the teachings of Mohammed and his followers. In particular, what has been called an "Islamic cultural crisis" is seen in the present-day confrontation between Moslem tradition and the culture of Western science and technology.

In the neighboring nation of Iran, the Moslem-controlled government bases public schooling on Islamic doctrine in an effort to promote a monolithic version of culture. Ferdows has concluded that

> The current socialization effort within the educational system is proving to be effective and will be even more so as time passes and a new generation appears. Success is found particularly among that segment of school children whose family environment is in harmony with the religious, cultural, and social ideology of the state. These children not only learn about veiling, motherhood, and different gender roles through schooling, but also personally observe, experience, and imitate their own parents and family members as role models. This reinforces what they are taught in school. (Ferdows, 1995, p. 335)

Three of the world's most populous nations—China, India, and Indonesia—are extremely heterogeneous by dint of their size and historical backgrounds. Each of these national societies includes hundreds of ethnic groups or tribes that speak separate dialects and abide by distinctive social customs. Societies that are becoming increasingly heterogeneous, primarily through immigration, are those of Great Britain, Canada, Germany, and the United States. Political, social, and educational practices in such countries are typically labeled *multicultural* in recognition of the populations being composed of diverse ethnic, religious, and social-class groups that demand to have their cultural traditions recognized and respected.

Compared with monolithic societies, plural societies are subject to greater cross-cultural confrontations as a result of the disparate cultural groups' efforts to gain greater power, rights, and privileges.

Transmitters of Culture

Because culture is learned, instead of being passed by genetic inheritance from one generation to the next, it requires transmission agents and methods. The process by which individuals learn their group's culture is called *enculturation*. Agents or mediators are individuals and groups in the society that seek to teach the young the knowledge, skills, and values that the agents hope to promote. Typical mediators include the family, children's companions, members of the community, teachers, religious workers, club leaders, law enforcement officers, social workers, and mass-communication media (books, magazines, radio, television, computer networks).

A distinction should be recognized between cultural influence and idiosyncratic influence on development. The term *cultural influence* is limited to the treatment of children that is typical of a culture group. In contrast, an *idiosyncratic influence* is the treatment given by a particular individual—treatment that is not representative of a group's practices. For example, a mother who slaps her child is engaging in an idiosyncratic act if such treatment of a child is not commonly approved by a group of which the mother is a member. Although theoretically we can readily draw the distinction between cultural and idiosyncratic influences, in practice it is often difficult to tell one from the other.

Cultural learning takes place in various settings—home, neighborhood, school, church, playground, public library, movie theater, and more—in which agents employ particular methods for transmitting cultural beliefs and practices. Those methods can include lecturing, advising, demonstrating, modeling, posing questions, offering problems to solve, displaying charts, showing motion pictures, requiring rote memorizing, drilling, threatening, punishing, and rewarding.

Multiple agents or mediators are operating at any given time. Hence, the growing child can receive diverse cultural messages from different messengers—parents, agemates, teachers, television programs, videos, and the like. The degree of consistency among the messages is affected by the degree of homogeneity of the society. In monolithic societies in which mediators agree on which cultural elements to teach and which to discourage, children are confronted with a more consistent array of beliefs than in plural societies where different agents seek to promote dissimilar beliefs.

Acculturation

Whereas the term *enculturation* identifies the process by which people acquire the culture of the group within which they are originally reared, the term *acculturation* identifies people's adopting cultural traits or social patterns of another group. Birman has distinguished between group and individual acculturation.

> At the group, or cultural level, acculturation is the process by which the collective culture of a group is changed through contact with another culture. Psychological acculturation, on the other hand, refers to the changes in behavior of individual members of such a group, who may differ with respect to the extent and type of acculturation. (Birman, 1994, p. 261)

Scholars have recognized several likely outcomes of cross-cultural encounters. Berry envisioned four possible results of the interaction of ethnocultural groups:

> *assimilation* (in which an ethnocultural group disappears by absorption [into the culture of the dominant group]), *separation* (in which an ethnocultural group sets out on its own), *integration* (in which an ethnocultural group establishes itself as an integral part of a pluralistic society), and *marginalization* (in which an ethnocultural group [clings to the edges of a dominant culture] and its members become demoralized). (Berry, 1994, p. 126)

Birman (1994) converted Berry's *integration* into *bicultural integration,* which recognizes contributions from both an individual's indigenous or home-taught culture and the newer cultural milieu into which that individual now fits. There are many ways and degrees of combining the two cultures, so that different persons can display different versions of biculturalism.

Throughout this book, in the discussion of each human development theory, our attention to acculturation appears under the headings *cross-cultural encounters* and *practical applications.*

Cultural Change

No culture remains the same with the passing of time. Every culture is continually in a process of change. However, the speed of change can differ markedly from one society to another, and various aspects of a given culture can display different rates of change.

One striking contrast in the pace of change over time is observed in the technology adopted for storing, manipulating, retrieving, and communicating information. For centuries prior to the invention of typewriters and Linotype machines near the end of the 19th century, information to be saved was written by hand or, in the case of printed materials, was typeset by hand. The products of these processes (documents, books) could then be stored on shelves and in filing cabinets, with brief descriptions of the stored items catalogued on cards organized in alphabetical order to facilitate the task of finding the saved items. However, by the 1990s these methods had been replaced with computer technology that effected a thousand-fold expansion in the capacity and speed of storing, manipulating, retrieving, and communicating data. In addition, computer technology itself progressed so rapidly that one year's most advanced equipment and methods became outdated a year or so later. Consequently, not only have the hardware and software for processing information changed at an accelerating rate, but such innovations have required parallel rapid changes in people's knowledge of how to handle information. Hence, the term *computer literacy* has taken its place beside reading, writing, and calculating as necessary skills in a modern world, with this new type of literacy placing new demands on educational theory and practice.

Compared with information-processing technology, other aspects of culture evolve at a very slow pace. Examples of far more stable cultural components are found in the domain of religion. Although the passing of time does bring change to certain aspects of religious belief, many facets of today's dominant religions are of ancient origin. Present-day Hinduism traces its beginnings and central creed back nearly 4,000 years, Judaism perhaps 3,500 years, Confucianism over 2,500 years, Christianity 2,000 years, and Islam 1,400 years.

Finally, among the cultural elements that undergo change are the kinds of theories of human development that are the central concern of this book.

Cultural Conflict

Cultural conflict results from the clash of incompatible cultural beliefs or practices. Conflict can be intergroup, intragroup, interpersonal, or intrapersonal.

Intergroup discord occurs when the convictions of one group collide with the convictions of another. As a result, battles are fought over territorial rights, religious doctrines, concepts of justice, language, and ethnic customs. For instance, observers of the unfortunate life conditions of many Native Americans often trace the American Indians' present-day plight to the past success of European immigrants and their progeny in wresting the Indians' land from them and, by government edict, confining Indians to bounded territories known as *reservations*. As illustrated by the U.S. government's traditional educational provisions for reservation children, the measures employed by a domineering cultural group to impose its culture on a dwindling indigenous population are frequently cloaked as philanthropy—as charity in the best interests of the defeated people—although the outcomes are judged as less than charitable by defenders of the domineered group.

> The destruction of Native American families was, in part, carried out through the coerced attendance of Native American children at boarding schools designed to forcefully remove Native American culture. The child had to live away from the parents for the duration of the school year and was not allowed to speak the

native language or engage in any activities that were remotely connected to the child's culture. The child was often forced to practice Christianity and was taught that any religious belief that s/he had from his/her own tribal belief was of the devil and was to be supplanted by the Judeo-Christian belief system. . . . For the most part the boarding schools were effective in their effort in destroying traditional Native American culture. (Duran & Duran, 1995, pp. 27-28)

Intragroup conflict involves differences of opinion within a cultural group. This occurs when subgroups of an overarching cultural entity wrangle over their differences in belief and practice. One such overarching entity is the Canadian nation, a sociopolitical and economic system under which people of varied ethnic backgrounds live. The most obvious subculture friction within Canadian national culture has been between French Canadians and Anglo Canadians, who see themselves as differing in language, ancestral origins, self-perceptions, traditions of law, and a variety of customs. Intranational conflict in Canada is further complicated by the presence of indigenous cultures (Indians and Inuits) and of a rapidly growing population of immigrants from many parts of the world.

Interpersonal conflicts appear when the cultural convictions of two or more individuals' clash. Such conflict can be observed in families in which mothers disagree with fathers over the issue of what religious training, if any, their children should receive. Or, on a jury in a murder trial, disputes can arise between individuals whose cultural backgrounds differ in regard to the morality of capital punishment.

Intrapersonal disharmony results when an individual suffers uncertainty and distress as a consequence of harboring incongruous cultural beliefs. A case in point is the problem a college administrator can face in deciding whether to support an affirmative-action policy in student admission practices. An affirmative-action policy advocates giving preferential treatment to applicants who are members of some designated social category—a category defined by ethnicity, gender, age, socioeconomic status, religious affiliation, or the like. Belief in affirmative action is founded on a principle of compensation: "Individuals whose ethnic group has suffered discrimination in the past deserve compensation for past wrongs by receiving special consideration—such as being allowed to have a lower level of academic attainment—in college admission decisions." In contrast, a non-affirmative-action policy is based on a principle of equity: "All applicants for admission to college should be judged on their individual records of academic performance, regardless of their particular ethnic, gender, age, socioeconomic, or religious affiliation."

Summary

For present purposes, *culture* has been defined as the collection of beliefs and practices held in common by members of a group. The group can be as broadly inclusive as *Latin Americans* or as narrow as *my immediate family.* A person may subscribe to all or to only a selected portion of a given group's commitments. Because everyone is a member of multiple groups, each individ-ual's cultural attributes represent an assortment of components drawn from the various cultures in which that individual participates. Every person's cultural characteristics are acquired through learning, that is, through observing other people or through being instructed by them—instructed either directly or else by media that the others have prepared (books, television programs, computer-network contents, and more). Theories of human development are useful for identifying which ways cultural influences contribute to young people's physical, cognitive, social, and emotional growth.

HUMAN DEVELOPMENT THEORIES

The term *theory of human development* or *model of human development,* as intended in this volume, refers to a proposed explanation of how and why people grow up as they do. The following is the definition of *theory* used for selecting the 25 models described in this book.

A distinction can be drawn between *fact* and *theory.* Facts or data are either discrete observations and measurements of people and events, or they are summaries of such observations and measurements. It is often convenient to organize facts by locating them at appropriate points along a scale that signifies the characteristic that those facts are thought to represent. Scales of this sort are usually called *variables, dimensions,* or *factors.* Among the thousands of variables researchers study are ones bearing such labels as *height, intelligence, emotional stability, moral values, prejudice, learning style, social skills,* and far more.

A theory is an explanation of how the facts fit together, particularly of how variables produce a particular outcome. In this book, that outcome is human development. All 25 models qualify as theories of *development,* because each one proposes variables whose interaction accounts for changes in the individual with the advancing years.

In sum, theorizing about human development means speculating about (a) which facts (variables) are most important for understanding how people grow up and (b) what sorts of relationships among the facts (variables) are most significant for producing that understanding.

Not everyone will agree with this definition of theory, because some people require that an explanation of development meet additional standards in order to be labeled a theory. For example, some require that theorizing include hypotheses derived from basic tenets and that the hypotheses be empirically testable by means of specified techniques. However, for the purposes of this book, the above definition is quite sufficient. All 25 models qualify as theories under our broadly encompassing definition.

No single theory attempts to explain all aspects of human thought and action. Instead, each theory addresses only one—or no more than a few—selected facets of development. Therefore, in order to illustrate the place assigned to culture in proposals about development, it has been necessary for me to include in this book, not just one model, but, instead, a variety of models, with culture assuming a somewhat different role in each theory. There are hundreds of theories bearing on development, far more than can be accommodated within the covers of a single book. Thus, the 25 presented in these chapters can do no more than hint at the great diversity of functions that different models assign to culture. The 25 that I selected are ones that reveal varied facets of human development and, at the same time, function as windows to a broad range of cultural characteristics. Obviously, these 25 are not the only theories that could fulfill such a purpose. Many others could serve quite as effectively. Thus, the models included in these pages should be viewed as only a sample of how theories reveal culture rather than as a definitive catalog of such phenomena.

What, then, were the criteria that guided my choice of these 25 from among the hundreds of available models? The answer is that two main standards served as my guides.

First, I wished to focus attention on (a) areas of interest that have been popular among researchers in the field of human development (Part I: Mental Processes and Contents) and (b) two features of theories that differ from one model to another (Part II: Structural Features of Theories). In Part I, the areas of interest are those of cognition (Chapter 2), learning (Chapter 3), and attitudes, emotions, and values (Chapter 4). Part II focuses on the differences among theories in their components (Chapter 5) and in conceptions of how such components interact to effect people's development (Chapter 6).

Second, I wished to present diverse viewpoints in each chapter so as to demonstrate the value of adopting different theoretical perspectives for understanding the influence of culture on development. For example, Chapter 2 offers six versions of cognition, and Chapter 6 describes four conceptions of how key variables in theories interact.

As implied in my earlier description of a peer-abuse model, the three features of theories that assume particular significance in this book are their key tenets, principal variables, and proposals about the role of culture in development.

The term *key tenets* refers both (a) to basic concepts on which a particular model of development is built and (b) to the theorist's mode of reasoning. Tenets also reflect which aspects of human thought and action a theory is designed to explain.

Entwined with its key tenets are a development model's *significant variables*. These are the factors a theorist believes account for why development operates as it does. The variables are assumed to form a chain or webwork of cause and effect. People who hope to influence the type of development on which a given theory focuses cannot effectively exert such influence without understanding the causal connections among the variables.

A bit of browsing through later chapters will reveal that the brief descriptions of theories reviewed throughout the book fail to depict the actual complexity of any theory in its complete form. It is also apparent that, under each of the theories, the descriptions of differences among cultures, of cultural encounters, and of practical applications are certainly not definitive. Rather, they merely illustrate a few of the cultural differences, types of encounters, and applications for a given theory. It has been necessary to thus limit such aspects of the 25 descriptions in order to keep the length of the book within reason.

Finally, my method of assigning a theory to a particular chapter has admittedly been a bit arbitrary, because the chapter titles are often not mutually exclusive. For example, a theory about intelligence could qualify for both the *cognition* and *forms of interaction* chapters. Likewise, a theory of how people acquire their gender characteristics might reasonably appear under either the topic *cognition* or that of *development configurations*. Therefore, my decision about where to locate a particular theory was based on two principal considerations: (a) which characteristic the author of the theory appeared to emphasize and (b) how many theories each chapter should contain in order to achieve some semblance of balance across chapters in terms of their length.

CAREPROVIDERS' INTERVENTIONS

The practical value of development theories lies in their ability to extract selected data from a great mass of observations about people and to organize those data in a manner that helps us understand how development occurs. This understanding can then be used to guide careproviders' attempts to promote children's and youths' optimal development. In effect, viewing cultures through the lens of a theory improves our ability to identify problems of development and to suggest solutions for those problems.

Throughout the book, the last three sections of each theory's description (*differences among cultures, cross-cultural encounters, practical applications*) are intended to help careproviders influence youngsters' ways of adopting cultural beliefs and practices. First, the purpose of describing differences among cultures is to alert readers to how variations from one culture to another can contribute to problems of child development. Next, the discussion of cross-cultural encounters adds greater precision to the analysis of such problems. Finally, the section on practical applications suggests how one or more of those problems might be resolved or at least ameliorated.

SUMMARY

This opening chapter has been designed help readers understand the next five chapters by (a) describing the purpose of the book, (b) portraying a theory of peer abuse so as to illustrate the pattern in which theories in subsequent chapters are presented, (c) defining the concept *culture* as it is intended throughout the book, (d) explaining how the term *theory* is used, and (e) suggesting ways that the book may help caregivers promote young people's development in terms of the influence of culture on development.

The principal contents of the volume are found in Chapters 2 through 6. Those chapters are sandwiched between this introductory chapter and the closing Chapter 7 that provides a retrospective overview of the 25 theories and offers an estimate of the future for development theories and for cultures.

Part I

Mental Processes and Contents

The 15 theories described in Part I are located within three chapters that focus on two sets of processes that have figured prominently in psychological research (*cognition* in Chapter 2 and *learning* in Chapter 3) and on three types of mental contents that have been of continuing interest to developmentalists (*attitudes, emotions*, and *values* in Chapter 4).

2

Cognition

The word *cognition,* as intended here, means both (a) mental activities—analyzing, synthesizing, evaluating, remembering—and (b) the beliefs about reality that those activities produce. Much of cognition is conscious, in that people recognize how and what they are thinking. In effect, they carry out their thinking with conscious intent. However, an undetermined quantity of cognition is unconscious or subconscious, consisting of mental operations that occur without the person's awareness, although the products or outcomes of such thought may be apparent. Thus, people may recognize what they have decided and then express the decision verbally without being aware of the process by which they came to their decision.

Cognition is too complex to be captured in its entirety by a single theory. Instead, the process and product of thinking must be viewed from a variety of theoretical perspectives, with each perspective revealing a different facet of cultural influence on development. A hint of that complexity is provided by the six models inspected in this chapter. Those six are Piaget's stages of mental development, Gardner's structure of intelligence, Vygotsky's proposal about the influence of action on thought, D'Andrade's social-construction conception of mentality, Jackson's phenomenological anthropology, and Jung's interpretation of dreams.

STAGES OF MENTAL DEVELOPMENT

Title: A Theory of Intelligence, as conceived by Jean Piaget, a renowned Swiss developmental psychologist.

Key tenets: In one version of Piaget's scheme, mental growth advances through four principal levels: sensorimotor (birth to about age 2), preoperational thought (about age 2 to 7), concrete operations (about 7 to 11), and formal operations (about 11 to 15). Beyond the midteens, thought patterns move from a condition of egocentrism and idealism to a growing recognition that people do not operate solely on the basis of pure logic but they also are influenced by life's social realities. The following are chief characteristics of the stages:

Sensorimotor Period (Birth–2). The infant advances from performing only reflex actions to finally representing objects mentally and thereby cognitively combining and manipulating them.

Preoperational-Thought Period (2–7). This stage is divided into two levels. The first (ages 2–4) is characterized by egocentric speech and primary dependence on perception, rather than on logic, in problem solving. The second (5–7) is marked by an intuitive approach to life, a transition phase between the child's depending on perception and depending on logical thought to solve problems.

Concrete-Operations Period (7–11). In this stage children can perform logical mental operations on concrete objects that either are directly observed or are imagined. An important feature of this period is the child's developing greater ability to recognize which aspects of an object remain unchanged (are *conserved*) when the object changes from one form to another. For example, when a large ball of clay is divided into a series of small balls of clay, the typical preoperational child will not recognize that in this transformation the weight and mass of clay remain the same. The concrete-operations child, in contrast, will understand that weight and mass have been conserved.

Formal-Operations Period (11–15). During adolescence the typical child is no longer limited by what he or she directly sees or hears, nor is he or she restricted to the problem at hand. The adolescent can now imagine various conditions that bear on a problem—past, present, and future—and devise hypotheses about what might logically occur under different combinations of such conditions. By the end of this final stage of mental development, the youth is capable of all the forms of logic that the adult commands. Subsequently, further experience over the years of youth and adulthood fill in the outline with additional, more complex concepts so that the adult's thought is more mature and freer of lingering vestiges of egocentrism than is the thought of the adolescent. (Summarized from Piaget & Inhelder, 1969)

Principal variables: Piaget proposed that human development results from the interaction of four variables: (a) heredity, as displayed in the maturation of the physique and nervous system; (b) physical experience; (c) social transmission (education); and (d) equilibration.

Piaget said that heredity establishes a time schedule for new development possibilities to open up at periodic points throughout children's growing years. This is the internal-maturation function of one's genetic endowment. Each maturational change comes at about the same time in each child's life, with the order of the changes identical for all children, thereby accounting for the universally observed sequential development stages of Piaget's theory. However, maturation alone does not guarantee that the possibilities will materialize. The extent to which such potentialities are actually realized is determined by the sorts of experiences children have with their environment. So internal maturation is a necessary but not a sufficient condition for development.

Unlike most theorists, Piaget separated the child's trafficking with the environment into two varieties: (a) direct and generally unguided experience with the world's objects and events that is called *physical experience* and (b) the guided transfer of knowledge (education in a broad sense) called *social transmission*. In their physical experience, children directly manipulate, observe, and listen to objects and events to discover what occurs. Physical experience provides the necessary basic understandings on which social transmission (instruction, teaching) will build.

To account for the coordination among maturation, physical experience, and social transmission that is necessary to produce integrated development, Piaget posited a fourth causal factor that he labeled *equilibration* or *equilibrium*.

In sum, Piaget's genetically timed maturation provides the foundation for stage-wise development, physical experience is necessary for actualizing the potential offered by maturation, social transmission equips children with learnings that have evolved in their culture, and equilibration keeps these three factors in balance.

Whereas Piaget is generally dubbed an *interactionist*—crediting heredity and environment with complementary roles in development—the strong influence he attributed to heredity has caused some observers to place him in the hereditarian camp. Critics have charged that by deriving his theory solely from observations of European children caused him to improperly diminish the influence of culture on children's development. For instance, Jacques Vonéche has questioned Piaget's assertion that the succession of stages through which cognitive development progresses is determined by a genetically controlled time clock that produces an invariant stage sequence in all cultural contexts.

> I am currently working on how developmental psychology has continuously "scientized" stages of ontogenic development that were initially literary or social ones. Greeks, with their system of "ages of life" based on the number 7 —in which age 7 marked the attainment of reason, age 14 that of adolescence, and age 21 that of majority and so on—were not too far from modern psychology. Apparently, one of two possible reasons makes this concordance possible: either the Greeks already had an elaborate developmental psychology, which is factually false, or the ages correspond to an inescapable biological sequence. In fact, since unschooled populations of the non-Western world do not exhibit such a sequencing of development, it is not a fact of nature but one of culture. . . . For Piaget, the institutional fact [of curriculum sequencing in the school] became a fact of nature [genetically determined pacing]. (Vonéche, 1987, pp. 78-79)

Differences among cultures: Many investigations have been conducted in diverse cultures to find answers to a trio of questions about Piaget's theory: (a)

Are the stages of mental growth that Piaget derived from his studies of Swiss children the same in kind and sequence as stages through which children in other cultures progress? (b) Do children of other cultures advance through the stages at the same rate as the Swiss children? (c) What causes differences in mental functions among individuals and cultures?

The universality of Piaget's stages. As noted above, Piaget contended, on the basis of his original interviews with European children, that the stages of his model were determined primarily by a genetic pattern universal throughout humankind. The young in one culture could be expected to advance through the same stages and in the same sequence as those in any other culture. However, later cross-cultural comparisons suggested that the dominant beliefs about childrearing in some cultures are more compatible with Piaget's stress on maturation and physical experience than are such beliefs in other cultures, and these differences influence what is regarded as *intelligence.* To illustrate, Levy (1996) compared parents' notions of learning and teaching in a Tahitian village with parents' notions in a Nepalese town. Tahitian beliefs proved far closer to Piaget's position than Nepalese beliefs. The Tahitian adults assumed that children learn to perform tasks chiefly by themselves, in keeping with the gradual maturational unfolding of their abilities. Thus, differences in development were attributed to differences in children's inborn natures. From a Tahitian perspective, no one teaches children very much.

> [Children] learn by watching and by playful trial and error that the adults often find amusing but sometimes annoying. . . . In a learning situation—as opposed to a simple direct command—to tell a child what to do (as opposed to the occasional what *not* to do) . . . is intrusive and taken as a sign of unjustified adult mood-driven irritability and impatience. (Levy, 1996, pp. 128-129)

In contrast to Tahitians, the Nepalese adults that Levy interviewed saw verbal instruction—Piaget's social transmission—as a necessary vehicle for learning even the most basic behaviors, such as walking, eating, speaking, and bladder control. The ability to use and understand talk was thought to be an essential part of all training, a necessary condition of task mastery.

> In [Nepal] the untaught child would be incompetent not only in his or her physical skills but in his or her moral nature. As one man puts it, "Unless parents control and educate children, children will have bad characters." [So] the "natural man" is not only inadequate in his skills but morally problematic. In Tahiti, the child who learns by itself "naturally" achieves both task and moral competence. (Levy, 1996, p. 132)

The rate of progress through stages. Not only did Piaget postulate four major stages of general intellectual development, but he also proposed successive modes of thought about the causes of phenomena that children offer on their way from *precausal, magical* thinking toward *causal, rational, scientific* explanations. Particularly during Piaget's third stage of mental development—that of concrete operations (ages 7-11 or so)—children display an admixture of what Piaget would call *magical* and *objectively rational* thinking. During these years, the young seem "unsteadily poised between what is subjective and what is objective, between physical and mental, idea and object, sign and significance" (Nurcombe, 1973, p. 106). To investigate the pace at which primary-school-aged children in different societies make this transition, Nurcombe compared how Canadian and Australian Aboriginal children performed four typical Piagetian tasks (explaining the nature of life, the origin of dreams and of the night, and the movement of clouds). The results suggested that the Aboriginal children were "retarded" in comparison with Canadian children in their concepts of the nature of life and the origin of night. The Aborigines were somewhat less "retarded" in explaining the nature and origin of dreaming. And they were no different than the Canadian children in their comprehension of the movement of clouds. In attempting to interpret these results, Nurcombe questioned how much the magical accounts of the Aborigines were a function of cultural experience rather than of a genetically grounded deficiency or delay in concept development. As one likely answer, he proposed that

> Magical thinking evolves from a compelling need for a comprehensive determinism and for a systematization of that which is presented to the senses. Mythical thought is not merely a rudiment of the scientific approach; it is, rather, a separate, parallel, alternative development, a science of the concrete imagination. Scientific thinking and mystical thinking differ less in their form than in their sphere of application. (Nurcombe, 1973, p. 119)

Explanations of such phenomena offered by Aboriginal children featured a "complex interweaving of mythical thinking, finalism, divine artificialism, metaphor, and acute observation . . . which can be described as *paracausal thought*" (Nurcombe, 1973, p. 119).

> Paracausal thinking is separate from and parallel to the causal mode which Piaget posits as the pinnacle. Paracausal thinking is well suited to the improvisational requirements of a nomadic, hunting ecological niche, but it is inappropriate in a society characterized by the need for accumulation and technological prediction. Transitional cultures sustain a shifting balance between the two modes of thought. (Nurcombe, 1973, p. 121)

Causes of individual and cultural differences. Piaget intially accounted for children's progress through the four stages by the internal maturation of their nervous system as governed by their genetic endowment. However, a host of studies conducted in different social settings have suggested that the nature of individuals' experiences within their family and community must play an important role in forming their intelligence as it is revealed in behavior.

A common form of reasoning addressed by Piagetian tasks is the syllogism, used to test a person's ability to draw inferences from a stated premise. Competently handling syllogisms has been considered a characteristic of the formal operations level in Piagetian theory.   As an example of employing syllogisms to estimate mental progress, consider a task posed by the Russian psychologist Alexander Luria to illiterate peasants in Central Asia.

> [Psychologist's syllogism] In the Far North, where there is snow, all bears are white.   Novaya Zemlya is in the Far North and there is always snow there. What color are the bears there?
> [Peasant] We always speak only of what we see; we don't talk about what we haven't seen.
> [Psychologist] But what do my words imply? [Repeats syllogism.]
> [Peasant] If a man was 60 or 80 [years old] and had seen a white bear and had told about it, he could be believed, but I've never seen one and hence I can't say. That's my last word. Those who saw can tell, and those who didn't see can't say anything! (At this point a younger man [one with some schooling] volunteered, "From your words it means that bears are white.")   (Luria in Rogoff & Chavajay, 1995, p. 861)

In effect, literate participants solved the syllogisms in the desired manner, but nonliterate ones typically refused to accept the major premise as true and thus protested that they could only judge what they had seen.   In a similar research setting, Cole and his associates (1971) changed the form of the problem so interviewees simply evaluated the truth of conclusions given by the experimenter on the basis of the premises.   In that form, nonschooled individuals had far less trouble than when they were asked to offer their own conclusions on the basis of the premises.

> Verbal syllogisms represent a specialized language genre, differing from other genres, that becomes easier to handle with practice and with understanding of the specialized form of this kind of problem.   In school, people may become familiar with the genre through experience with story problems and other verbal problems in which the answer must be derived from the relationships presented in the problem.   They are supposed not to question the truth of the premises but to answer on the basis of the stated "facts."   Being willing to reason on the basis of a premise that one cannot verify is a characteristic of schooling and literacy. (Rogoff & Chavajay, 1995, p.862)

The fact that Piaget founded his theory on the responses of children who were all products of European schools could account for his failing to recognize cultural experience as highly influential in determining how children solved different sorts of problems.

Cross-cultural encounters: From the perspective of Piagetian theory, two noteworthy types of cultural encounters are ones that concern (a) conclusions drawn about the effect of genetic inheritance on the development of intelligence and (b) interpretations of the influence of enculturation on intelligence.

The power of genetic inheritance.   As already noted, Piaget considered genetic endowment a powerful determinant of the pace of children's advance through his mental growth stages and of the highest stage they would attain. Therefore, doctrinaire Piagetians could be expected to assume that children's progress in completing Piagetian tasks would be chiefly a reflection of the quality of those children's genetic inheritance rather than their cultural backgrounds. Ergo, in a typical North American school, there would be very little hope of expediting the intellectual growth of children of ethnic minorities whose performance on Piagetian measures was below average. In other words, teachers who adopted a traditional Piagetian view of genetic influence might consider it a waste of time to try elevating such children's mental development because the gene pool from which those children drew their inheritance was considered not conducive to intellectual excellence.

The power of encounters. The term *acculturation*, as introduced in Chapter 1, refers to the process of an individual's adopting cultural traits or social patterns of a group (*encountered culture*) other than those of the group into which the person was born (*original culture*). A considerable body of research (deLacey, 1973) supports the following—rather commonsensical—generalization:

> The influence of an encountered culture on an individual is greater whenever the encounter (a) occurs earlier in the person's life, (b) pervades more aspects of life, and (c) extends over a longer period of time.

Thus, a Vietnamese child adopted at age 3 by a Canadian family of Anglo Canadian heritage might be expected to reflect more of Anglo Canadian mental-development characteristics (those measured by Piagetian tasks) than would a Vietnamese who immigrated to Canada at age 21. Piagetians could account for the observed difference by citing two of the four causal factors in Piaget's system—(a) direct and generally unguided experience with the world's objects and events that is called *physical experience* and (b) the guided transfer of knowledge (education in a broad sense) called *social transmission.* In effect, the Canadian cultural context would furnish a different set of opportunities for both physical experience and education than would the indigenous Vietnamese context.

Practical applications: Many educators and psychologists have founded instructional and evaluation procedures on Piaget's theory.

One group of proposals has used Piaget's scheme for choosing the school's instructional goals and learning activities. From this perspective, the central purpose of schooling is not to teach particular facts and concepts, nor is it to teach solutions to personal and social adjustment problems. Instead, the purpose is to promote the optimal development of thinking skills appropriate to each stage of mental growth as defined in Piaget's theory. Thus, the learning aims and activities to pursue at each age level are defined by the Piagetian stage of mental development for that age range (Biggs, 1976; Elkind, 1976; Furth & Wachs, 1975; Peel, 1976).

Another group of Piaget's followers have been critical of traditional methods of assessing intelligence that involve the use of such tests as the *Stanford-Binet* or *Wechsler-Bellevue* scales. Such instruments, critics contend, tell only whether a child can give a correct answer to specific questions. What is needed, instead, is a way to assess children's thought processes as they generate answers to questions. This need, they say, is fulfilled by Piagetian tasks, which involve children revealing how they think while they are being interviewed during the process of solving problems posed by an interviewer (Phillips, 1975, p. 162).

FRAMES OF MIND

There are many theories of intelligence. Most qualify as *folk psychology*—as informal beliefs that people "naturally" hold about the form and source of mental ability. A smaller but growing number of theories are formal models proposed by psychologists, anthropologists, and sociologists. Theories of both kinds can differ from each other in two main ways: (a) whether intelligence is a single general ability that affects a person's entire mental activity or whether it is composed of a series of different abilities that are only slightly correlated, if at all, and (b) the degree to which manifest intelligence is inborn—the result of genetic inheritance—rather than the product of experience or learning.

The following discussion, rather than attempting to review many specific conceptions of intelligence, presents one formal present-day model, then shows how notions of intelligence in various cultures compare with that model.

Title: Frames of Mind, as proposed by Howard Gardner, a Harvard University psychologist.

Key tenets: Intelligence is not a singular, unified personal power that operates with equal effectiveness in all aspects of life. Instead, intelligence is more accurately conceived to be seven separate types of ability or *intelligences* that make their separate contributions to the adequacy of people's performance in life's endeavors. The seven focus on (1) use of language, (2) logical-mathematical analysis, (3) spatial representation, (4) musical thinking, (5) the use of the body to solve problems or to make things, (6) an understanding of other individuals (a form of social intelligence), and (7) an understanding of oneself (Gardner, 1983).

> Where individuals differ is in the strength of these intelligences—the socalled *profile of intelligences*—and in the ways in which such intelligences are invoked and combined to carry out different tasks, solve diverse problems, and progress in various domains. (Gardner, 1991, p. 12)

The amount or strength of a particular intelligence is partially the result of the person's genetic endowment, that is, the individual's biological inheritance. Inheritance provides a base of potentiality that must then be nurtured by the person's experiences with the world, that is, by environmental factors. Without constructive learning opportunities, genetic potential will not be realized to its fullest capacity.

> This view of intelligence may serve as a critique of "general intelligence" approaches . . . [and is] a challenge to the Piagetian view of intelligence, where general operations are assumed to underlie work across disparate domains. In contradistinction to each of these approaches, it is claimed here that each intelligence has its own genesis and can evolve according to its own rules of processing. . . . For instance, musical memory may operate in a different fashion from, and have no intrinsic link to, a keen memory in the spatial, logical-mathematical, or interpersonal realms. (Gardner, 1995, p. 231)

Any role in society may utilize a combination of several of the intelligences, and any single intelligence can contribute to the performance of different sorts of activities.

An important feature of environments is the selection of activities most valued and fostered by the culture in which the child grows up. In effect, each culture emphasizes activities that promote the development of some intelligences more than others. These differing emphases are observed in the family, the school, occupational settings, and in such mass-communication media as books, magazines, and television.

Principal variables:　An understanding of the function of culture in relation to Gardner's multiple intelligences requires information about four main sets of variables: (a) the nature of the seven forms of intelligence and how they are assessed, (b) a society's activities that utilize different intelligences, (c) which forms of intelligence are most valued within the society, and (d) opportunities provided by the society for nurturing each sort of intelligence.

Differences among cultures: Variations across cultures in the styles of life they encourage result in differences in the types of intelligence fostered in those societies. Facets of life particularly significant in determining which intelligences are most valued include a culture's occupational structure, social organization and governance, social-class patterns, and recreational pursuits.

The occupational structure of hunter-gatherer tribes places high value on the space-perception, body-strength, and physical-agility skills required for spotting and capturing animals and for recognizing and harvesting edible plants. Thus, much time and energy are invested in exercising spatial and physical types of intelligence. Demonstrated aptitude in these two forms contributes to people's survival and earns rewards of prestige and material wealth. In contrast, cultures that depend heavily on sophisticated communication and abstract-knowledge skills, as found in postindustrial "information societies," esteem language and logical-mathematical talent. Consequently, those two sorts of intelligence are stressed in the formal-education institutions of such societies, and people who exhibit particular talent in applying those aptitudes can enjoy high status and prosperity.

The social organization and mode of governance of societies is often conveyed by such terms as *autocratic, democratic, socialistic, communistic, feudal,* and the like. Such systems can differ in the social roles that citizens are expected to assume. For example, a democracy requires political participation on the part of all citizens, since everyone is expected to make informed decisions at election time. In contrast, a feudal structure or autocracy requires political decisions only by the top leaders, with the remainder of the populace expected simply to fulfill their assigned duties. Therefore, the sort of social intelligence (understanding other individuals) and personal intelligence (understanding ourselves), and how the two are valued and nourished, can differ in keeping with the nature of societies' dominant styles of governance.

Related to a society's modes of governance are people's convictions about proper power and privilege relationships across age levels. In the Nyansongo community in the Gusii region of Kenya, East Africa,

> Obedience rather than enterprise or initiative is considered to be the key to success. . . . Smartness or brightness by itself is not a highly valued characteristic, and the Nyansongo concept of intelligence includes respect for elders and filial piety as vital ingredients. An obedient child, according to Nyansongo thought, is also responsible, that is, he performs the tasks and chores regularly assigned to him by his parents with a minimum of supervision. (LeVine & LeVine, 1963, p. 181)

Among the Djerma-Sonhai in Niger, West Africa, the term *lakkal* (often translated into English as *intelligence*) refers to practical know-how, particularly knowing how to live according to social norms. *Lakkal*, a form of social intelligence in Gardner's system, is considered a gift of God that is inborn but not apparent until after age 7. A child who does not have *lakkal* by then will never acquire it (Segall, Dasen, Berry, & Poortinga, 1990, p. 104).

Each society also exhibits a particular social-class system, with people located across various levels of social classes that are usually distinguished from each other by types of occupations, amounts of income, quality of housing, education, and friendship alliances. The different levels may also vary in such subculture characteristics as language usage, style of dress, and recreational preferences. Which types of intelligence are best suited to a given social-class level can vary according to the cultural requirements of that level. The notion that differences in tested intelligence between cultural groups depends more on environmental influences than on genetic endowment has been supported by a study of classification skills among Australian children from four experiential backgrounds—(a) high-socioeconomic European heritage, (b) low-socioeconomic

European heritage, (c) Aborigines having high contact with European culture, and (d) Aborigines having low contact with European culture. In testing the four sets of children with a series of Piagetian tasks that required classifying objects, deLacey (1973) demonstrated a consistent relationship between the children's cultural milieus and their classificatory performance. The higher the socioeconomic level of children of European ancestry, the better they succeeded with the tasks. The greater the contact of Aborigines with European culture, the better the Aborigines performed.

> It seems to be sufficient to explain the differences in classificatory performance in terms of environmental differences. . . . The results of this study also imply that the parallel development between additive and multiple classificatory abilities reported by Inhelder and Piaget might occur only where the child's environment provides a favourable opportunity for cognitive growth [of the sort measured by the Piagetian tasks]. (deLacey, 1973, p. 68)

Since the classification tasks used in these studies were ones derived from a European tradition, it would seem desirable also to test the four groups' skills in classifying phenomena important in the daily lives of Aboriginal children, such as classifying indigenous animals, tools, types of plants, weather conditions, kinship relations, and the like. The results of such testing could help resolve the question of the influence of cultural familiarity on classificatory abilities.

The recreational activities in which people engage are also related to the forms of intelligence in which they excel. Individuals who are avid readers of history, philosophy, and classical literature can be expected to possess advanced aptitudes for language and logical analysis. Ones who spend long hours listening to or producing music are expected to have strong musical intelligence. Those skilled at woodworking, sewing, bowling, hiking, or playing tennis count on their physical-coordination intelligence. Ones adept at landscape painting, sculpture, or fabric design (as in Balinese wood sculpturing and Javanese batik designing) depend on their aptitudes for both space perception and manual dexterity. Furthermore, it is apparent that cultures vary in how much they value and reward these different sorts of activities.

In a society's folk psychology, the components of intelligence often differ not only from Gardner's seven varieties but also from other societies' commonsense beliefs as well.

> In a comparative study of Chinese and Australians, Keats (1982) asked informants to designate the characteristics of an intelligent person. Results showed that the two groups equally often mentioned having an inquiring mind, creativity, originality, problem-solving skills, and the possession of knowledge. [However,] the Chinese chose imitation, observation, carefulness, and precision of thought, whereas the Australians more often mentioned communication and linguistic skills. The personality traits associated with an intelligent person by the Chinese were perseverance, effort, determination, and

social responsibility, whereas the Australians emphasized confidence, happiness, and effectiveness in social relations. (Segall, Dasen, Berry, & Poortinga, 1990, p. 106)

Among Indians of the Southwestern United States, Apaches have traditionally placed high value on learning ability (particularly on adeptness in memorizing ceremonial practices), initiative, aggressiveness, and leadership (Goodwin, 1942/1969, p. 540). As another example, a study by Berry (1994) identified two core characteristics of intelligent behavior valued by the Cree Indians of Northern Ontario, Canada. Cognitive competence among the Cree emphasized (a) deliberation, that is, listening carefully and weighing alternatives before drawing a conclusion, and (b) self-sufficiency, in the sense of not depending on others but taking personal responsibility for one's thoughts and actions.

Some cultures place high value on competencies that appear to combine more than one of Gardner's kinds of intelligence. An example in the language of the Baoulé society of West Africa's Ivory Coast (Coté d'Ivoire) is the concept *n'glouèlê,* a complex ability not easily translated into English. One component of *n'glouèlê* could be called "obligingness" or "willingness to help" as demonstrated in a child's voluntarily, and without urging or supervision, performing tasks helpful to the family, school, or community. This obligingness component, which could qualify under Gardner's social intelligence (understanding of other individuals), is supplemented by such skills as manual dexterity ("smart hands") and whatever language and mathematical-logical competencies the tasks require (Segall, Dasen, Berry, & Poortinga, 1990, p. 107-108).

A question can now be asked about how well do a culture's preference for different types of intelligence affect the fate of individual members of the society and of the society as a whole. As one answer, Gardner has criticized the schooling traditions in Western societies for (a) failing to accord equal esteem to each of his proposed seven intelligences and thereby (b) offering children and youths an unfavorably limited menu of learning opportunities.

> Our educational system is heavily biased toward linguistic modes of instruction and assessment and, to a somewhat lesser degree, toward logical-quantitative modes as well. . . . Students learn in ways that are identifiably distinctive [as demanded by their individualistic patterns of intelligences). The broad spectrum of students—and perhaps the society as a whole—would be better served if [scholarly] disciplines could be presented in a number of ways and learning could be assessed through a variety of means. (Gardner, 1991, p. 12)

Cross-cultural encounters: Problems can arise from confrontations between cultures that hold divergent notions of intelligence, of which varieties of intelligence are most admired, and of how those forms should be nurtured. Specifically, difficulties can occur when (a) children enter an education system whose practices are founded on a different theory of intelligence than that held in children's out-of-school environments, (b) educational practices from one culture are transferred to another culture that holds different assumptions about the nature of abilities and their development, and (c) people steeped in their own culture's conception of intelligence interact with people steeped in a conflicting view.

The schooling of immigrants. Teachers in societies that employ Western approaches to education typically base their judgments of students' intellectual abilities on three sources of evidence—direct observations of students' oral performances in class activities, the analysis of students' work products (projects, homework assignments, achievement tests), and the results of standardized intelligence or aptitude tests. Faulty conclusions about students' abilities can result if teachers fail to understand immigrant children's cultural backgrounds.

The sort of oral performance that teachers often regard as evidence of higher intelligence involves children (a) frequently volunteering answers to questions the teacher or classmates pose, (b) giving reasonable responses when called upon, (c) participating actively and relevantly in class or small-group discussions, and (d) asking thoughtful questions. Teachers may conclude that immigrant children have low mental ability if they rarely display these behaviors. However, such children may, indeed, be intellectually quite apt but are simply acting in accordance with the standards of their home culture. For instance, Samoan children may seldom participate in class discussions or ask questions because of cultural beliefs about status: "Low-status people (including children) are supposed to listen, not ask questions. To ask questions is to act above one's station, thereby challenging the statuses of both listener and speaker" (Pelissier, 1991, p. 87). Asking a lot of questions is also considered unwise in the culture of Pukapuka atoll in the Southeastern Pacific, since status rivalry makes it inappropriate to ask questions and thereby to lose face through publicly acknowledging ignorance.

Furthermore, Warm Springs Indian children in the U.S. Northwest may be regarded as "silent" and thus unintelligent by teachers in typical American schools because the habitual modes of organizing talk and interaction in the children's home life differ markedly from those of mainstream schools. The differences concern how a person takes a turn to talk, who is the leader, what sorts of responses are acceptable, and more (Pelissier, 1991, p. 85).

Immigrant children's unsatisfactory performance in discussions, on homework assignments, and on tests may be interpreted as reflecting low intellectual ability when it actually is the result of the immigrants' inadequate command of the school's language of instruction or their lack of acquaintance with such things as tests and written assignments.

Cross-cultural transfer of educational practices. Beginning in the 16th century, a variety of European nations aggressively competed in efforts to colonize all lands outside of Europe. The two principal aims of such endeavors were to enrich the colonizing nations and to "civilize" the residents of those lands. Also involved was the unstated goal of enhancing the Europeans' *national pride*—that sense of sovereign power gained from besting others physically, economically, or intellectually. The civilizing function consisted of teaching the local populations the "superior culture" of the Europeans, particularly by gathering the native peoples within the Christian fold. This task was assigned particularly to missionaries who either accompanied the conquering navies and armies or followed in their wake. Thus, missionaries and, in later times, secular teachers introduced European forms of schooling around the world, including the proper aims of education, methods and materials of instruction, and techniques of evaluation. In 1898 the United States, by dint of the Spanish-American War, formally joined the colonizing lists by wresting from Spain such territories as the Philippines, Puerto Rico, and a variety of Pacific Islands. Japan, which had adopted Western schooling practices in the mid-1800s, soon became a colonizer and furthered the extension of Western schooling practices.

After World War II, most of the formerly colonized territories won their political independence.   However, this did not halt the export of educational practices from Europe, North America, Australia, New Zealand, and Japan. Rather, the transport of a growing array of educational methods and materials took the form of foreign aid to developing nations. Today, the process continues at an accelerating pace as communications among societies via radio, television, and computer networks have become immediate and pervasive (Thomas, 1987).

Thus, from the perspective of Gardner's theory, millions of people have been taught by methods inconsistent with the traditional conceptions of intelligence held within their own societies. Under such an acculturation condition, two sets of consequences might be expected to result.

First, the greater the difference between the colonizers and the indigenous population in their conceptions of intelligence and in the sorts of intelligence fostered in the society, (a) the greater the difficulty indigenous people experience in adopting the colonizers' culture and (b) the greater the colonizers consider the local people's aptitudes and culture inferior to their own.

Second, the patterns of acculturation displayed by members of the colonized population can differ from one individual to another, apparently as determined by three principal conditions: (a) the frequency and intensity of their encounters with the colonizers, (b) their inherited aptitudes for each of Gardner's intelligences, and (c) their motivations, that is, how strongly they desire to adopt the for-eigners' ways in comparison to maintaining their own culture's practices. Consider, for example, these two likely acculturation patterns.

Youth One: This 16-year-old lad has been intimately engaged with the colo-nizers since early childhood (attended their schools, employed by them), has high genetic aptitude for developing a wide array of intelligences, and is strongly motivated to be accepted in both the imported society and native society. Thus, he is the somewhat rare individual who acquires the skills and knowledge of both cultures at a high level of mastery and succeeds socially in both cultures.

Youth Two: This 18-year-old woman has had little direct contact with the colonizers (has led a sheltered life within her own village), has an inherited aptitude principally for music and social-interaction skills (a high propensity for empathy and estimating other people's motives), and wishes to please her parents by adhering to their traditional ways. Therefore, she does not acquire the modes of logic and mathematical skills valued in the colonizers' culture. However, she finds it easy to reproduce the melodies and rhythms of Western music that she occasionally hears on the radio.

Culturalcentric views of intelligence. A common feature of how people estimate others' intelligence in Western societies—particularly in asking test questions—is a set of tasks requiring respondents to draw inferences from data, including inferences from observations of other people. From noting what other people say and do, an individual is asked to judge what those people are thinking and how they are likely to behave. But such an approach to assessing intelligence depends on the respondent's conception of knowledge, a conception about how a person comes to know what others think; and that conception can differ from one culture to another. During anthropological studies in the Samoan Islands in the mid-1920s, Margaret Mead's efforts to get Samoans to give character sketches of members of their families were met with the universal response, "I don't know." From this experience, Mead (1928/1937) concluded that Samoans had only a rudimentary understanding of the behavior of others and, therefore, were an intellectually simple and personally undifferentiated people. However, Eleanor Gerber's (1985) more recent investigations in Samoa, which elicited the same responses to questions like Mead's, led her to change her mode of questioning, a change that produced elaborate answers and thus furnished quite a different picture of Samoans' intellects. Rather than asking why someone had done a certain thing (which drew the answer "I don't know"), Gerber asked, "But why do *you* think, in your own mind, that he did this?" Such queries produced detailed estimates. In explanation, Gerber wrote:

> What prevented my informants from answering the first question was not a lack of interest in motivation, but a belief about knowledge. Samoans frequently say . . . "We cannot tell what another person is thinking." Given this idea, it becomes very difficult to state with assurance what another person's motives in fact *are,* especially when the question "why" is apparently interpreted as calling for nothing but the truth. As a consequence, the only possible answer to this question about matters internal to another person is "I don't know." (Gerber, 1985, p. 133)

Incorrect conclusions about intelligence can also be drawn by people who base estimates of students' ability solely on students' verbal descriptions. It is apparent that some cultures emphasize learning in practical "on-the-job" settings, without attaching much significance to what learners can tell about the tasks they do. In such cultures, intelligence is commonly judged in terms of how adeptly students carry out tasks rather than in how fluently they describe task performance.   For instance, observed performance provides the basis for assessing learners' aptitudes for ocean navigation in Micronesia, for tailoring in Liberia, and for canoe building in Tonga.

Practical applications: According to Gardner, the aim of schooling should not be to teach subject matter for its own sake but, rather, to use subject matter as a vehicle for improving the learners' command of his seven types of intelligence. As he demonstrates in *The Unschooled Mind* (1991), a given set of learning activities can be designed to simultaneously promote the development of several of the types.   For instance, a classroom of ten-year-olds who are studying Brazil can strengthen their:

1. *Language competence* by reading about life in Brazil, writing reports and stories, discussing what they have studied, and learning some Portuguese language phrases.

2. *Logical-mathematical analysis* by calculating distances, comparing the sizes and growth rates of the populations of various Brazilian states, and predicting the likely future status of the Amazon rain forest if current agricultural slashing and burning practices are continued.

3. *Spatial-relations skills* by locating sites on maps and creating maps of their own.

4. *Musical thinking* by listening to Brazilian music and comparing it to music from other cultures.

5 *Body-movement skills* by drawing maps and pictures (manual dexterity) and practicing Brazilian dance forms (large-muscle coordination).

6. *Social intelligence* by working in small groups on projects related to the unit on Brazil—such projects as painting a mural of life in an Amazon Indian village, building a model church, and producing a simulated radio drama about the home life of a Brazilian family.

7. *Self-understanding* by assessing the quality of their own participation in the unit on Brazil.

A SOCIOHISTORICAL CONCEPTION OF INTELLIGENCE

Title: Soviet Theory of Cognitive Development, created by Lev Semenovich Vygotsky and such colleagues as D. B. Elkonin and A. R. Luria.

Key tenets: During the early years of the Soviet Union as a political state, psychologists endeavored to devise a theory of intellectual development suited to the social philosophy of Karl Marx's dialectical materialism on which the Soviet Union was founded.   In the mid-1920s a suitable theory was proposed by Vygotsky and, over the following 65 years, was further refined and embellished by other Soviet psychologists.   In recent times this theory has been embraced, either wholly or in part, by social scientists in various parts of the world.

A fundamental conviction on which the theory is based is that, as children advance in age and experience, they engage in an increasing variety of activities. Their participation in those activities generates the contents of their minds. In effect, a person's higher mental functions are social before they are internalized by the individual, and they become internalized by means of social interactions. Thus, what people do—their activities—are not just a result of what they think. Rather, what and how they think is a result of what they do. However, the pathway from activity to mental contents is not exclusively a one-way street; instead, the process operates in a cyclical fashion. Activities lead to thoughts; then thinking about the activities can lead to revising the conduct of future activities. In this way, contemplation and evaluation influence activity, with the resulting activity affecting further thought contents and processes.

Central to the Soviet model is the concept of a hierarchy of types of activities, with a dominant or *leading activity* at the top of the hierarchy at each stage of development. In effect, each period of children's development is motivated by a particular leading activity. The change from one leading activity to another brings about a change in the person's perception of life and signifies the transition from one mental stage to the next. A leading activity is marked by three features: (a) it is the chief factor establishing a given period in the child's psychological growth, (b) it is within the field of this activity that particular psychic functions emerge, and (c) the climax of the activity forms the foundation for the next leading activity.

Therefore, successive leading activities signify the focus of development over the passing years and form a series of developmental stages. The best-known version of this series has been described by V. V. Davidov (1990, pp. 96-97).

1. *Intuitive and emotional contact between child and adults (birth to age 1):* The kinds of development resulting from this contact include the infant's feeling a need for interacting with other people, expressing emotional attitudes toward others, learning to grasp things, and displaying a variety of perceptual actions.

2. *Object-manipulation activity (early preschool years, ages 1 to 3):* Children adopt socially accepted ways of handling things. Through interaction with adults, they develop speech and visual-perception thinking (memory images).

3. *Game-playing activity (later preschool years, age 3 to 7):* Children engage in symbolic activity and creative play. They develop some understanding of how to cooperate with others in group activities.

4. *Learning activity (primary school years, 7 to 11):* Children develop theoretical approaches to the world of material things, a function that involves their considering objective laws of reality and beginning to comprehend psychological preconditions for abstract theoretical thought (intentional mental operations, mental schemes for problem solving, reflective thinking).

5. *Social-communications activity (early adolescence, ages 11 to 15):* Adolescents acquire skills of initiating types of communication needed for solving

life's problems, for understanding other people's motives, and for consciously abiding by group norms.

6. *Vocational-learning activity (later adolescence, ages 15 to 17):* Older adolescents develop new cognitive and vocational interests, grasp elements of research work, and attempt real-life projects.

The transition from one stage of development to the next disrupts the stability of the child's modes of thought and ways of interacting with the world, thereby producing crises in the young one's effort to master the next leading activity. As a result, development is characterized by cycles of stability interspersed with transitional crises.

Three features of particular importance in the Soviet model are its proposals about the influence on development of (a) the society's history, (b) the child's individual history, and (c) a hypothesized *zone of proximal development.*

Traditionally, the unit of analysis in studies of cognition had been the individual person, whose mental development was considered to be the product of the individual's biological inheritance interacting with the immediate environment. However, Vygotsky contended that understanding the nature of the social environment required the study of how history had fashioned the cultural characteristics of the society in which the child grows up. He further suggested that it was important to focus on the individual child's developmental history, since each new step in development—that is, each new encounter with the environment—is affected by the child's present condition of receptivity, which itself is a product of past events in the child's life.

The *zone of proximal development* is defined as "the set of actions that the child can perform when helped by another person, but which are not yet available to the child in his individual acting" (Valsiner, 1987, p. 233). In Piagetian theory, children cannot profit from instruction until they demonstrate that they have already spontaneously acquired mental structures (perceptual lenses) necessary for grasping a new concept or activity. However, Vygotsky disagreed with this notion, proposing instead that the child need only be progressing toward such a level of maturity in order to profit from instruction. In other words, a child in the *zone of proximal development* could—with the aid of the teacher—learn the new concept or skill.

Principal variables: Explanations of why people think the way they do require information about (a) the society's historical evolution, which accounts for the society's dominant patterns of production and consumption of goods and services, (b) a worldview, values, and social institutions (government, family, occupations, modes of education, artistic pursuits, and the like) that accord with those patterns, (c) typical stages of human development within such a society, and (d) the individual person's developmental history.

Differences among cultures: The most fundamental assumption on which Marx founded his social theory was the conviction that a given people's culture is determined by the dominant system of producing and distributing goods and services in their society. In effect, people's social relationships, values, and beliefs derive from the ways of behaving dictated by that society's production and consumption patterns. In a feudal social structure, a small social elite (aristocrats) own and manage production facilities (principally agricultural land), while a large labor force of have-nots (serfs) work the land for the profit of the aristocracy. In a capitalistic social structure, a relatively small corps of factory and landowners (the bourgeois) depend on a large population of propertyless workers (the proletariat) to labor at a low wage for the profit of the owners. In a state-socialist (communist) social structure, all production facilities are owned in common by the entire populace, whose members manage and work those facilities; then the production output is distributed fairly among the citizens as guided by the motto: "From each according to his or her ability, to each according to his or her need." In Marx's opinion, not only can societies differ in such major ways as those reflected in the terms *feudalism, capitalism,* and *state socialism* or *communism,* but many other subforms of these societal patterns exist as well, as determined by the particular histories of different societies.

Cross-cultural encounters: When societies can differ markedly in their modes of production and consumption, and if people's ways of thought—their *intelligences*—are fabricated from their participation in those modes, then we can expect that the dominant physical and mental skills, values, and perceptions-of-life held by people of one culture will differ from those held by people of another culture that evolved along a different sociohistorical route. Therefore, we could expect to witness in cross-cultural encounters (a) a variety of misunderstandings and (b) differences in the ability and willingness to compete and cooperate. In the 1990s' reunification of Germany, the reported conflicts in attitudes and skills between East and West Germans might be interpreted as providing at least modest support for this Marxist thesis. During the four decades between 1950 and 1990, East and West Germans lived under opposing sociopolitical systems which, according to Marxist theory, would affect the mental development of people growing up in the two societies (Adler & Brayfield, 1996; "Eagle's Embrace," 1995).

Practical applications: One obvious implication of Marxist theory is that efforts should be made in cross-cultural encounters to explain to the contending parties the sociohistorical bases for the skill, value, and attitude differences they display and thereby reduce the negative consequences of the encounters.

As for Vygotsky's version of Marxist theory, perhaps the most far-reaching application of his proposal has been the influence his viewpoint has exerted on the perspectives scholars adopt when designing their research. Prior to the 1960s and 1970s, the dominant focus in the study of cognition was on the individual person's mental skills as determined by genetic endowment interacting with the immediate environment. However, in recent times an expanding corps of researchers have accepted

> Vygotsky's analysis of the interrelated roles of the individual and the social world [that] includes individual and environment together in successively broader time frames from momentary learning, to individual life-course development, to generations in a society, to species history (respectively, microgenetic, ontogenetic, sociocultural, and phylogenetic development). Development over the life course takes place within developmental processes occurring over both the course of cultural history and of phylogenetic history. (Rogoff & Chavajay, 1995, p. 871)

A further influence of Vygotsky's model is seen in a growing number of educators' incorporating into their teaching methods his notion of a zone of proximal development. Rather than waiting for children to display a particular form of reasoning before attempting skills and knowledge that depend on that form, teachers who follow Vygotsky's lead will attempt to teach the new learnings somewhat before the time that children might exhibit their readiness spontaneously.

THE SOCIAL CONSTRUCTION OF REALITY

Title: Propositions About Culture and Cognition, as conceived by Roy D'Andrade of the University of California, San Diego.

Key tenets: Rather than furnishing a formal theory, D'Andrade has offered a series of propositions about the relations between culture and human cognition, propositions that might comprise elements of a formal model. The propositions and implications they hold for understanding cognitive development can be illustrated with two of his proposals. But first, it is useful to learn D'Andrade's conviction about how *culture* is properly defined.

> Culture consists of learned and shared systems of meaning and understanding, communicated primarily by means of natural language. These meanings and understandings are not just representations about what is in the world; they are also directive, evocative, and reality constructing in character. Through these systems of meanings and understandings, individuals adapt to their physical environment, structure interpersonal relationships, and adjust psychologically to problems and conflicts. (D'Andrade, 1990, p. 65)

Now consider two examples of D'Andrade's postulates:

First proposition. "Language differences in the way objects are categorized and distinguished are paralleled by cognitive differences in the perception of similarity between such objects, and in the degree to which these objects are accurately remembered" (D'Andrade, 1990, p. 69).

Second proposition. "Category systems that bring together definitional attributes from a number of domains, such as emotion terms, have the capacity to reinforce certain values. Typically, these systems bring together representations of situations, actions, and the self along with a strong evaluational component" (D'Andrade, 1990, p. 74).

It should be apparent that D'Andrade's propositions can fit comfortably within the theory Vygotsky proposed.

Principal variables: The sources of the culturally shared meanings that people display are the social institutions with which people habitually interact, such as the family, the school, the church, the peer group, the neighborhood, and mass communication media (television, radio, books, newspapers, magazines). The dominant modes of thought conveyed in those institutions are the ones people typically adopt. However, D'Andrade adds that such culturally shared meanings are not the only factors that affect what people think and do. Other influential variables are social conditions (economic prosperity or depression, war or peace, crime rate) and environmental conditions (climate, abundance of natural resources), how influence or power is distributed in the society, economic opportunity, individuals' personality characteristics, their genetic endowment, and more.

Differences among cultures: The effect of cultural traditions on individuals' cognitive styles has been demonstrated in a host of studies. For instance, the impressive speed and accuracy of mental calculations among Japanese and Chinese abacus experts are attributed to the experts' visualizing multiple-digit problems as patterns of abacus beads, enabling them to recall as many as 15 digits either forward or backward (Rogoff & Chavajay, 1995, p. 865). A somewhat similar mental skill was observed in the African nation of Liberia among Moslems who practiced the Arabic language by spending hundreds of hours memorizing the Islamic holy book, the Qur'an. Compared with other Liberians not well versed in Arabic, these Arabic-literate Moslems were superior in remembering a string of words in order, as one word was added to the string on each successive trial, a task much like that of memorizing the scriptures (Scribner & Cole, 1981).

Cultural traditions also influence the way people interpret test situations that are intended to reveal their mental abilities. Students in Western-style schools are accustomed to answering questions posed by adults. In such societies, when the young give either incorrect answers or no answers at all, adults feel warranted in concluding that such responses are evidence of a child's misconceptions or ignorance. However, in some societies children can fail to answer questions even when they know the correct responses. They may do so in order to avoid showing disrespect for the adult who has asked a question whose answer seems apparent (Why embarrass the adult by exposing his ignorance?). Or they may feel that the adult is trying to trick them, since the correct answer appears obvious; by not answering at all, the youth avoids falling for the trick and appearing to be a fool.

Cross-cultural encounters: If we accept the notion that reality is a social construction, then each individual's beliefs about the nature of the world will typically reflect the general conception of reality held within that individual's culture. Thus, moving to a different cultural setting may well contribute to people's personal/social maladjustment in their new environment.

In way of illustration, Levy (1996) has described the worldview of people in Piri (a remote village in the Tahitian Islands), a view dominated by what people directly see and experience in their daily lives, unaffected by the complex and conflicting beliefs found in metropolitan settings. Such villagers become confident that their culturally shared conception of the world is the truth about reality. As a result, when they

> move into new situations—move to modern Tahiti, Europe, or America, or as the village changes around them—it takes a generation or two for the new worlds to affect their village-based sureness, and in the meantime, they appear to others as provincial, and intellectually constricted, simple, stubbornly closed off, sim-plistically old-fashioned or other-fashioned. (Levy, 1996, p. 138)

Among the more dramatic examples of the social-construction thesis are the differences across cultures in the causes that people cite for events in their lives. The process of attributing cause involves two stages of reality construction. At the first stage, individuals identify particular things as being real or true. At the second stage they identify a relationship between those things as also being true. In that relationship, one of the things is thought to cause the other. For example, consider the matter of pregnancy. In most present-day societies, an act of sexual intercourse that results in the male partner's sperm cell merging with the female partner's ovum is believed to be the cause of pregnancy. But such a conviction is not universal. Among traditional Trobriand Islanders of the South Pacific, pregnancy is believed to result from one ancestral spirit inserting another ancestral spirit into the mother's womb. This action, they contend, is most readily accomplished if the opening to the womb has been enlarged by intercourse, hence explaining why women who have frequent intercourse become pregnant more often than those who do not (Malinowski, 1948, p. 236). In effect, among informed members of many present-day societies, spermatozoa and ova are real things—part of a shared cultural reality—and the process of intercourse that joins sperm and ovum is a relationship that is assumed to result in pregnancy. In contrast, among traditional Trobriand Islanders, ancestral spirits are real things whose behavior is responsible for women bearing offspring. Thus, it is hardly surprising that misunderstanding and disagreement are likely to result when people reared under such contrasting social-construction conditions reveal their beliefs to each other.

Practical applications: One application of social-construction theory assumes the form of a reality-clarification activity. Just as values-clarification sessions are intended to reveal the values people hold, so reality-clarification sessions are designed to reveal people's beliefs about what is real. One way to conduct such sessions with a group of counselees or a classroom of students is to build the discussion around a sequence of six questions, with members of the group taking turns answering the questions. The questions focus on beliefs about causes of events and on the likely consequences of people's responses to the events as founded on their estimates of cause.

Question 1. What do I believe happened? This question is about a specific event, either an event in the speaker's own life (a high mark on a math test, the death of a relative, finding a 10-dollar bill on the street, a dream) or an event witnessed directly (an argument between classmates about religion) or reported in the mass-communication media (a person winning a large amount of money in a lottery, a child making a miraculous recovery from a near-fatal illness, an earthquake that destroyed a large city).

Question 2: Why did that happen? What caused it? The intention of this query is to reveal the factors that the speaker believes were responsible for the event, with each of these factors serving as something real to that individual and with the proposed connections among the factors reflecting the speaker's view of causal reality.

Question 3: Why do I hold such a set of beliefs? That is, where or from whom did I get such a way of explaining the event? The aim of this step is to elicit the speaker's opinion about the origins of this conception of reality and to identify which parts of the conception have been socially constructed—that is, which parts are embedded in cultural traditions.

Question 4: How do I feel about that event? What emotions, if any, does it generate? The intent at this point is to elicit the emotional content generated by that speaker's conception of the reality of the event.

Question 5: How might I act in response to that event? This question is designed to show what action, if any, the speaker might intend to take, thereby revealing the behavior that could result from the speaker's portrayal of reality.

Question 6: What consequences for my life or for the lives of others could result from my actions? The purpose of this final step is to elicit the speaker's prediction of how the behavior at step 5 might influence his or her own life and the lives of other people.

It should be clear that the aims of this six-step process are (a) to encourage participants to verbalize their beliefs about causes of events, (b) to illustrate how one person's views of reality can differ from another's, (c) to suggest which beliefs are social constructions, shared by members of a cultural group, (d) to reveal how such beliefs may or may not lead to overt behavior, and (e) to identify how that behavior could influence the lives of both the person who held the beliefs and other people in the speaker's life.

PHENOMENOLOGICAL CONSTRUCTIONS OF REALITY

Title: A Phenomenological Anthropology Theory, as presented by Michael Jackson, a professor of anthropology at Indiana University.

Key tenets: Jackson defines his version of phenomenology as:

> the scientific study of experience. It is an attempt to describe human consious-
> ness in its lived immediacy, before it is subject to theoretical elaboration or
> conceptual systematizing. . . . [It consists of] prioritizing lived experience over
> theoretical knowledge. . . . Phenomenology seeks a corrective to forms of
> knowledge and description that, in attempting to isolate unifying and universal
> laws, lose all sense of the abundance and plenitude of life. (Jackson, 1996, pp.
> 2, 6, 7)

As noted in our earlier discussion, a theory of social construction focuses on
the meanings created and shared within a group. In comparison, a phenomenological theory focuses on meanings constructed by the individual person,
resulting in a pattern of mental contents and processes that includes some
meanings that are shared and some that are unique to the individual. Therefore, a
phenomenological theory of cognitive development should account for the
accumulation—or more precisely, the sequential construction—of an individual's
mental contents or meanings as produced by that person's encounters with a day-
by-day succession of social and physical environments. Those meanings
constitute the individual's evolving *lifeworld.*

The goal of phenomenological research is to "disclose the fugitive ways in
which the seemingly fixed forms of custom are actually lived in both consciousness and activity" (Jackson, 1996, p. 11). The researcher thus avoids forcing the
events of people's daily lives into a preconceived theory of cause, such as
offering an estimate of how hereditary and environmental factors have contributed
to or "caused" the event. Instead, the investigator judges the meaning of events
in terms of their consequences by asking: What were the experiencing person's
thoughts and actions that appeared during—or as a result of—those events?

> The phenomenologist suspends inquiry into the hidden determinants of belief
> and action in order to describe the implications, intentions, and effects of what
> people say, do, and hold to be true. (Jackson, 1996, p. 11).

In other words, the phenomenological researcher "follows the data" rather than
using the data to illustrate a theory of what the data might mean. Hence, the
attempt is to understand life from the experiencing person's perspective rather
than from the researcher's vantage point. Therefore, if each person's experiences
are a combination (a) of shared beliefs and actions (cultural learnings) and (b) of
beliefs and actions unique to the individual, then we might assume that the
meanings of life events (in the sense of beliefs and actions resulting from those
events) would be unique to that individual.

At this point we encounter the difficulty (not mentioned by Jackson) of
determining how accurately the researcher has been able to identify and convey
the investigated person's meanings. The question becomes: Does not the
researcher's own perceptual lens, which represents his or her own lifeworld, color

the way he or she reports and interprets someone else's cultural and personal meanings? Some phenomenologists, existentialists, and postmodernists answer *yes,* it does indeed color the report; so they seek to solve the problem by recounting the events of another person's life in that person's own words and actions without adding any of the researcher's interpretation regarding what those words and actions "really mean" (Denzin, 1997; Hammersley, 1992). Such accounts fulfill the aim of phenomenological theory as "detailed descriptions of how people immediately experience space, time, and the world in which they live" (Jackson, 1996, p. 12). In effect, the report depicts the other person's condition "in its lived immediacy, before it is subject to theoretical elaboration or conceptual systematizing." However, in his application of phenomenological theory, Jackson moves beyond description, since he infers generalizations from one or more individuals' experiences. He then submits his inferences as explanations of the beliefs and actions of a class of persons that the observed person seems to represent. For instance, in his study of witchcraft among the Kuranko people of Sierra Leone in West Africa, that class consisted of self-proclaimed witches who were facing imminent death.

> One must consider how the beliefs [in witches] are actually used by the women who confess to witchcraft during terminal illness—as desperate stratagems for reclaiming autonomy in a hopeless situation. The self-confessed witch . . . actively uses the imagery of witchcraft to give voice to long-suppressed grievances, coping with suffering by declaring herself the author of it. . . . Thus, she determines how she will play out the role which circumstance has thrust upon her. She dies deciding her own destiny, sealing her own fate. (Jackson, 1996, pp. 11-12)

In a further example of adding interpretation to description, Jackson asserts that storytelling among the Kuranko serves the function of "reconfiguring" people's perceptions of their lives, thereby enabling them to bear the dilemmas and tensions of their daily existence. However, this interpretation is marred by his admission that "it is difficult to capture the kinds of transformed awareness that storytelling or ritual effects" (Jackson, 1996, p. 21).

Hence, such phenomenological investigators as Jackson are not simply objective recorders of others' experiences. They also function as interpreters, willing to assign meanings that would seem to reflect something of their own worldviews while, at the same time, they attempt to offer explanations that are true to the perspective of the persons they are studying. So Jackson's examples of how to apply phenomenological theory should be seen as descriptions of people's words and actions followed by the researcher's inferences about what those behaviors mean for a given class of people. The inferences are proposals about shared (cultural) meanings, without regard for nuances of meaning that might distinguish one individual from another within that culture. In effect, Jackson's application of phenomenology is designed to identify the cultural (shared) portion of an individual's lifeworld, leaving the uniquely individual portion unexplored.

Finally, given phenomenology's intention of capturing the pattern of experiences of individual persons' lives, the preferred research method becomes a form of ethnography—a report of an individual's life encounters and a portrayal of how those encounters function in that person's daily living. Thus, for achieving the aim of phenomenological theory, such research methods as conducting surveys, polls, historical analyses, or controlled experiments are inappropriate.

Principal variables: Investigations reflecting Jackson's phenomenological perspective derive their nature—that is, their likenesses and differences—from a combination of five variables: (a) the particular culture of the people who have been studied, (b) researchers' methods of collecting evidence (interviews, observations, autobiographies), (c) researchers' ways of reporting results (direct quotations, detailed behavior descriptions, behavior summaries, inferences), (d) the extent to which a report focuses on individuals (revealing both the studied person's shared cultural beliefs and that person's unique beliefs) or focuses on a class of persons (revealing only shared beliefs), and (e) the extent to which investigators offer interpretations of what their data ostensibly mean.

Differences among cultures: What we know about differences among cultures depends on what descriptions of cultures are available to us. This point is readily illustrated with published studies deriving from such a theoretical position as phenomenological theory. Research conducted from a phenomenological viewpoint usually focuses either on (a) a class of people who share cultural beliefs and practices or (b) individual persons who hold both shared and uniquely personal beliefs and practices. Therefore, some studies permit only comparisons across cultures whereas other studies permit comparisons both across cultures and among individuals within cultures.

Focus on cultural meanings. The concern of this kind of investigation is with a culture's modes of promoting cognitive development and with the shared meanings that result from those modes. The following cases illustrate three ways investigators have sought to discover the phenomenological meanings resulting from such modes.

When Devisch (1996) was living among the Yaka people of Southwest Zaire, he sought to understand the shared Yaka lifeview by "intensive participation in the daily life scene and activities of the Yaka. In the village setting, my attempt was to adopt a status of full membership, not that of a visitor or guest" and thereby reveal "the heart and womb of Yaka culture" (Devisch, 1996, pp. 94-95). His investigation focused on Yaka oral lore, kinship structure, hunting practices, the council of elders, divinatory seances, intiatory and healing dramas, and cosmology, thereby permitting a comparison of these phenomena with similar phenomena in other societies. Devisch's account of his research is organized as several generalizations. Here is one: "Village, forest, and savanna, day and night, as well as origin and end are key polar concepts that differentiate between the realms of inhabited and noninhabited space." Devisch proposes that each generalization expresses the essence of a Yaka conception of reality. Each generalization is then detailed with descriptions of Yakas' shared beliefs about the content of the generalization. In effect, the generalizations are inferences that the visiting anthropologist has drawn from participating in village life, proposed as accurate revelations of "major dimensions of Yaka culture accessible within the framework of its own arrangements, within the terms of its own epistemological locus." At the same time, Devisch admits that "my assumptions and questions . . . may sometimes be at odds with those of my hosts" (Devisch, 1996, pp. 94-95). His report contains no direct quotations from the Yaka or descriptions of individuals but, rather, consists entirely of summaries of types of events and group viewpoints.

Focus on meanings constructed by individuals within cultures. Investigations of this type typically draw from autobiographies, biographies, or vignettes in individual people's lives that reveal how they see themselves fitting into the surrounding culture. The following three examples demonstrate how the cluster of principal variables can differ among such studies.

Abu-Lughod's (1996) case of a young Bedouin woman in Egypt uses interviews conducted with the woman along with self-revealing essays she has written to show how she both abides by some traditional expectations of her culture and rebels against others. Abu-Lughod's presentation of the case consists mainly of direct quotations from the young woman, of some behavior summaries by the author, and of relatively few author interpretations.

Another ethnographic study focusing on one girl's words and actions is Herzfeld's (1996) analysis of the tape-recorded public lament voiced by a 15-year-old daughter as she walked in the funeral procession to the burial of her 90-year-old father. The incident, which occurred on the island of Crete, featured the traditional Greek practice of a funeral mourner, enroute to the cemetery, uttering an extemporaneous dirge in poetic meter and imagery, honoring the deceased and decrying the ill fate that is now to be suffered by the living as a result of the loss. In contrast to Abu-Loghod's treatment of the Bedouin case, Herzfeld's consists primarily of his tracing the history of funeral laments, their style and imagery, and with what the girl's elegy possibly revealed about her conception of her social condition and her unstated intentions. In effect, Herzfeld's rendition is short on direct quotations from the lament and long on his interpretation of what the lament implied. For example, in the Cretan male-dominated society,

> She was not only categorically protesting her lot as a woman, she was also protesting, and rejecting, the categorical definition of herself as a woman limited by her gender. . . . [And when she later arranged a marriage for her younger sister,] she had to adopt the social role of a man . . . and took pride in this aspect of her actions. (Herzfeld, 1996, p. 163)

Thus, throughout the case analysis, Herzfeld not only identifies features of traditional culture but also illustrates one girl's method of pursuing her own purposes by acceding to some cultural expectations and deviating from others. Finally, in rationalizing the multitude of underlying meanings that he assigns to the incident of the girl's lament, Herzfeld admits that his account is only one possible interpretation, so it should be considered "suggestive" rather than necessarily correct.

> I have here tried to establish certain connections between a biography and a performance and to suggest that these converge in a symbolic vocabulary that is rich with past communal experience. The links I have advanced, while suggestive, would certainly be very difficult to "prove." That my analysis is provisional respects the uncertainty the mourners themselves experience in interpreting events. (Herzfeld, 1996, p. 164)

A further pattern of principal variables appears in Desjarlais's (1996) portrayal of life in a publicly operated shelter for socially displaced and mentally disturbed homeless adults in Boston. The shelter has its own culture—its defined ways of operating—into which its transient visitors must fit. Desjarlais's account is organized as a series of his interpretations of what shelter life means to its residents, interpretations illustrated liberally with quotations from residents and with Desjarlais's own observations of the occupants' appearance and actions. Thus, the study identifies both cultural themes and differences among individuals in the meanings they construct around those themes. Desjarlais admits that his analysis, like every other investigator's account, is necessarily incomplete, since human experience cannot be fully captured in words. "[Experience] eludes social science analysis and resists symbolization. The import of experience is inexhaustible because experience . . . carries forth a wealth of meanings that can never be conclusively interpreted" (Desjarlais, 1996, p. 74).

Cross-cultural encounters: People can react in diverse ways to the differences between the life view they acquired from their original culture and the life views displayed in cultures with which they come into contact. At one extreme, some individuals will cling tenaciously to their traditional beliefs, condemning the beliefs of other cultures as blatantly false. At the opposite end of the scale, people may gradually abandon their traditional views in favor of those of the newly engaged culture. Or they may pretend to adopt the new culture's notions of reality in order to be accepted by its members, yet at the same time secretly adhere to their inherited conceptions. On the other hand, many will seek to combine elements of their traditional culture with those of the newly encountered society, thereby producing an admixture of cognitions that may be somewhat unstable.

Practical applications: From the vantage point of Jackson's theory, individuals within any culture can suffer personal-social distress as the result of the differences between their own beliefs and the beliefs of people around them.

This is true even when individuals remain in their original culture and subscribe to most aspects of that culture's dominant worldview. That is, each person's genetically based propensities, when combined with an individualized pattern of life experiences, produces a somewhat unique perspective on life. And if anguish can derive from conflicts between personal belief systems even within a familiar culture, that anguish is likely to be far greater when the person interacts with people whose culturally patterned notions of reality are markedly different from his or her own.

Attempts to alleviate such distress frequently take the form of psychotherapy. Hence, this question can be posed: Which of the many available styles of psychotherapy will be most compatible with a phenomenological anthropology conception of reality? An obvious choice would be *client-centered therapy* or *person-centered therapy* as pioneered by Carl Rogers (1951). In his person-centered approach, the task of the counselor is to elicit the client's expression of beliefs and feelings, to listen attentively, to mirror those feelings, to display a nonjudgmental understanding of the client's situation, and to encourage the counselee to move through the steps of analyzing his or her problems, of suggesting solutions, and of appraising the worth of the potential solutions. The therapist allows counselees to select their own life goals, to express any opinions they wish, to generate their own options for action, and to assess their own progress. In a pure form of this approach, therapists do not criticize clients' conceptions of reality, do not furnish information or advice, and do not offer any assessment of the success of the counseling endeavor. Hence, the counselor is expected to display acceptance of the client, genuineness and understanding. Therefore, the therapist serves only as a catalyst that mediates the clients' process of alleviating the distress resulting from cross-cultural engagements (Meador & Rogers, 1979).

Compared to Rogers' client-centered therapy, Albert Ellis's *rational-emotive therapy* would be unsuitable, since its basic tenets are incompatible with Jackson's phenomenological model. From the rational-emotive perspective, the client's problems derive from a faulty conception of reality. Ellis asserts that "people's emotional disturbances and dysfunctional behaviors largely (not completely) stem from their irrational and unrealistic thinking and can be efficiently helped by their making a profound philosophic change." The therapist, in contrast to the client, accurately recognizes reality and is obliged to transmit this conception of life to the client by means of several "cognitive methods—including scientific disputing of irrational ideas, the use of coping statements, cognitive distraction and focusing methods, modeling techniques, semantic procedures, and several psychoeducational techniques" (Ellis, 1985, p. 3139).

DREAMWORK

So far in this chapter, all of the theories have been founded on the assumption that cognition is principally, if not exclusively, a conscious activity—the belief that, in the main, people are quite aware of what they are thinking and can intentionally guide their thoughts. This assumption includes the belief that people's ability to direct their thinking increases over the first two decades of life and continues throughout most, if not all, of adulthood.

However, it is widely recognized that thought can also take place on a subconscious level, traveling through curious byways without the person's supervision. Perhaps the most obvious and intriguing product of such unconscious cognition is the dream. Hence, using dream theory as a lens for viewing people's beliefs and behavior can be useful in showing ways that dreaming is understood in different cultures. The model inspected in the following pages is one proposed by an early colleague of Sigmund Freud, a colleague who departed from the psychoanalytic camp in the early 20th century to launch his own analytical-psychology theory.

Title: Analytical Psychology, as formulated by Carl Jung, whose psychiatric practice was located primarily in Zurich, Switzerland (Campbell, 1971; deLazlo, 1959; Hall & Nordby, 1973; Mattoon, 1981).

Key tenets: The human psyche or personality operates on both conscious and unconscious levels. Jung defined *conscious* as the part of cognition that functions under the control of the ego. *Unconscious* is the remaining part not under ego control. Most mental operations are unconscious and consist of many kinds of contents that can vary from one person to another and from time to time in the same person. Some contents are products of people's individual experiences *(personal unconscious),* some are the result of cultural experiences—events and traditions common to the group—*(cultural unconscious),* while others seem generally held throughout the entire human species (*collective* or *racial unconscious*). Jung derived the evidence to support his collective-unconscious proposal from his own and other people's dreams, visions, and fantasies—with *dreams* defined as images that appear during sleep, *visions* as images appearing spontaneously without conscious intention while the person is awake, and *fantasies* as people's purposely generated images when awake. Jung also believed that certain symbols and *archeypes* found in diverse societies were reflections of unconscious contents held in common throughout humankind. Examples of archetypal images are fairy tales and myths that have almost identical motifs in widely separated cultures.

Jung's writings imply that, with the passing of years, dream images increase in diversity as the person accumulates an increasingly abundant array of experiences and memories.

Principal variables: Three categories of variables important in Jung's dream theory concern (a) the sources of dream content, (b) the nature of symbols, and (c) functions of dreams.

Sources of dream content. Dream images can originate from three main sources—current environmental stimuli, memories from the past, and recent everyday experiences.

Environmental stimuli that impinge on the sleeper can generate dreams designed to rationalize the environment's intrusion into the sleeper's awareness. The noise of wind rattling a door may produce the dream image of a carpenter hammering on a wall or a wolf jumping against a cupboard. An overheated room may induce an image of the person being in a fire or hot shower.

Dreams may also derive from memories of past experiences, such as episodes during childhood that were too painful to retain in conscious memory and were thus repressed into the unconscious. Or the images may be based on experiences that were not important enough to be preserved in active memory but, nevertheless, were of sufficient note to be retained in the unconscious.

A major source of dream images is the complex of recent events in the dreamer's daily life—the illness of a parent, the expense of repairing a washing machine, or the unexpected arrival of a letter from a long-lost friend.

In Jung's opinion, the source of a dream is unimportant. What is significant is the dream's psychic meaning, that is, the function of the dream in the person's life.

Functions of dreams. Jung proposed that dreams reflect people's basic nature, in the sense that "Dreams are impartial, spontaneous products of the unconscious psyche . . . they show us the unvarnished natural truth" (Jung in Hall & Nordby, 1973, p. 118).

Freud contended that the function of dreams is to satisfy the sleeper's unfulfilled wishes. Jung accepted this proposal as accounting for some dreams, but he also contended that many dreams serve to compensate for psychic imbalance. He believed the human personality strives to retain an equilibrium among instincts, self-perception, and environmental reality. When an individual's conscious perception of these matters is distorted, then the unconscious aspect of the psyche seeks to correct the imbalance. Jung explained that:

> I expressly use the word "compensatory" and not "opposed," because conscious and unconscious are not necessarily in opposition to one another, but complement one another to form a totality, which is the *self.* (Jung in deLaszlo, 1959, p. 147)

Dreaming provides the needed correction by either confirmatory or oppositional compensation. In confirmatory compensation, the dream verifies one's conscious view of a life situation—supporting one's impression of reality.

However, far more often the dream counteracts one's distorted conscious perception.

> Some dreams compensate the dreamer's conscious attitude by presenting it in exaggerated form; other dreams deviate only a little from the conscious situation and thus suggest but slight modification. Still others take a view that is generally opposite to consciousness; such dreams occur when the conscious attitude is inadequate or wrong. (Mattoon, 1981, p. 256)

Although most dreams are of a compensatory nature, a few are prospective, traumatic rehearsal, or extrasensory.

A dream interpreted as prospective or anticipatory can guide people to act differently than if the dream had never taken place. In Jung's opinion, this guidance function derives from the fusion of a variety of the dreamer's perceptions, feelings, and thoughts that had resided in the unconscious and now can be useful in directing the individual's conscious decisions.

Traumatic dreams are recollections of actual frightening experiences, such as an attempted rape or a battlefield scene, whose strong emotional residue generates images of the episode that reoccur until the intensity of the distress surrounding the memory diminishes.

Extrasensory dreams have a telepathic/prophetic or clairvoyant function, as in a dream of someone's death prior to the individual's actual demise or a dream about an environmental disaster—flood, volcanic eruption, forest fire—before the disaster occurs.

The nature of symbols. Jung agreed with Freud that:

> Images are the language of dreams [with] grammar unlike that of waking thoughts. The language is likely to be figurative and often fantastic. A dream image may express a thought but rarely directly. (Mattoon, 1981, p. 247)

Whereas Freud said symbols were universal, carrying the same underlying meaning for everyone whose dreams contained those images, Jung thought the symbols in different people's dreams would imply different meanings that depended on each individual's experiences. Whereas any projectile-shaped dream image—such as a tower or carrot—was interpreted by Freud as universally signifying a penis, Jung would seek to learn what such an image meant in the particular dreamer's life. The two theorists' conflicting beliefs about dream symbols become particularly important in the interpretation of the dream contents of people from different cultural contexts. Freud would apply his universal-symbol notion to interpreting dreams from people of all cultural backgrounds, whereas Jung would find it necessary to understand the individual's cultural and personal experiences before estimating the meaning of that person's images.

Jung conceived of two sources of symbols. The most prominent are a person's current and past experiences. Less frequently, symbols originate in the collective unconscious as archetypal signs embedded in the cultural or species unconscious and thus are ones found throughout a cultural group or in all humankind.

Differences among cultures: Two features of Jung's theory that he believed are influenced by culture are dream symbols and functions attributed to dreams.

Kinds of symbols. As a class assignment at Keravat National High School in Papua New Guinea, 17-year-old students (70 boys and 38 girls) wrote essays titled "Recently I Had a Dream." Epstein's (1998) analysis of the essays revealed universal themes of wish fulfillment, such as to gain wealth or fame, that were cast in symbols specific to the students' cultures.

> In many societies of Papua New Guinea wealth in shell-valuables, shell money, or pigs was a sine qua non of leadership. So, for example, when a student from the Western Highlands had a dream about pigs it was, as he acknowledged, a pointer to his political ambitions and his wish to become a "big man." (Epstein, 1998, p. 9)

Epstein also found that dreams reflecting intense anxiety included traditional images of ogres and demons known as *tabaran*—"malevolent beings of fearsome appearance whose domain is bush and forest and to whose attacks human beings are forever vulnerable" (Epstein, 1998, p. 9).

Among the Foi people in the southern highlands of Papua New Guinea, a dream of sexual intercourse is interpreted to mean future success in hunting. Dreaming of a house falling down in disrepair means imminent death, and a dream of red bird feathers means success in acquiring valuable pearl shells (Weiner, 1991, pp. 27-28).

In some cultures, dreams are not regarded as symbolic. What is seen and heard in a dream is accepted as exactly what it appears to be. According to Hallpike (1977), such is the case in the Tauade society of Papua New Guinea. Although the Tauade know that what occurs in dreams does not affect their body, they are convinced that dream events happen to their soul, which has left their body during sleep. Several senses—sight, hearing, touch, pain, smell—may be involved in the experience.

> I was being carried along in a stream, and a bad spirit with a diseased skin seized me and put his hand over my mouth. I bit his arm, so he bit me in return. . . . I ran away and climbed up a tree and sat in the fork and looked down to see if he was following. He was sniffing my tracks like a dog. He went away, and I went back to my place, but he followed me there, and I killed him with my axe. I chopped his body into pieces and flung the bits into the bushes. . . . There was a terrible stink. My bush knife stank. I wiped the knife in the ground to get rid of the blood and the smell. (Hallpike, 1977, p. 262)

Functions attributed to dreams. As explained earlier, Jung proposed five functions of dreams—wish-fulfilling, compensatory, prospective, traumatic-rehearsal, and prophetic. Cultures often differ in (a) which of these roles—or others—are assigned to dreams and (b) the relative importance or frequency of an assumed function.

The Yuma Indians of the Southwestern United States illustrate a culture in which dreams are assumed to play two principal roles; Jung included one of the roles (prophesy) in his theory but not the other (power enhancement). The Yuma have traditionally believed that dreams foretell events and endow the dreamer with extraordinary abilities. Thus, bands of raiders and large war parties were typically led by men who were thought to have derived supernatural powers from their dreams. In many American Indian societies, smoking tobacco by pipe or in the form of cigars has been an integral part of the culture, with medicine men in some tribes imbibing a potent narcotic form of tobacco to generate prophetic visions and dreams (Terrell, 1971, pp. 25, 296).

In Epstein's Papua New Guinea study, animals that often appeared in students' dreams were the cassowary, crocodile, shark, snake, and bats—animals that "all featured prominently in local oral traditions where it is their aggressive proclivities which are emphasized" (Epstein, 1998, p. 10). The function here was not Jung's rehearsal of an actual traumatic episode from the dreamer's waking life but, rather, the function of symbolizing anxiety—reflecting fear based on some unidentified current cause but with the cause disguised as a customary image.

Among the Chikabumi Ainu people of Japan's Hokkaido Island, dreams can furnish advice, notifying people that they should say prayers as offerings for the dead person who appears in a dream or informing them of where to locate a new dwelling (*chisei*).

> A man who was looking for a good place on which to build a *chisei* erected a tripod on some chosen spot and slept under it for one night. He was to dream there. Or he planted an *inau* there and slept at home. If he had no troublesome dream during the following three to five nights, he built his *chisei* on the spot he had chosen. (Hilger, 1971, p. 130)

The Ainu also consider some dreams telepathic, providing news of a crucial event in the life of the dreamer, such as the death of a loved one in an accident.

In the Kaulong society of New Britain Island in the Southwest Pacific, dreams are believed to serve an important educational function. During sleep, the self (soul or psyche) can detach itself from the body and travel about, engaging in new experiences and accumulating new knowledge, thereby promoting the dreamer's development. The dream serves as an image or running record of the journey.

> Normally among adults, such a detached self remains under some degree of control, returning to its usual container at the conclusion of sleep. Certain individuals develop unusual powers of self-control and are able to direct their wandering self in deliberate fashion in order to seek out, discover, see, or hear

that which is desired by the person. Such individuals are often hired to find lost possessions . . . or to spy on the activities of enemies. (Goodale, 1995, p. 39)

Among the Foi of New Guinea, dreaming is seen as a talent or art whose use can be enhanced by fasting and abstaining from sexual intercourse. A person skilled in divining the meaning of dreams becomes privy to the dreams' "hidden prescient messages [that] are sent by ghosts, the disembodied souls of the departed. Dreams are the only way in which the deceased can communicate directly with the living" (Weiner, 1991, p. 2). To illustrate the educational role of dreaming, Weiner (1991, p. 1) tells of the spells that should be uttered during the construction of a Foi men's communal longhouse. Weiner's Foi informant, an elderly scion named Dabura, explained that long ago he had learned the spells from an old man who appeared to him in a dream and who had "assured him he would have a long life. Dabura continued to contact the ghost through dreams over the ensuing years."

In summary, the foregoing examples:

1. Offer support for Jung's rather than Freud's conception of dream symbols. That is, symbols do not have universal meanings across all cultures but, instead, are specific to a given society's traditions or to people's individual experiences.

2. Show that, in regard to the roles that dreams are assumed to play in people's lives, some of Jung's proposed functions are found among the sampled cultures (wish fulfillment, prophecy), but a number of other functions in those cultures were not ones recognized in Jung's theory (educational, informational, advisory, symbolized anxiety, personal power-enhancement). Furthermore, in none of those societies was it assumed that dreams play the compensatory role that Jung postulated as the main function of dreaming.

Cross-cultural encounters: In social intercourse between people from differing cultures, misunderstanding and conflict can result if members of one group act on the basis of convictions about dream symbols and functions that are not shared by members of other cultural groups. In way of illustration, consider the following contrasts in cultural beliefs about dream functions.

Interpersonal difficulties can occur when individuals from a culture that subscribes to an advice function of dreams interact with people from a culture which holds that dream functions are limited to wish fulfillment and anxiety reflection. The behavior of a person who believes in advice that is inferred from dreams may follow such advice when choosing a marriage partner, taking a trip, investing money, buying an automobile, lending money, selecting a vocation, and the like. Those decisions are not likely to sit well with people who reject dreams as proper guides to behavior in real-life situations.

In a similar way, differences between cultures in beliefs about the prophetic function of dreams can also result in interpersonal conflicts. People who believe that dreams of disaster are prophetic will not be disposed to take action to avert the expected calamity because it is accepted as inevitable. In contrast, people who reject the notion of prophetic dreams will be disposed to take action to avoid potential disaster.

Practical applications: As a psychotherapeutic technique to be used with markedly disturbed individuals, or simply as a device for promoting a person's self-understanding, Jung's method of dream interpretation represents one practical use of his theory. Five of the steps in Jungian dream analysis are those of:

1. Describing the dream structure in terms of: (a) the dream's place, its people, and their initial situation, (b) the plot as it advances, (c) a decisive event that causes a significant change, and (d) the final result or solution to the dream problem.
2. Establishing the dream context, including (a) the personal or achetypal associations of the dream images, (b) the dreamer's immediate and long-term conscious beliefs, and (c) the dream series in which this dream occurs.
3. Recognizing that (a) the dream is not a disguise but a set of psychic facts, (b) the personalities of the dreamer and the dream interpreter can affect the interpretation, and (c) the dream probably does not tell the dreamer what to do.
4. Estimating whether the dream is compensatory, prospective, traumatic rehearsal, or telepathic/prophetic.
5. Testing the reasonableness of the interpretation by reviewing the dream facts, by the dreamer's immediate response (confirming or not confirming the interpretation), and by subsequent events. (condensed from Mattoon, 1981, p. 265)

In applying this five-step formula, the analyst need not be restricted to the dream functions that Jung included in his theory. Rather, other functions appropriate to the dreamer's own cultural background can profitably be employed as well.

SUMMARY

The substance of this chapter can be summarized in relation to the role assigned to culture in each of the six models.

Although Piaget primarily credited the child's inherited genetic time clock for determining both the pace and the extent of intellectual development, he did recognize a dual role for the environment. In his view, when internal maturation readies the child to achieve a further intellectual advance, the potential that such internal growth provides can only be realized by means of the child's interacting with the world. The initial stage of that interaction consists of children drawing conclusions—extracting lessons—through their own unguided observations of the world about them. The second stage, which requires the first as a foundation, consists of children advancing intellectually by means of instruction, in the sense of formal and informal education.

During the early decades of his studies, Piaget appeared to ignore the influence that differences between cultures exerted on mental development. Perhaps he assumed that the aspects of culture that significantly affect intelligence are common to all cultures. However, as critics have since pointed out, such an assumption is ill founded. In his later years, Piaget did admit some influence of variations in environments, but still considered genetically controlled maturation to be the primary force behind mental development.

In contrast to Piaget's scheme, Vygotsky's model—in keeping with Marxist social philosophy—assigns a society's historically fashioned culture a far stronger role in determining people's cognitive styles and the contents of their minds. According to Vygotsky, the way children learn to think is to a great extent acquired from the way they are taught by their elders, who have already been enculturated into the patterns of thought of their particular society.

D'Andrade's social-construction view of cognitive development is more compatible with Vygotsky's model than with Piaget's, since D'Andrade envisions people's dominant modes of thought as products of the ways of thinking shared throughout a culture, ways that are continually modeled by the adults and taught to the young.

Gardner, in his frames-of-mind theory, has assumed that the potential for developing all seven of his types of intelligence is shared throughout humankind. He also has assumed that some individuals' genetic inheritance equips them with greater potential than other individuals for developing certain of the seven types. However, the extent to which any given type actually will be realized in a person's life depends on whether and how that type is nurtured. Thus, differences in the typical patterns of intelligence from one culture to another can be expected if certain kinds are emphasized and practiced more often in one culture than in another.

Jackson's phenomenological model emphasizes the individualized modes of thought that people develop from a combination of culturally shared ways of knowing and idiosyncratic ways that are unique to a particular person. Therefore, whereas culture is an important formulator of people's cognitive styles and the contents of their minds, it is not the only formulator. Because it is difficult, if not impossible, for one person to comprehend the idiosyncratic aspects of another person's mental operations, the only aspects that other members of a culture can readily understand are the culturally shared features. The task of discerning how someone else thinks is even more daunting for people who lack an intimate knowledge of that someone's culture.

In Jung's theory of dreams, culture contributes to dreaming in two main ways. First, long-established cultural symbols ostensibly become embedded in people's genetic structures so that individuals can inherit cultural meanings in the form of a cultural unconscious. Second, daily cultural experiences that are accompanied by strong emotion—fear, guilt, anxiety, shame—can generate dreams that perform such functions as compensation and traumatic rehearsal.

3

Learning

The concept *learning*, in its broadest sense, can be defined as "the process of acquiring knowledge and new behaviors as a result of encounters with the environment." Therefore, to qualify as a product of learning, what people know and are able to do must have been acquired through daily experiences rather than simply through changes within their bodies that have been determined by genetic factors. Although the genetically designed internal maturation of the body—and particularly of the nervous system—provides a necessary foundation for learning at progressive stages of a person's life, gaining knowledge and new behaviors still requires transactions with environments. Because environments are heavy laden with cultural elements, culture exerts a great influence over what people learn.

It is true, of course, that creative learning can involve a person manipulating ideas and information that are already in mind, that is, manipulating memories to produce novel insights without the need for new input from environments. Because those memories are products of the person's earlier engagements with environments, my definition of learning as a process requiring environmental encounters still holds true.

Learning, like cognition, is an extremely complex activity that has not been represented completely by any single theory. Consequently, diverse theories have been created to illuminate different aspects of the learning process and thereby serve as alternative windows on cultural influences, as illustrated by this chapter's five models. The first four models are organized in terms of four steps in the learning process, with each theory treating a different step: (a) *attention*—the act of focusing on some aspect of the environment, (b) *perception*—interpreting what that aspect means, (c) *imitating models*—copying the behavior of someone else, and (d) *consequences of actions*—experiencing the outcomes of behavior as either reward or punishment. The chapter's fifth theory, an attempt to explain autism, is an example of learning gone wrong.

THE FOCUS OF ATTENTION

Title: Attention Theory, as formulated by Eleanor Gibson, a professor at Cornell University.

Key tenets: *Attending* means "perceiving in relation to a task or goal, internally or externally motivated. To be described as attending, a person must be set to do something, be motivated to perform a task or to achieve some end" (Gibson & Rader, 1990, p. 2).

Three types of attention can be labeled *captured/involuntary, self-directed-voluntary*, and *other-directed*. The first type consists of a person's awareness being attracted by salient stimuli in the environment. A curious noise or strange sight lures the person's mind from what he or she was thinking about at the time. Advertisers depend on captured/involuntary attention techniques as means of forcing or enticing potential customers to notice their products.

The second type—self-directed, voluntary attention—derives from individuals' concerns and needs at the moment.   Attention is self-directed when people purposely center their awareness on certain aspects of the environment in preference to other aspects. The hungry child interrupts her doll play to seek out the cookie jar. The teenager, stranded at school after football practice, hunts for a telephone to ask his parents for a ride home.

The third type, other-directed, is found chiefly in child-rearing and educational settings in which learners are obliged to heed what the instructor intends to communicate—either personally or in the form of reading matter, tape recordings, motion pictures, or computer programs.

> Good attention refers to perception that meshes with performance by efficiently picking up the information that has utility for a particular task. . . . Developmentally, attention changes toward greater specificity of correspondence between information pickup and utility of that information (one learns to perceive affordances—[useful objects and techniques]—and to define tasks); and developmentally, attention tends toward economy. As affordances for action are perceived more efficiently, the perceiver's task can become more complex, more information can be picked up, and superficially speaking, the "span" of attention increases. (Gibson & Rader, 1990, p. 8).

In the process of growing up, children develop knowledge structures in the form of mentally organized beliefs that are strongly influenced by direct experience and education. With the gradual accumulation of beliefs about which causal factors produce which effects in the world, children's attention becomes more specifically directed.   Hence, development equips children with more precise expectations about which features of the environment will be most useful for accomplishing the task at hand.

Not only does specificity of expectation improve with experience, but so also does flexibility of choice, in the sense of the child's recognizing a greater variety of ways (affordances) for accomplishing a task. When motivated by a desire to perform a given activity, a teenager will attend to more alternative affordances than will a toddler.

A further aspect of attention is preparedness. People can be more attentive if they know what to expect and thus what to look for. As the young develop, they acquire more knowledge, organize it in terms of what they already know, and add it to their increasingly systematized cognitive filing system, that is, to their long-term memory. This means that with the passing of time individuals become more adept at expecting which sorts of things in their environment or in memory will be most useful in performing a given task.

Principal variables: Two general categories of variables important in attention theory are (a) tasks that people are motivated to perform and (b) objects and methods useful for accomplishing tasks. But it is not enough to know only kinds of tasks or goals to pursue and kinds of objects and activities. As a third category, it is also necessary (c) to identify which activities and objects are most effective for achieving which goals. Therefore, to identify which things deserve attention, people need to know the degree of causal correlation between particular objects or events and particular tasks or goals. This knowledge enables them to answer the question: "If I want to accomplish this particular end, to which things should I direct my attention?"

As children mature, their pool of specific items in each of these three categories increases, and the relationships among them assume more complex patterns. Therefore, if children's caregivers are to be successful in efficiently directing a child's attention at successive levels of maturity, they need an understanding of the capacity for attention in individuals' development.

Differences among cultures: Cultures can vary markedly in the contents of each of the principal factors because of cultural differences in (a) the dominant goals pursued in different societies, (b) the objects and activities commonly employed in pursuing such goals, and (c) beliefs about cause—that is, beliefs about which activities are most appropriate for reaching which goals. Cultures can also vary in (d) people's notions of when to offer instruction to the developing child. The following examples illustrate such differences in representative societies.

Dominant goals pursued. The goals that guide people's attention can be captured/involuntary, self-directed, or other-directed. From the viewpoint of culture, the most significant goals are the *other-directed* varieties. *Self-directed* goals, while still influenced by culture, are more likely to be idiosyncratic—more specific to the individual.

One way to view the influence of culture on goals involves dividing goals into *basic* and *adopted* types. Basic goals are intentions (needs, drives) common to virtually all humans. Adopted goals, on the other hand, are more specific aims whose fulfillment contributes to achieving basic goals. To illustrate, two typical basic goals are those of gaining prestige and of becoming freed from physical and psychological pain or disability. Cultures can differ in their preferred ways of achieving such outcomes.   Those preferred ways are the culture's adopted goals.   For instance, in present-day America, greater prestige accrues to young women who are slim than to ones whose bodies are bulky. Thus, the adopted goal of many American females is to become slimmer, so they concentrate on diet and exercise.   In contrast, conventional Hawaiian and Samoan cultures have accorded prestige to women whose bodies are well filled out.   Since becoming slim is not a traditional Hawaiian or Samoan women's aim, they pay little or no attention to fat-free foods and aerobics.

In people's pursuit of freedom from pain, cultures can vary in the adopted goals worth individuals' attention.   In European societies influenced by psycho-analytic theory, a young man who displays extreme fear of open spaces can be diagnosed as suffering from agoraphobia caused by his having being abandoned by his caretakers in early childhood.   His therapist focuses attention on the man's recovering the repressed memories of that early experience so the patient can intellectually and emotionally relive the experience in a constructive light and thereby dispel the phobia.   However, the same fear in a member of an Amazonian tribe in South America can be diagnosed as the result of either (a) the soul of the patient having been carried off by spirits or (b) a magical object having been introduced into the victim's body.   In the case of the former cause, the tribal shaman's adopted goal is to recover the soul by exiting from his own body and entering the underworld in search of the abductor.   Specifically, in Ainaye Indian culture the shaman goes to the land of the dead people who are thereby stricken with panic and flee, enabling the shaman to capture the patient's soul and bring it back to the body (Eliade, 1964, p. 327).   In this instance, attention has focused on events in a supernatural world that can be seen only by the tribal healer.

Activities for achieving goals. People who have identical adopted goals are often obliged to engage in quite different goal-fulfilling activities as a result of their contrasting cultural environments.   Consider the same adopted goal held by two 23-year-old bilingual primary-school teachers during the mid-1970s.   One teacher lived in an American metropolis (Los Angeles), the other in an Indonesian village (Situ Raja) in the hills of West Java (Thomas, Hanafiah, Sumantri, Sudiadi, & Shiflett, 1975).   Note how these two cultural contexts influenced the activities on which the women focused attention as they pursued the same goal—that of teaching their pupils in a manner that enabled each child to achieve his or her academic potential.

The American teacher's third-graders came from diverse ethnic backgrounds. Among them were several children recently arrived from Mexico with a meager command of English, thereby obligating the teacher to offer instruction in a combination of English and Spanish.   Because in Situ Raja everyone was of Sundanese ethnic origin, all of the third-graders spoke the Sundanese language at home.   But since the third grade in Indonesian schools is a time of transition from local dialects to the country's national language (Bahasa Indonesia), the teacher needed to use a combination of Sundanese and Bahasa Indonesia. Consequently, to achieve their goal of providing understandable instruction, both teachers were obliged to focus attention on a pair of languages, but the languages differed from one culture to the other.

In aspects of teaching other than language, the aim of providing quality instruction in the two third-grade classrooms required attention to quite different matters because of the material culture in the two settings. The American class was well supplied with learning materials—textbooks; a classroom library; weekly newspapers for children; radios and television sets for each classroom; and a variety of posters, maps, and charts. Therefore, much of the teacher's attention concentrated on showing the 25 pupils how to use the materials in individualized learning activities. However, in Situ Raja the third graders had only three reading textbooks to be shared by the 39 pupils, so they took turns reading aloud to their classmates. Arithmetic lessons had to be taught with problems the teacher wrote on the blackboard. And because there was no electricity available in the village and thus no lights in the schoolroom, on cloudy days pupils had difficulty seeing the problems. Therefore, the teacher's attention during much of the school day focused on lecturing—orally furnishing information that the children were expected to memorize—and on disciplining inattentive class members.

How well students achieve the goal of academic success can also be affected by the culture's dominant child-rearing activities prior the child's entering school. For example, throughout North America, Native-American children have been consistently less successful in academic achievement than children of other ethnic groups. Some observers have proposed that such substandard performances result from Indian and Inuit children's entering school poorly prepared intellectually for academic success, either because of inferior genetic inheritance or unfavorable experiences during early childhood. However, the assumption that such children bring inferior analytic intelligence to the formal school setting has been cast in doubt by a study of Inuit children (kindergarten through Grade 2) in the Nunavik community of Canada's Arctic region. When tested for analytic intelligence with the internationally popular nonverbal Raven Coloured Progressive Matrices, Inuits scored at or above the norms for other North American ethnic groups (Wright, Taylor, & Ruggiero, 1996). One explanation of this admirable performance comes from Berry's (1971) ecological model, which proposes that certain features of the environment, such as the Arctic context and Inuits' cultural activities, foster the development of highly acute spatial and visual skills. From a young age, Inuit children join their elders in hunting and traveling about the region. Such hunting and navigating activities in an Arctic setting are seen as intimately linked to the intellectual skills of recalling visual patterns and judging spatial relationships. Hence, according to Berry's model, prior to entering school, Inuit children will have learned to pay careful attention to visual features of their environment and thus be able to score well on the Raven matrices.

The complex features of an environment that can require attention can be illustrated by the search skills that must be learned by the successful hunter in the Miyanmin culture of New Guinea. In a single day, a lone man, accompanied by his dog, can explore 10 to 15 miles of rough, untracked, steep terrain, seeking out edible land animals and birds.

> [The hunter] searches the ground for spoor, food remains, feces, wallows, nests, and disturbances indicating a burrow. The trunks of standing trees are examined for claw marks. Tracks may be followed and feces examined for information about the immediate diet and feeding places of the animal. Fruit-bearing trees and shrubs are also sought out and those close to fruiting are noted for such future action as the building of a ground blind or arboreal hide, or a moonlit ambush. At the same time the stalker is alert to movement in the undergrowth and the canopy of the forest, listens for calls, and is ready to be distracted long enough to stalk a single lizard or small bird. (Morren, 1986, p. 120)

A city dweller, lacking the attention training of the Miyanmin hunter, could hardly hope to thrive in such a setting.

Beliefs about causal relations. The term *causal relations* refers to people's opinions about what conditions will produce a particular outcome. Or, stated as a question: Which causes generate which effects? Here are six such beliefs:

> When atmospheric temperature descends below zero degree centigrade, water changes into ice.
> A democratic form of government in which all citizens have the vote results in the best kind of life for the majority of the people.
> Spare the rod and spoil the child.
> Kindly, obedient children are ones raised with lots of love.
> People's thoughts are the result of electrochemical interactions among billions of brain cells.
> An omnipotent God created the universe.

An important function of any society's formal and informal education procedures is to disseminate throughout the populace the convictions about cause and effect that are components of the culture. In at least two ways, these beliefs influence how people direct their attention.

First, when an event occurs, people typically ask what caused it. For most events, the culture provides an answer, and that answer directs a person's attention to the feature of life believed to be the cause. When water changes to ice, attention focuses on a decrease in temperature. When people display irrational thought processes, attention focuses on brain chemistry.

Second, if the event—as an outcome—is one that a person would like to change, then attention is directed to the condition that tradition teaches as the way to alter such a cause. Thus, from one cultural perspective, a fractious child can be rendered biddable by applications of the rod. Or, from a contrasting perspective, treating fractious children with love and tenderness is the way to render them amiable and obedient.

The ways cultural beliefs about cause influence which phenomena attract people's attention can be illustrated with examples from Bene Nsamba and Zulu traditions.

Religious explanations of cause often derive from people's inability to identify mundane explanations of events, particularly of unwelcome events. In the absence of readily apparent causes, supernatural spirits or conditions are postulated as causes, thereby satisfying the human desire to account for why things occur as they do. Consequently, at times of crisis, people's attention often focuses on imagined supernatural forces. Booth (1936) has described this phenomenon among the Bene Nsamba of what was then the Congo/Belgian Congo (today the Democratic Republic of the Congo).

> The Bene Nsamba find themselves surrounded by too many troubles. There are pain, sickness, and death. The crops fail. The hunt is not successful. Other people are hostile. There is so much to fear. In religion they seek the help of unseen forces in averting or overcoming these calamities. . . . Causes are not evident for the effects which are seen. Religion gives courage to face these unknown mysteries. . . . To the Bene Nsamba, religion is a means of getting what they want. In groups, the people ask the Spirits for victory in conflict, for rain, for fertility in land and animals, for salvation from diseases and wild beasts. . . . As individuals they seek boons from the Spirits in deliverance from all sorts of ills and in success in every imaginable kind of venture. (Booth, 1936, pp. 40, 42)

Zulu culture in South Africa envisions an unbroken continuity between people currently alive and the spirits of departed senior relatives, especially of relatives who were held in high esteem when on earth. It is therefore important for the living to refer frequently to such revered progenitors and make them feel that they are a continuing part of the family and clan. Such continuing recognition is important, because if the ancestral spirits are displeased, they may turn their backs on the living in times of crisis and cause misfortunes—illness, drought, hostility within the community, and more. Therefore, the attention of the living is periodically directed toward placating the departed by means of sacred rituals (M'Timkulu, 1977).

How and when to teach children. Alan Howard's comparison of parents in the United States and in Rotuma (a South-Central Pacific island north of Fiji) led him to conclude that Americans and Rotumans have different ideas about how to direct young children's attention to new learnings. Howard concluded that Rotumans, more often than Americans, depend on children's *captured /involuntary* and *self-directed/voluntary* interests as guides to when the young are ready to be taught a given skill or bit of knowledge.

[Rotuman parents] seemed to have a natural sense of a developing child's curiosity, and they taught him things after his attention had determined the focus. It was as if they did not want to intrude on their children any more than was necessary for socialization, but were prepared to provide information at the child's discretion—in contrast to American parents, who seem to feel that knowledge is something like medicine—it's good for the child and must be crammed down his throat even if he does not like it. (Howard, 1970, p. 37)

Cross-cultural encounters: Among a variety of results of cross-cultural encounters, two that attract widespread interest involve language usage and political aims.

Language usage. The mistakes people make while learning an unfamiliar language are often the result of their failing to pay attention to factors significant in speaking the new language correctly but not significant in using their native tongue.   A Frenchman eating rice in a Malaysian restaurant hears that the Malaysian word for rice is *nasi.* But he later misuses *nasi* by applying the term to rice growing in a field.   This is because he had not attended to the fact that, unlike the French, Malaysians apply different words to rice in its different states and locations.   Rice is *padi* in the field, *beras* in the market, and *nasi* on the table.

A Spaniard newly introduced to English may say "a ranch large" because her attention has not been drawn to the fact that, contrary to Spanish usage in which *rancho grande* would be correct, the English language generally locates adjectives in front of, rather than behind, the nouns they modify.

A German conducting research on the island of Java may understand that the Javanese language is socially stratified, with different vocabulary and grammar used by an upper-class person when speaking to a peer than when addressing someone of lower status, and vice versa.   However, the German may not know how to distinguish the social status of one person from that of another and therefore may behave in a manner quite inappropriate to the people he meets. The difficulty lies in his not attending to the significant clues of status in Javanese culture.

Political aims. Conflicts can occur within a society when competing cultural groups adopt political agendas that influence the kinds of research and opinion to which they turn their attention.   A case in point is the controversy in U.S. American society about which factors influence people's intelligence-test scores. Results of testing programs have shown that certain ethnic groups earn higher average scores on traditional measures of general intelligence that do other ethnic groups.   For example, on the average, youths of European ancestry achieve higher scores than do youths of African American and Latin American heritage, whereas youths of East Asian ancestry achieve higher scores than youths from European backgrounds. In an effort to explain these differences, observers from European backgrounds often assert or imply that the chief cause is genetic inheritance—that the Anglo European gene pool equips children with greater general intellectual capacity than does the gene pool from which African-Americans and Latin-Americans draw their potential. In keeping with this viewpoint, such people tend to focus on genetic research (Hernstein & Murray, 1994; Jensen, 1972, 1973). In contrast, defenders of African American and Latin American interests usually reject a genetic-inferiority interpretation and contend, instead, that social disadvantage (cultural deficit) is the cause of the lower average scores received by African Americans and Latin Americans. To support their position, they focus primary attention on sociological studies and interpretations (Garcia Coll, et al., 1996; Ogbu, 1994).

Practical applications. The suggestion offered here for applying attention theory is founded on the following conviction: The scope of what people learn from events is expanded whenever they are obliged to focus their attention on aspects of events that they would not naturally see or hear. The word *naturally* in this context refers to a person's habit of what to look for in a given situation. This application proposes substituting a form of *other-directed* attention for someone's established form of *self-directed-voluntary* attention. The technique consists of the familiar teaching device of posing attention-directing tasks for the learner, tasks that serve to elucidate aspects of the environment that the learner would not usually notice. Here are examples from the realms of speech, navigation, and baseball.

An English visitor in Spain attempted to speak the Spanish language that he had learned in secondary school, but he failed to trill the double *r's* in such words as *perro, correo,* and *tierra.* To help him acquire this skill, a Spanish companion focused the Englishman's attention on how to place his tongue and how to expel his breath so as to enunciate the double *r's* properly.

Passengers in a Polynesian outrigger canoe can be mystified by the boatman's ability to navigate accurately beyond the sight of land and without the aid of such instruments as a compass or a sextant. The mystery is solved when the boatman describes the types of waves, currents, winds, and objects in the water and sky from which he draws clues when guiding his vessel from one island to another.

Foreign spectators at baseball games appear to attend almost exclusively to where the ball is at the moment, thereby missing nuances of the game that can significantly affect the outcome. One way to expand a spectator's purview is to pose such tasks as this: Watch the runner on second base to see how the locations of the shortstop and second baseman influence the amount of lead the runner takes from the base.

CYCLES OF OBSERVING AND ACTING

Title: A Theory of Perceptual Learning, as devised by James J. Gibson (1979) and Eleanor Gibson (1997), a husband and wife team at Cornell University.

Key tenets: The word *perception* refers to the process of interpreting sensory information—of picking up information (through seeing, hearing, touching) and making sense out of it (Gibson, 1997).

Three concepts central to the Gibsons' theory are *tasks, reciprocity,* and *affordance.*

Tasks are goal-directed behaviors that can be either overt (outwardly observable actions) or covert (mental acts). Individuals' daily lives consist of tasks whose performance influences their development.

Reciprocity assumes two forms—child/environment and perception/action. The term *child/environment reciprocity* refers to the way children's interpretation of their physical and social environments is a result of the mutual influence between a child's present developmental state and the immediate surroundings. The term *perception/action reciprocity* refers to progressive cycles of perceiving (getting information) and acting. The child perceives an environment, then acts on that perception. The action serves to confirm or disconfirm the original interpretation, either strengthening or altering the interpretation and thereby influencing successive perceptions that are then also assessed through the child's subsequent actions. This perception/action process, played over and over, constitutes development.

> Perception obtains information for action, and action has consequences that inform perception about both the organism [child] itself and the events that it perpetrates. Perception, which has the function of obtaining information, is active and exploratory. Action is both exploratory and performatory: exploratory in the sense of foraging for information and performatory in the sense of controlling environmental consequences. (Gibson, 1997, p. 25)

In effect, people do not act on the basis of objective reality, that is, on the grounds of what their physical and social environments are "really like." Instead, they act on their perception of their environments, on their interpretation of what the environments "seem to be like."

Affordance means the fit or match of a child's perceptual state and an environment, a relationship in which the child has the equipment and ability to take advantage of the opportunities the environment offers. Those features of a context that serve as opportunities for one child will not represent the same opportunities for another child who has different goals and abilities. Therefore, an affordance is

> the possibility for action on the part of an actor in an environment. The constraints of the actor and the constraints of the environment mutually contribute to such possibilities for action. . . . Accordingly, perception of the environment is necessarily perception of the self. In the course of development, perceivers tune their actions by differentiating the information that is relevant in the environment for the purpose of some action or activity. . . . Action is

guided by perception and action over time informs perception. (Tudge, Gray, & Hogan, 1997, pp. 79-89)

Children's daily lives can be seen as an ever-shifting kaleidoscope of child-and-context engagements. A child's state of development is never static but always undergoing some degree of change.

Principal variables: Five factors that influence development from the viewpoint of the Gibsons' theory are (a) the child's present state of development (interests/goals and abilities), (b) the environments the child encounters, (c) the affordances offered by the child's engagements with those environments, (d) the child's perception of those affordances, and (e) the child's actions in response to such perceptions.

Differences among cultures: As explained above, affordances are environmental conditions that people interpret as opportunities for achieving goals—in other words, opportunities for satisfying needs. Societies can differ in both (a) the kinds of physical and social environments they offer and (b) the methods of using such environments that are culturally approved. Cultural differences can be illustrated with examples relating to people's pursuit of two kinds of goals, those of sex-drive release and occupational choice.

Sex-drive release. Achieving the aim of sex-drive release requires a person to decide how best to satisfy sexual needs without suffering undesired consequences. The task of identifying suitable sex-drive affordances can involve a complex perceptual process in which a variety of considerations participate, including (a) the developmental state of the individual at the time he or she is scanning the environment, (b) kinds of available people or objects that might provide sex-drive satisfaction, (c) approved conditions of sexual activity, (d) suitable methods of employing people and objects, and (e) consequences to be expected from such methods. Cultures can differ in each of these features.

Developmental state. Factors influencing a person's developmental readiness to seek sexual expression include (a) the maturation condition of the person's sex organs and glandular system and (b) present and past encounters with physical sexual stimulation and with titillating visual and auditory images. Both of these factors can be influenced by cultural traditions. An example of culture affecting the condition of the sex organs is the tradition of female circumcision as widely practiced in the Middle East and North and Central Africa. According to Ciaccio and El Shakry (1993), the intent of removing part or all of a girl's clitoris and labia is to preserve female premarital virginity and chastity during marriage.

Circumcision is believed to protect women from "losing their honor" by quelling their incipient sexual desires. . . . Women are not expected to derive pleasure from sex; in fact, they are often physically prohibited from doing so. They are socialized to believe that their sexuality is something to be ashamed of and hidden. Indeed, this view is reinforced constantly throughout the childhood of females and is epitomized by circumcision. . . . Female circumcision still exists in Egyptian society despite governmental decrees. According to conservative figures, 75 percent of Egyptian women are circumcised. This figure may be as high as 98 percent among the lower rural classes. (Ciaccio & El Shakry, 1993, pp. 49-50)

As for titillating images, cultures vary in the opportunities they offer the young to witness sexual activities and their descriptions. Children whose entire family inhabits a one-room structure are liable, from their earliest years, to witness adults engaging in sexual foreplay and copulation. In more advanced industrialized societies, an increasing range of sexual scenes and descriptions has become available to the young on television and computer networks.

Objects of sex-drive satisfaction. Either by written law or by custom, cultures dictate (a) which affordances are acceptable and which are unacceptable for satisfying sexual appetites and (b) consequences to be expected for abiding by or violating those dictates. For instance, Jewish law, as portrayed in the holy scriptures (the *Torah*), specifies *shoulds* and *should nots* among potential sex-drive affordances. The single *should* is copulation involving husband and wife. The multiple *should nots* include copulating with: persons of one's own sex, other men's wives, animals, menstruating women, one's mother, one's father's wife, one's son's daughter, a woman and her daughter, one's father's sister, or any other kinswoman (Maimonides, 1967). Transgressors can expect to be punished with immediate sanctions applied by the clergy or by the government and with eternal sanctions applied by God after the offenders' earthly demise.

In contrast to Jewish law's forbidding copulation between persons of the same sex, a variety of cultures approve of homosexuality. For instance, Denmark and Sweden have laws in which the same-sex partners enjoy property and inheritance rights, a policy that gay- and lesbian-rights activists in the United States have urged state governments to adopt (Belser & Clark, 1992).

Centuries-old controversy continues in many cultures over the issue of prostitution. Should people who provide sex-for-pay be acceptable objects of sex-drive satisfaction? Some societies openly accept prostitution by not having legislation designed either to eliminate or control prostitutes. Others seek to regulate the practice by licensing prostitutes, requiring them to have periodic health examinations, and prosecuting those who violate the licensing rules. Such a law legalizing sex-for-sale in Thailand was enacted in 1992 with the proviso that women could become licensed prostitutes only at age 18 or above, although many girls at ages 13 and 14 were already in the trade ("Thailand: Sense About Sex," 1992). Subsequently, Thailand's 1996 Prostitution Act stipulated that people paying for sex with children under age 15 could be jailed for up to 6 years and fined up to $4,800. However, the law was seldom implemented ("Thailand: Women and the Law," 1997).

Still other societies pass laws prohibiting prostitution but they neglect to enforce the laws, so that prostitution continues to be widely practiced. An example is Japan, where "sex and sexual relations are not viewed as moral issues as they often are in Western countries, and in the United States in particular. Rather, sex is viewed as a natural phenomenon, like eating, to be enjoyed in its proper place" (Morrison, 1998, p. 8). In keeping with this tradition, until the mid-1950s the government licensed prostitutes. But in 1956 social reformers, led by women members of the national legislature (the Diet), forced the abolition of licensed prostitution and passed the Prostitution Prevention Law.

> Notwithstanding the Antiprostitution Law, prostitution in Japan is a well-established industry, accepted as a fact of life by most Japanese, including the police. While exact numbers are not available, estimates indicate that as many as 300,000 women work in the prostitution industry nationwide . . . primarily in the same locations as before passage of the Antiprostitution Law. (Morrison, 1998, p. 8)

Approved conditions. Cultures do not all concur about the circumstances under which sexual intercourse can properly take place. Two conditions that are often the source of disagreement are those of age and marital status of the participants.

Gress-Wright addressed both age and marital status in the contrast she drew between Sweden and the United States in the two cultures' views of teenage sex behavior.

> In 1974, the Swedish sex-education curriculum was officially revised, [thereby eliminating] "the general recommendation of restraint when young." The curricular reform commission, accommodating and encouraging changes already taking place in popular opinion, directed that teachers emphasize to students that sex is natural; that a person without a developed sexuality is deficient; that premarital sex is to be expected; that cohabitation and childbearing outside of marriage are acceptable; and that even adultery is tolerable. The new curriculum constituted a decisive repudiation of all Judeo-Christian teaching on sex. (Gress-Wright, 1993, p. 17)

In such a cultural climate, the rates of teenage pregnancy and abortion are lower than in the United States and Great Britain, an outcome that Gress-Wright traces partly to "continued cultural ambivalence about chastity, childbearing, and working [in the U.S. and U.K.]. . . . Black and white [American teens] are both too liberated—they have sex—and not liberated enough—they don't use contraceptives. Those who make policy must decide whether the conservative approach—abstinence—or the liberal approach—providing contraceptives—is more desirable in the local context" (Gress-Wright, 1993, p. 25).

The difficulty within a culture of determining acceptable ages for sex partners is illustrated in the application of statutory-rape laws in the United States. The term *statutory rape* refers to sexual intercourse between an adult and a minor, usually an adult male and a young girl. All 50 U.S. states have statutory rape laws on their books. In most states, the "age of consent" that defines minority status has been 18 years, though in some states it is 16. Thus, a 20-year-old male who copulates with a female under "the age of consent" is guilty of statutory rape, whether or not the female willingly agreed to the act. In the past, few states bothered to prosecute such incidents. However, when welfare-reform laws were passed in the mid-1990s, the federal government urged states to bring such cases to trial, in the hope of deterring teenage girls and their partners from engaging in intercourse, thereby reducing the incidence of teenage pregnancies. In California, between 1995 and 1998, 1,454 offenders were prosecuted and 5,000 additional cases were under investigation. The typical ages of the individuals in such cases was illustrated in San Diego County where the males averaged 25.7 years and females 14.4 years (Lynch, 1998). In an effort to express a current American-culture view of this problem, Lynch wrote:

> Few people would place a consensual relationship between a 17-year-old girl and a 19-year-old boy in this [criminal-statutory-rape] category, and any laws that attempt to do so will surely languish in the same disuse that marked the statutory rape legislation for many years. But nearly everyone would place a relationship between a 13-year-old girl and a 20-year-old man in the criminal category. Thus the debate is over where to draw the line and what to do once the line is drawn, not whether to draw it in the first place. (Lynch, 1998, p. 16)

Cultures often hold contrasting standards for males than for females, with the standards applied differently before than after marriage.

> Before marriage, Japanese men freely engage in premarital sex, whereas women may do so but must be discreet. This phenomenon is described as *honne* (true situation) and *tatemae* (front). The *honne* is that young women do have premarital sex, and the *tatemae* is that neither they nor their families admit this. Once a couple is married, the sexual double standard becomes more entrenched. Women are expected to remain faithful to their husbands regardless of their husbands' behavior. In contrast, men are given far more sexual freedom. (Morrison, 1998, p. 8)

Cultures may also fail to agree on the conditions under which sexual matters can properly be discussed. This issue is perhaps most clearly displayed in various societies' attitudes toward sex education. Sweden and Denmark are alike in the openness of their sex-education policies in the schools, policies intended to encourage sexual pleasure for youths and, at the same time, protect their health, educational, and social welfare. Obligatory sex-education classes in Belgium and the Netherlands also promote open discussion of sexual issues, with the key aim being that of preventing teenage pregnancy (Friedman, 1992). Before the dissolution of the Soviet Union, any sex education that was offered focused exclusively on the biology of the human reproductive system. However, during the 1990s, classes that focused on personal and social concerns gained ground, with the educational program of the Russian Sexology Association including 238 classroom hours of sex education in Grades 5 through 11 (Popova, 1996).

Methods of sexual satisfaction. The types of sex acts regarded as admissible can also vary across cultures. In Malaysia, sodomy is punishable by up to 20 years in prison and lashes with a whip ("Ousted Official," 1998). In contrast, under the penal code of the State of California, neither sodomy or nor oral copulation between consenting adults is unlawful, although sodomy or oral copulation by an adult with a child or with anyone intoxicated or under threat of harm is punishable by several years in prison (Calligan, 1992, pp. 86-90).

In summary, how people perceive the available affordances relating to sex-drive release is influenced in multiple ways by their culture's traditions.

Occupational choice. The term *occupation* refers to an individual's livelihood—the way a person makes a living. Occupations not only include wage-paying jobs but also subsistence farming and fishing, homemaking, retirement on a pension, and the like. The perceptual process affecting an individual's choice of occupation can be complex, involving consideration of such variables as (a) the array of available occupations, (b) types and levels of material compensation, and (c) the relative prestige of different occupations.

The availability of a vocation depends not only on whether a given occupation exists in the culture, but also on the number of openings for new aspirants and the conditions that affect a particular individual's chances of being accepted into the occupation. Subsistence-agriculture societies have many openings for farm work of a type rather easily learned and repetitive in nature. Industrialized societies, in their moderately mechanized form, provide many openings to specialized factory jobs that involve repetitive activities in the mass production of commodities. More advanced technological societies require higher-level skills for monitoring the operation of automated machines that perform the manufacturing jobs done by manual labor in less advanced industrial settings.

Whether or not individuals are accepted into a given vocation can be influenced not only by the available openings, but also by an applicant's age, education, social class, religious status, family influence, geographical location, and the existence of a guild or union that controls access to the vocation. Cultures can vary in their customs regarding each of these conditions.

How individuals perceive the job opportunities depends partly on the available modes of communication about occupations. Being limited to direct observation and word-of-mouth as sources of vocational information in a Himalayan village offers very different perceptual affordances from those in a North American metropolis that furnishes vocational counselors in secondary schools, employment bureaus, newspaper want ads, and easy access to the World Wide Web.

Two forms of compensation affecting people's perceptions of occupations are those of material goods and social status. These factors are closely linked and strongly influenced by cultural values, since the significance of compiling worldly wealth can vary across societies. One consideration in a person's choosing an occupation can be physical comfort—obtaining enough wealth to buy healthful housing, clothing, food, medical care, convenient transportation, and entertainment. But beyond "bare necessities" or "creature comforts," people often seek wealth for social purposes, such as to impress others by displaying an opulent lifestyle, to wield power by financing political or philanthropic movements, to control other people's behavior through hiring employees, and to enjoy the freedom of not having to work for a living.

Some cultures reward both the accumulation and retention of material wealth. In such environments, the person who acquires wealth and preserves it is respected. Other cultures reward the accumulation of goods, but mainly so the goods can be given away, as in the *potlatch* tradition of the Indian tribes of northwestern Canada and the United States and, to a lesser degree, in the periodic *selamatan* celebrations of the Javanese and the elaborate funerals in Bali and in Toradja society of the Central Celebes. Still other cultures honor the rejection of material goods, as in Christian monastic orders, Buddhist tradition, and the Hindu stage of mature adulthood when a person abandons all belongings to live an ascetic life in the forest and later to wander about as a homeless mendicant (Marek, 1988; Thomas, 1988).

Occupations within every society vary in the status attributed to them by the populace. There is some measure of agreement across many cultures in the prestige assigned certain occupations. Medical doctors, high-level public officials, and university professors generally rank near the top of the prestige hierarchy, whereas trash collectors, day laborers, and people engaged in unlawful activities (thieves, street-walking prostitutes, muggers) rank near the bottom (Thomas, 1962). However, in addition to such accord, there are also significant differences across cultures in both the relative rank of particular vocations and in the level of esteem in which they are held. Consider, for example, the butchering of animals. In the Dassanetch society of South-West Ethiopia, slaughtering cattle is a highly honored activity, an essential component of a ceremony in which killing cattle contributes to an individual's social standing.

> The greater [a man's] status and prestige, the more animals he is required to kill in order to live up to his role as a "notable" and host. The older a man becomes, the more animals he slaughters. . . . [In addition,] slaughtering concerns situations of occult attack. A man protects himself and the members of his household from a threatening misfortune by slaughtering a sheep or a goat. . . . The appearance of bad omens as well as real misfortunes can lead to the performance of *ai fasiet*, in which the blood of the carcass is allowed to drip over the bodies of the members of the household in the belief that blood prevents the misfortune because it is antithetical to demons. (Almagor, 1978, pp. 56-57)

In most European and North American cultures, butchering is a respectable occupation, accorded a moderate level of esteem similar to that of brick laying, carpentry, shoe repairing, and clerking in a small store. But in India, Hindu doctrine holds the slaughtering of animals in very low regard; butchering is a vocation suitable only for "untouchables"—for members of the despised scheduled castes or *dalits* (McDonald, 1994).

Cross-cultural encounters: As children grow up, they learn the meanings typically attributed in their culture to people's appearance and actions. When such children subsequently perceive people from different cultural backgrounds, misunderstandings often result.

Consider, for example, the culturally conditioned gender behavior taught in different Papua New Guinea tribes.

> Whereas the Nakanai expect boys to be stoical and girls to be volatile, the Arapesh permit only boys to weep and indulge in fits of rage. The Wogeo and Siuai reproach girls for any displays of violence, reserving such behaviour for boys, while the Senseng teach baby girls to chase and beat boys in anticipation of the later courtship patterns. (Ryan, 1972, p. 162)

Imagine, then, the interpretation that the Nakanai would draw when they see an Arapesh boy crying in disappointment, or the opinion the Wogeo would hold about a girl who pursues and bludgeons a boy.

In the realm of sex-drive expression, interactions between people from contrasting cultures may yield either satisfying or frustrating outcomes for the participants. An Irish youth from a traditionally orthodox Catholic home can be delighted—though somewhat conscience stricken—when he settles in Holland and gradually adopts the liberal perspective toward sex that the Dutch hold about intercourse between unwed young people. On the other hand, an 18-year-old Danish girl attending art school in Paris can be distressed when her 22-year-old Algerian boyfriend refuses to use a condom as the pair plan to spend the night together. Whereas the young woman is willing to have sex with a man to whom she is not married, her Danish sex-education background warns her to protect herself from unwanted pregnancy, possible venereal disease, and potential AIDS infection, so she insists that her male partner use a condom. In contrast, her Algerian companion considers it both insulting and sexually unfulfilling to use such a device, with the result that their intended *affaire d'amour* goes unconsummated.

In the area of occupational choice, cross-cultural problems can arise when people's perceptions of the status of occupations differ between cultures. The 19-year-old son of an Indonesian family that recently emigrated to Western Canada became friends with a Canadian youth (the son of a lawyer) who had become a ranch hand so he could learn the ranching business as preparation for owning his own ranch in the future. When the Canadian introduced his Indonesian companion to ranch life, the Indonesian decided that he, too, would like to learn ranching. His family, however, rejected the plan on the grounds that being a "cowboy" was a "dirty hands" job, a vocation fit only for peasants and thus beneath the dignity of their family whose patriarch, while in Indonesia, had been a minor government official doing a white-collar job. In effect, the Indonesians could not understand the attitude that Western Canadians, who came from pioneer stock, held about ranching and about getting their hands soiled in their occupations.

Practical applications: Two counseling techniques that draw on the Gibsons' theory can be referred to as *predict-and-review* and *alternative-affordances* approaches. The predict-and-review procedure is based on the Gibsons' notion, described earlier, that

> *perception/action reciprocity* consists of progressive cycles of perceiving (getting information) and acting. The individual perceives an environment, then acts on that perception. The action serves to confirm or disconfirm the original interpretation, altering or strengthening the interpretation and thereby influencing successive perceptions that are then also assessed through the person's new actions. The perception-action process, played over and over, constitutes development. (Gibson, 1997, p. 25)

In the counseling setting, the client is asked to suggest how he or she intends to behave in an upcoming encounter—such as in a meeting with his or her teacher or spouse or employer—and to explain why that seems like a profitable way to act. Following the encounter, the client returns to the counselor and reviews the episode by describing the extent to which the encounter had resulted in the predicted outcome. If the encounter is judged to have been at all unsatisfactory, then the counseling session focuses on identifying the likely causes of such a result and on considering other ways of behaving that might have produced a more acceptable result. Hence, the task of proposing other kinds of behavior is that of generating alternative affordances. A variety of sources of such options can be used, such sources as clients themselves, the counselor, other clients in group-counseling sessions, books and magazines on human relations, and videotapes of person-and-person interactions.

THE ACQUISITION OF GENDER ATTRIBUTES

Title: Social-Learning Theory (or Social-Cognition Theory) as formulated by Albert Bandura, a professor of psychology at Stanford University. Although social-learning theory in its broadest application endeavors to explain how people acquire all sorts of beliefs and behaviors, the brief version offered here is limited to explaining how children and youths acquire their gender traits.

It is important to distinguish between how the words *sex* and *gender* are intended throughout the following discussion. Whereas *sex characteristics* refers to biological features that distinguish females from males, *gender characteristics* refers to social-psychological traits that typify females and males within a given culture.

Key tenets: Bandura's (1986) social-learning theory emphasizes the way children's copying other people's behavior can serve as a window to a society's beliefs about which people display characteristics worth copying.

In Bandura's opinion, most of children's learning results from their actively imitating what they see or hear other people say and do. Consequently, the term *modeling (observational learning* or *vicarious learning)* means that children add to their repertoire of actions by observing someone else perform an action rather than by overtly carrying out the behavior themselves (Bandura, 1969, pp. 118-120). Imitation can be direct, as when a child personally witnesses someone else's behavior, or indirect, as when a child adopts actions depicted in either biography or fiction as presented in books, television programs, stage dramas, and the like.

The process of learning from models consists of five main functions: (1) paying attention to the model, (2) coding the model's actions so as to place the results in memory, (3) retaining the results in memory, and (4) carrying out the remembered material in actions. All four of these steps require (5) motivation, which is influenced by the consequences experienced by the observed model and by the child himself or herself when attempting the action.

Principal variables: Important features of modeling include (a) *goals* the child hopes to achieve, (b) the *availability* of models who are apparently attempting to reach such goals, (c) the *methods* that models employ, (c) the degree of *success* models appear to enjoy in terms of the consequences that result from their actions, (d) the ability of the child to *copy* the model's behavior, and (e) the *consequences* the child experiences when applying the modeled actions in her or his own life.

Difference among cultures: Societies can vary in which behaviors they encourage in males and in females. Hofstede (1996), from her comparison of national characteristics among the citizens of 40 nations, identified a masculinity/femininity factor that distinguished one national culture from another.

> Masculinity stands for a society in which social gender roles are clearly distinct; men are supposed to be assertive, tough, and focused on material success, whereas women are supposed to be more modest, tender, and concerned with the quality of life. The opposite pole, Femininity, stands for a society in which social gender roles overlap; both men and women are supposed to be modest, tender, and concerned with the quality of life. . . . Countries scoring high on Masculinity included Japan, Germany, the United States, Britain, Mexico, and the Philippines; countries scoring low on Masculinity (feminine) included the Nordic countries, the Netherlands, France, Portugal, Costa Rica, and Thailand. (Hofstede, 1996, pp. 533-534)

Within a society, encouragement to adopt particular gender characteristics is fostered by the culture's dominant models of male and female behavior and by the consequences people experience when they copy those models. Discouragement is fostered by the punishment suffered by people who copy culturally disapproved models.

Conveying desired gender characteristics to the young by both personal example and instruction can be illustrated with childrearing practices in the village of Khalapu, India, where females are taught to be kindly and subservient to men, and men are expected to be aggressive and vindictive in their relations with people with whom they compete, particularly with people of status lower than their own.

> Daughters will soon marry out of the village and play no active role in village life, but the sons must be taught the patterns of loyalty and hatred which define the social groupings with which they must live throughout their lifetime. Therefore, whereas the wives usually do not extend their quarrels to their children and may welcome in the courtyard the offspring of families with whom their husbands are feuding, the men pass their animosities to the next generation [by identifying] the trustworthy, the untrustworthy, the relatives, the enemies, the false friends, and the neutrals who make up the participants in the intricate web of village factionalism. . . . [Furthermore] aggression training is given traditional sanction through the occasional reading of the Ramayana and the Mahabharata [Hindu epic poems] and the relating of stories about the bravery of Rajput warriors. (Minturn & Hitchcock, 1963, pp. 350-351)

As seen in the traits of heroes and villains in the Hindu epics, the analysis of such transmitters of culture as books or dramas can suggest which beliefs about gender are fostered by the society's dominant social-political groups. In Ferdows' study of the portrayal of genders in Iranian school textbooks (Grades 6-12), she noted that out of a total 10,922 references to people, 6.8% were to females and 93.2% to males.

> This implies [that] children can learn little from women, their lives, and contributions. In some way, this finding poses a contradiction since the Islamic Republic's leadership continuously urges women to participate in religious and political functions and sponsors . . . conferences to study the position and role of women in Islamic society. . . . [The texts support] the general proposition that the Iranian/Muslim woman is primarily expected to be a devoted mother and kind, caring wife. She is present to feed, groom, and protect her children. Her education prepares her to be a capable childrearer and to assist her children in understanding the different gender roles. (Ferdows, 1995, p. 332)

Cultural distinctions are often found in adults' beliefs about differences in traits that boys and girls should exhibit at particular age levels. Dorsky and Stevenson reported that in the northern Moslem-Arab villages of the Republic of Yemen, children are not thought to be capable of self-control, rationality, responsibility, or significant learning until at least the age of 4; and the two genders are expected to differ in the time such characteristics appear.

In women's views, males are much slower to develop in these areas. What [such women] do not appear to recognize is that the time lag can be accounted for, [not by innate male biology, but rather] by differential treatment of boys and girls. For example, male toddlers are permitted to hit and kick their mothers or sisters practically until they tire of doing so or can be distracted from the aggression. Not only are older sisters expected to tolerate painful abuse from younger brothers, but they must also start pitching in and helping their mothers in many ways from an early age . . . while boys are largely free of such responsibilities. Boys have more leisure time and are less closely supervised than girls. (Dorsky & Stevenson, 1995, p. 313)

In traditional Apache culture in the Southwestern United States, men consider themselves superior to women in judgment, breadth of knowledge, and mental stability, with this attitude conveyed to children through modeling and remarks. As a result, "Small boys playing with girls their own age are hardly ever subservient, [though] they do not consciously seem to exert the superiority that a man does toward women" (Goodwin, 1942/1969, pp. 539). By age 11 or 12, boys are reluctant to play with girls for fear of being ridiculed by their friends.

In traditional European and North American cultures, the models of masculinity and femininity that have been encouraged result in differences between males and females in their sense of competence. Jean Block, after reviewing the psychological literature on gender differences and self-efficacy, concluded that

Males describe themselves as more powerful, ambitious, energetic, and as perceiving themselves as having more control over external events than females. . . . The self-descriptions of males, more than those of females, include concepts of agency . . . efficacy . . . and instrumentality—all reflections of a self-concept in which potency and mastery are important components. In contrast, females describe themselves as more generous, sensitive, nurturing, considerate, and concerned for others. . . . The self-concepts of females emphasize interpersonal relations and communion . . . and do not emphasize competition and mastery. (Block, 1983, pp. 1339-1340)

Within every culture, the task of molding children's concepts of proper gender characteristics begins early in life, as shown by the ways children are dressed, the toys and gifts they receive, and the types of play they are encouraged to pursue. In later years, gender preferences are reflected in the school subjects considered most suitable for females and males.

During infancy, cultures often distinguish girls from boys in the colors selected for clothing and blankets. The most common designation is pink for girls and blue for boys, as observed in such diverse settings as Australia, Britain, France, Peru, Russia, Singapore, South Africa (among whites), and the United States (Adler, 1993). In Hong Kong, pink and red are for girls, blue and gray for boys. Koreans prefer pink and red for girls, blue and brown for boys. In Canada, color coding "could even include the baby's disposable diaper, which, according to one current television advertisement, can be obtained in blue Oxford stripes for a boy or pink rosebuds for a girl" (Davis, 1993, p .31).

The extent of discrimination between the genders in the behaviors encouraged during early childhood can vary from one culture to another. In traditional Australian aboriginal villages,

> When old enough to run around, boys were free to play, to remain with the women and girls, or to watch their fathers and uncles making tools and weapons. Girls were expected to help with food collecting, which was constant, to look after the younger children, and to learn skills such as net making and weaving. For all, work and play went hand in hand. (O'Neill, 1993, p. 4)

In Poland—where boys are urged to be active, brave, and resistant to pain—

> crying for help and tears are punished by peers and by parents. The usual way of punishing small boys is to tell them that they behave like a woman or like a crybaby. Girls are considered fragile and are taught to be polite, quiet, and helpful to others. If they display some physical, aggressive behavior toward people or objects, they are rebuked, such as, "You behave like a bully." (Grzymala-Moszczynska, 1993, p, 272)

Most cultures model pastimes judged suitable for boys and those suitable for girls, but with the specific types of toys and games varying across cultures. In rural areas of Haiti, boys' toys are usually handmade objects, such as fishing poles, kites, and slingshots, whereas girls' toys are hand-sewn dolls (Douyon, Philippe, & Frazier, 1993, p. 102). Boys in Hong Kong have more assertive kinds of toys (cars, building blocks, weapons) while girls play with passive kinds (dolls, stuffed animals, playhouses, cooking sets) (Yu, 1993, p. 111). Japanese boys between ages 2 and 6 play a variety of ball games, whereas girls more often draw pictures and assume pretend roles. During the primary school years, Japanese boys engage in more physical play, such as sumo wrestling, while girls pursue more static, elaborate pastimes, including *origami* paper folding (Sukemune et al., 1993, p. 177).

> [In Korea,] cars, toy guns and sporting goods are chosen for boys, while musical instruments, dolls, and play dishes and utensils are given to girls. Boys play with building blocks or with toy cars, which develop their sense of space and analytical skills; with toy guns, which enhance aggressive and independent characters; or with mechanical toys, which contribute to their intellectual development. In contrast, girls play with musical instruments, dance, play with dolls, or play house in order to develop emotional capacities and social skills. Accordingly, 95 percent of young girls have dolls, while the same percentage of young boys are prohibited from playing with dolls. (Lee in Kim, 1993, p. 190)

During infancy, the gender-typing of toys is rare in Peru, but "becomes highly emphasized in the preschool years" with action toys (cars, airplanes, boats, war-related playthings) furnished to boys, and dolls, houseware, and beauty-related items for girls. "Toys that are more gender-neutral include bicycles, tricycles, roller skates, and educational, computer, and electronic games" (Ragúz & Pinzás, 1993, p. 249).

In France, although children receive some encouragement to play with toys that are stereotypically associated with the opposite gender, the dominant pattern is for parents and older siblings to reinforce traditional gender roles through toys and gifts that the young receive (Davido & O'Donoghue, 1993, p. 79).

For centuries, virtually all societies that provided formal schooling drew a distinction between males and females in the amounts and kinds of education available to each gender. Males always received more opportunities for schooling, and the subject fields they were encouraged to enter usually differed from those provided for females. Although a dramatic reduction in these male/female discrepancies has occurred over the past century, modeling of such culturally embedded distinctions continues to different degrees in different societies. Variability from one society to another is displayed in statistics on literacy and school enrollments, which reflect cultural attitudes about the relative importance of formal education for the two genders.

First, consider two countries' academic-field enrollment patterns. In Finland, where more than half of university graduates today are women,

> Mathematics, computer science, and engineering are the only male-dominated subjects. Female-dominated subjects include teacher training, humanities, medicine and health, home economics, and domestic science. In all other studies neither sex exceeds 60 percent of all students. (Husu & Niemelä, 1993, p. 67)

In Poland's rural areas, three times as many men as women enter universities, whereas in cities more women than men are university students. Women are in the majority in universities, teachers colleges, and medical academies. Men more often attend polytechnic institutes and agricultural academies (Grzymala-Moszczynska, 1993, p. 274).

Next, consider female/male literacy comparisons in six nations for people age 15 and over (Education, 1998, pp. 880-885).

Nations	Male % Literate	Female % Literate
Afghanistan	47.2	15.0
Botswana	80.5	59.9
Denmark	100.0	100.0
Japan	100.0	100.0
Malaysia	89.1	78.1
United States	96.7	95.3

Yu (1993, p. 113) reports that in Hong Kong, as the level of schooling of females has continued to rise, young men have still been encouraged to pursue studies related to medicine, science, technology, and business. Nonacademically oriented males usually have been directed into industrial or work-related apprenticeships. Their female counterparts have been counseled to become secretaries and clerks, while the more capable young women have entered teacher training, nursing, social work, or business education. However, high-achieving females have been pursuing science and technology studies at an increasing rate.

Cross-cultural encounters: One important consequence of cross-cultural information exchanges has been an increasing dissatisfaction expressed by females in various societies over their traditional rights and roles. This dissatisfaction is to a great extent the result of rapidly expanding communication facilities (books, magazines, radio, television, the computer Internet) through which knowledge of the recently intensified feminist movements in America and Western Europe has spread worldwide. When the disappointment causes an individual to adopt new gender attributes that lead to a more positive self-image and life fulfillment, then the outcome can be judged constructive. However, if there is no way for the person to break the bonds of tradition, she may then suffer greater misery than she would have if she had never been introduced to other cultures' role possibilities.

Whenever contact with another culture motivates persons to adopt an aspect of that culture's gender behavior, those individuals may thereby alienate themselves from family members and acquaintances who have remained true to their culture. A Korean doctoral student attending the University of California told me that when she returned home during the summer vacation, her mother had arranged separate meetings with four other mothers and their unmarried adult sons. In keeping with Korean tradition, the aim of the meetings was to introduce a young man to a young woman in the hope that they would prove well matched for marriage. In this case, the aim was unfulfilled, because all four men wanted a traditional Korean wife, submissive and satisfied to dedicate her life to bearing children and supporting her husband's endeavors. To the distress of mothers and sons alike, this young woman was clearly an unsuitable candidate, since she was educated far beyond their desires; and from copying the females whom she observed during her sojourn abroad, she had adopted an assertive demeanor and vocational ambitions that would be acceptable in North America but not in traditional Korean culture.

In cross-cultural marriages, problems often arise because of the different concepts of proper husband and wife roles brought to the union by the man and woman. Consider, for example, the potential for conflict in a marriage between a traditional Mexican man and an "emancipated" U. S. American woman. First, observe the Mexican cultural expectations for the husband and wife roles as sketched by Diaz-Guerrero and Rodriguez de Diaz (1993, pp. 201, 205).

> The dynamics of the Mexican family are rooted in two fundamental proposi-
> tions: (1) the absolute supremacy of the father and (2) the necessary and absolute
> sacrifice of the mother. The mother's role has always implied abnegation,
> which involves the denial of any and all possible selfish aims. . . . Soon after
> the honeymoon, the husband passes from slave to master, and the woman enters

the hardest test of her life. . . . The husband must work and provide. He knows nothing, nor does he want to know anything, about what happens in the home. He demands only that all obey him and that his authority be unquestioned. Often, after working hours, he joins his friends and leads a life no different from that he led when unmarried.

Next, note the characteristics of a typical emancipated U.S. American woman. She expects to have a respected occupation outside the home—at least part-time—whereas inside the home she expects her husband to share housekeeping and child-care tasks. When work is finished, she expects that the two of them will frequently participate together in recreational activities.

Practical applications: A counseling strategy based on Bandura's theory can be used to raise an ofttimes subconscious psychological process to a conscious level and thereby equip the counselee to wield intentional control over the process. The nature of the process is perhaps most easily explained when contrasted to a competing interpretation offered by B. F. Skinner's radical behaviorism, which will be the next theory we inspect in this chapter.

The process has to do with the way the consequences of an event influence a person's future behavior in events of a similar type. According to Skinner, when a consequence that follows an individual's action is reinforcing (experienced as a reward), then in similar circumstances in the future the person's tendency to act that same way will be automatically strengthened. But if the consequence is nonreinforcing (experienced as of no importance or as punishment), the tendency to act that way again will automatically be weakened. This automatic process is assumed to be the same for all species—laboratory rats, pigeons, chimpanzees, and humans alike. However, Bandura has disagreed.

> Although the issue is not yet completely resolved, there is little evidence that reinforcers function as automatic shapers of human conduct. . . . A vast amount of evidence lends validity to the view that reinforcement serves principally as an informative and motivational operation rather than as a mechanical response strengthener. (Bandura, 1977, p. 21)

By *informative* Bandura means that the consequences—either rewarding or punishing—tell the person under what circumstances it would seem wise to try that particular behavior in the future. In other words, the consequences improve the person's prediction of whether the recently attempted act (a behavior the person either directly tried or copied from someone else) will likely lead to pleasant or unpleasant outcomes on a later occasion. When Bandura speaks of the *motivational* role of consequences, he means that people will more likely try to learn modeled behavior if they value the consequences that such behavior seems to produce. In sum, Bandura sees consequences as regulators of future behavior—they regulate by furnishing individuals information about likely future consequences and by motivating them to act in one way rather than another so as to obtain the results they desire. Consider now how this conception of the consequences-effects process can be applied in counseling.

Two necessary assumptions underlying the technique are these: (a) The information and motivation process is usually intuitive, operating at a subconscious level and may therefore be inefficient, in the sense of failing to guide future decisions in the most constructive manner. (b) Raising the information process to the conscious level enables a counselee to consider different interpretations of events and to decide which version is the most reasonable. The motivation for future action then derives from the preferred interpretation.

The resulting counseling technique can be used with clients who are distressed about many kinds of events. However, in keeping with our present interest, the following example addresses types of apparent gender discrimination that cause clients to seek counseling. Typical discrimination incidents are ones related to admitting persons to places or positions (employment, educational programs, recreation sites), promoting individuals to a higher status (job, school, athletic team), making invidious remarks about individuals, and more. The counseling approach consists of a pattern of questions intended to transform a client's intuitive information-processing habit to a conscious level of control. One such pattern is the following:

—Can you describe the incident? Who was there? What did they say and do? And what did you say and do?
—How did you feel about how it turned out?
—If you should be in a similar situation in the future, what are some different ways you might act? That is, what are some different things you might say and do? (The counselor may add other options to those suggested by the client.)
—For each of these ways of acting, how might things turn out? Which of those outcomes do you think might be best, and why?

BEHAVIOR AND ITS CONSEQUENCES

Title: Radical Behaviorism, as formulated by B. F. Skinner, a Harvard University psychologist.

Key tenets: As children grow up, they accumulate an increasing array of ways to behave in different life situations. In other words, for any situation, children and youths develop a variety of ways they can respond. These ways form their repertoire of behavior options. Which option they will choose to adopt on any given occasion is determined by the consequences that have followed the use of that option on similar occasions in the past. Rewarding consequences (*reinforcers*) that have accompanied an action strengthen the likelihood that such an action will be used in the future in similar circumstances. Nonrewarding or aversive consequences (*nonreinforcers* and *punishments*) that have followed a behavior serve to weaken the probability that such a behavior will be adopted on similar future occasions (Skinner, 1974).

Thus, the way to alter an individual's conduct is to manipulate the consequences that accompany such conduct—arranging for approved behavior to be followed by reward and disapproved behavior to be followed by nonreward or punishment. In effect, to modify people's ways of acting, it is unnecessary to understand what they "have in mind"—their beliefs, theories, and intentions—because all behavior is controlled by consequences, not by unobservable thoughts. Since there is no agreement among psychologists about the structure, content, or operating principles of *mind*, dwelling on such matters merely distracts people from the publicly observable controllers of behavior—the rewarding and punishing consequences.

Principal variables. The four variables of chief importance in radical behaviorism are (a) the kinds of occasions on which a behavior is called for or elicited, (b) the kinds of behavior a person exhibits on those occasions, (c) the types of consequences accompanying each kind of behavior, and (d) an identification of which sorts of consequences increase a given behavior in the future and which sorts decrease or eliminate that behavior on subsequent occasions.

Differences among cultures: From the vantage point of radical behaviorism, cultures vary in four main ways: (a) the kinds of behavior that are approved and disapproved, (b) the degree of approval and disapproval (ranging from slight to extreme) of each kind, (c) types of consequences considered appropriate for encouraging approved acts and for discouraging disapproved acts, and (d) the effectiveness of the various types of consequences for influencing behavior. These forms of cultural variation are illustrated by the following examples.

Approved and disapproved kinds of behavior. The importance of children abiding by cultural rules can differ from one type of behavior to another. This difference is usually reflected in the sorts of consequences adults apply for infractions and the consistency with which they actually carry through with threatened sanctions or promised rewards. Gaskins's (1996) observations of life in a Mayan village in Mexico illustrate one cultural pattern of adjusting sanctions to the assumed significance of various types of behavior.

> Many parents feel that the only way that they can assert authority is through the use of threats and the occasional use of force. Corporal punishment is therefore quite common, although many parents (especially mothers) express a dislike for hurting their children. The common wisdom is that if your children are not afraid of you, they will not obey you. The ideal method of sustaining their fear is to threaten often and impressively but follow through only when absolutely necessary. This leads to a style of interaction between many parents and their children of testing and asserting limits endlessly (often with loud voices and with great dramatics on the part of the parent) on trivial matters, often ending with the children's inappropriate behavior going unpunished, but virtually complete compliance by children regarding important rules. (Gaskins, 1996, p. 356)

Gaskins suggests that the pressure of public approval and disapproval serves to standardize such practices in village culture: "A parent who beats his children regularly is not well regarded in the community, but a parent who allows his children to defy his authority on some important issue and go unpunished is even less well regarded" (Gaskins, 1996, p. 256).

Howard (1970) observed marked cultural differences between the opinions of North American and Rotuman parents about which acts on the part of children warrant serious concern. Whereas Americans often use punishment to protect the young from harmful activities, parents on the Pacific Island of Rotuma allow children to

> engage in the most dangerous pursuits without being stopped. It is common to see a three- or four-year-old tot swinging a razor-sharp machete in imitation of his elders. No one shouts in horror or even urges him to put the implement down, as long as he is handling the tool reasonably well. In general, Rotumans seem to be optimists regarding childhood accidents. . . . They simply do not seem to have a sense of impending danger. . . . Whereas American middle-class parents tend to punish children for damaging household property, Rotumans are very permissive in this area. Children are allowed to handle almost any item belonging to the household, and even the destruction of valuables rarely arouses anger or brings punishment. (Howard, 1970, pp. 35-36)

However, young Rotuman children who damage a neighbor's property or fight with peers outside their own family invite immediate, severe punishment because such behavior threatens the village's social amity. "Thus aggression is not bad for its own sake, but only when it has disturbing effects on personal relations" (Howard, 1970, p. 43).

In Rotuman society, one of the greatest offenses is to show off or act proud *(fakman'ia)*. The typical punishment for behaving in a conceited fashion is ridicule —"Look at how silly he is, acting like a showoff and making a fool of himself in front of everyone" (Howard, 1970, p. 35).

Degrees of approval and disapproval. One way to judge the degree to which a behavior is disapproved is by how far a person will go to ensure that a child or youth complies with a command. For instance, observations of mother-child interactions in the Okinawan village of Tiara showed that

> A boy, looking after a younger child, is more likely to abandon or neglect his charge than a girl. In families where there are several children of caretaking age, each is assigned a specific share of time. Inevitably the girls find themselves with the greater or entire portion of this duty, for the boys either simply refuse or evade assuming their share. This shirking of duty is partly supported by the mother, who, by her failure to enforce assignments, displays passive acceptance or approval of the boys' actions. A girl, however, invites censure not only from her mother but also from other girls for similar actions. (Maretzki & Maretzki, 1963, p. 519)

Appropriate types of consequences. Three of the more dramatic ways in which societies differ are in their customs governing (a) the proper combination of positive and negative responses to children's behavior, (b) corporal punishment, and (c) public exposure as means of discouraging objectionable conduct.

Positive/negative consequence ratio. A cultural contrast in the amount of positive (complimentary, rewarding) and negative (critical, punishing) treatment of children is found in Levy's comparison of general childrearing practices in a Tahitian village and a Nepalese town. Children in Tahiti were allowed to go about their business of growing up without much verbal direction by adults; and when Tahitian parents did apply directive verbal interventions, their remarks were primarily negative: "Don't do this" or "Stop doing that." In Nepal, parents offered much verbal guidance to their offspring as the children were learning to perform a new task, and this guidance was usually in positive, encouraging terms. Only after a child had achieved a measure of mastery would negative remarks appear, and then in a moral form, such as "It's not right to do that," rather than, "Don't do that" (Levy, 1996, p. 134).

> In Asian cultures, praise for good performance is rare, whereas punishment in the form of ridicule and shaming the child is quite frequent. Praise is given only for exceptional achievement or other virtues, but it is seldom given publicly. In such an environment reward has a high motivating effect on learning outcomes. (Mishra, 1997, p. 161)

The ratio of positive and negative responses to children's behavior can also vary by age level. In the Mexican village of Juxtlahuaca, very young children were generally indulged, with parents offering frequent nurturant responses to children's behavior. However, by age 6 or 8, all this had changed.

> Whereas in early childhood, rewards and nurturance for compliance were the major techniques for training, in late childhood, punishment for lack of compliance becomes more prevalent. The child is now considered capable of understanding and is therefore punished for failure to carry out requests or commands, as well as being subjected to withdrawal of nurturant responses by the parent. . . . [For example, after eight-year-old Helena has collected the turkeys, as her father had ordered, she] approaches her father and looks at him. He does not speak or recognize her presence by any overt move. . . . Any expectation she may have had of appreciation for her behavior was disappointed. Similarly, Juanita received no overt special thanks for her work. (Romney & Romney, 1963, pp. 666-667)

Corporal punishment. The term *corporal punishment* means inflicting bodily harm for unacceptable behavior, with the types of punishment ranging from the most painful and debilitating to the gentlest and least offensive. Hence, varieties of corporal punishment can extend from the extreme of cutting off the hands of a thief to the inconsequential mild slap on the buttocks of a sassy 5-year-old.

Whipping has been a popular mode of corporal punishment over the ages, with the type of whip and number of lashes usually intended to reflect the seriousness of the transgression. A cat-o'-nine tails (nine braided leather or rope strands hooked to a short handle) has often been used to flog criminals and disobedient seamen and soldiers. The Islamic Qur'an, as dictated to scribes by the Prophet Mohammed in the 7th century, prescribes whipping as punishment for those who engage in sexual intercourse outside of marriage.

> As for the fornicatress and fornicator, flog each of them, giving a hundred stripes, and let not pity for them detain you in the matter of obedience to Allah, and let a party of believers witness their chastisement. (Shakir, 1975, p. 334)

In countries influenced by British tradition, the word *caning* identifies the practice of striking a recalcitrant child or youth with a cane or switch. Newell (1972, pp. 9-19) has reported that the use of such punishment in schools was outlawed in Poland as early as 1783, by Holland in the 1850s, France in 1887, Finland in 1890, Norway in 1935, Sweden in 1958, and Denmark in 1968. Following World War II, Israel and Japan, along with the Soviet Union and its satellite countries of Eastern Europe, denied teachers the use of the cane. In contrast, corporal punishment by school personnel is still permitted in Australia, Canada, Great Britain, New Zealand, South Africa, certain school districts of the United States, and a variety of other countries.

Cultural views about the appropriateness of corporal punishment are often linked to conceptions about the maturity level of children. For instance, in Nyansongo, a Gusii community in Kenya, 85% of mothers considered caning suitable punishment for misbehavior among children ages 3 to 6, but less than half would use caning for those beyond age 6 because

> the major alternative to caning—food deprivation—is considered too cruel for small children [under age 3], who "lack the sense" to understand why they are being refused what their mothers always grant them. Another reason for less frequent caning of older children is that the behavior of the child himself may make it unnecessary or ineffective. If the child of 6 or older has learned to be "good," that is, obedient, then he can be corrected by the verbal warning or rebuke of his mother; she need no longer beat him to enforce compliance. . . . Nyansongo parents disapprove of continuing the use of physical punishment on a child who does not respond to it: "After all, I don't want to kill him!" (LeVine & LeVine, 1963 p. 167)

Other than caning, popular ways of punishing the misbehavior of children and youths in Gusii culture included depriving of food, reprimanding, chasing from the house overnight without a blanket, withholding clothes, and assigning laborious chores.

Public exposure.   Public exposure as an imposed consequence consists of widely proclaiming a person's wrongdoing. Over the centuries public exposure has assumed various forms. Individuals accused of committing acts proscribed by church law have commonly been condemned from the pulpit. Until well into colonial days in America, locking wrongdoers in stocks in the village square submitted them to the ridicule of passersby. In Nathaniel Hawthorne's novel *The Scarlet Letter,* the adulterous Hester Prynne was forced to wear a red letter *A* on her bodice for everyone to see. A recent method of branding drunk drivers has involved a judge's ordering them to display a bumper sticker on their autos announcing that the driver had been convicted of driving while under the influence of alcohol or drugs. In certain jurisdictions, sex offenders have been required to post signs in front of their residences proclaiming their crime.

Schools can differ in the extent to which they reveal students' admirable and deplorable behavior. Advertising admirable behavior can take the form of children's names on honor rolls displayed on a classroom bulletin board, printed in a newspaper, or announced during an assembly program. Wrongdoers' misconduct can be publicized by their being required to leave the classroom or sit in a corner, to have their names listed on the chalkboard, or to wear a sign identifying their misdemeanor.

Effectiveness of different types of consequences. How successful different kinds of consequences are in altering behavior is a matter of great debate. In Western societies, certain behaviorists—including Skinner—assert that punishment is not an efficient means of permanently eliminating individuals' unacceptable acts. Although they recognize that aversive consequences might deter people from misconduct while the punishing agent is present, they believe that the unacceptable act remains in the wrongdoer's repertoire of options, reappearing when the agent is absent (Thomas, 1996, p. 174). However, other learning theorists disagree that punishment is merely a temporary suppresser. They contend that punishment can be effective in extinguishing undesired acts (Hilgard & Bower, 1975, pp. 223-225).

Whatever the truth may be, it is apparent that cultures can vary in the extent to which their members are convinced that certain kinds of consequences are more effectual than others in altering various types of behavior, with this conviction reflected in the rewards and punishments they mete out to children and youths.

Cross-cultural encounters: Frequently, foreign educators studying in North American universities have carried the Skinnerian model back to their homelands. However, the desirability of transporting the preferred modes of reinforcement of one society into another has been a matter of considerable disagreement. This issue was brought to my attention when I was working on educational research projects in American Samoa. My closest Samoan coworker (a school principal who also held the position of talking chief in the Samoan social structure) was highly critical of educational authorities from the U.S. mainland banning corporal punishment from American Samoa's public schools. He asserted that from their earliest years, Samoan children learned that misbehavior would be met with a physical response—a handful of coral rocks cast at the offender, a slap across the buttocks or side of the head, and the like.   Simply warning the miscreant without adding some physical mode of reinforcement, he insisted, was of little avail.

Not only do methods of reinforcement generate cross-cultural controversy, so also do the kinds of behavior that warrant reward or punishment.   Howard's (1970) study of schooling in Rotuma revealed that most Rotuman parents dispense unconditional love to their children, punishing the young only for violating a limited number of well-defined rules.   Therefore, at home Rotuman children do not need to perform at a prescribed level of skill in order to receive their parents' approval.   But such is not the case in the Western sort of school that was first brought to the Pacific Islands by Christian missionaries in the 19th century.   Schools demand that pupils pursue imported academic goals, ones that most children do not find intrinsically appealing.   Unlike the Rotuman home, the school requires that learners reach prescribed levels of mastery if they are to avoid punishment and win their teachers' respect.

Questions of appropriate types of punishment can also lead to international political conflict, as illustrated by charges of the abuse of human rights brought against governments by such organizations as Amnesty International. A much publicized example is the case of an American youth attending high school in Singapore, where he joined companions in disfiguring two autos with eggs and spray paint. His arrest and conviction drew a $2,200 fine and six months in jail as well as a traditional form of punishment inherited from British colonial times—flogging with a rattan cane. U.S. authorities objected to the Singapore government, contending that the large fine and jail term were beyond reason and the flogging was inhumane.   The Singapore government responded that it not only had the right as a sovereign nation to determine its own penal practices, but such punishment had traditionally proved effective for encouraging citizens to obey the law ("Six Lashes in Singapore," 1994).

Practical applications: Perhaps the most widely adopted use of Skinnerian theory has been the process popularly referred to as *behavior modification*.   The aim of behavior modification is to replace people's unacceptable habits with desirable ones by manipulating the consequences of their actions in ways that cause them to find it more rewarding to adopt appropriate behavior than to continue in their current unacceptable pattern.   The behavior-modification process can be summarized in four basic steps:

1. Identify the specific behavior your wish to have the person substitute for his or her objectionable behavior.
2. Arrange for the person to try this new, desirable behavior.   There are several ways this can be done: simply wait for it to occur spontaneously, provide a model, verbally explain the desired behavior, reward gradual approximations of the behavior, or several of these together.

3. Determine what sorts of consequences will be strongly rewarding to the individual and what sorts will be punishing.
4. Manipulate the consequences so that the desired behavior, when it appears, will be more rewarding (less punishing) than the objectionable acts. In effect, arrange the consequences so the person will be convinced that it is profitable to adopt the new behavior and abandon the old.

The kinds of consequences that modify behavior can differ from one culture to another because of traditional cultural beliefs about which outcomes should be interpreted as rewards and which interpreted as punishments.

TWISTED LEARNING: AUTISM

In the context of this book, *twisted learning* refers to a process gone awry— the process of acquiring and expressing knowledge, skills, attitudes, and values. There are many ways learning can go wrong, and there are numerous terms created to distinguish one way from another—dyslexia, dyscalculia, attention-deficit disorder, pervasive developmental disorders, multiple complex developmental disorders, and more. The theory chosen in the following pages to illustrate twisted learning is one intended to explain autism.

The label *autism* and the symptoms to which it applies are of rather recent origin. The credit for recognizing and labeling the signs of this handicap in children goes to an American psychiatrist, Leo Kanner, who, in the 1940s, first noted :

> There is from [birth onward] an *extreme autistic aloneness* that, whenever possible, disregards, ignores, shuts out anything that comes to the child from the outside. Direct physical contact or such motion or noise as threatens to disrupt the aloneness is either treated "as if it weren't there" or, if this is no longer sufficient, resented painfully as distressing interference. . . . The children's aloneness from the beginning of life makes it difficult to attribute the whole picture exclusively to [parents' early relations with such children]. We must, then, assume that these children have come into the world with innate inability to form the usual, biologically provided affective contact with people, just as other children come into the world with innate physical or intellectual handicaps. (Kanner, 1943, pp. 33, 42-43)

The most apparent symptoms of autism are (a) impaired sociability, language, and communication, and (b) a constricted range of interests and activities. Autistic children are also often mentally retarded (Rapin & Katzman, 1998). Baron-Cohen (1995, p. 60) notes that "social and communication development are clearly abnormal in the first few years of life, and the child's play is characterized by a lack of the usual flexibility, imagination, and pretense." In short, the autistic fail to learn the communication and social skills that normal children acquire.

In addition to the genetic explanation for autism implied in Kanner's remarks, a variety of alternative interpretations have been proposed by other theorists. Bettleheim (1967), as a psychoanalyst, blamed autism on parents' unconscious hostility toward their children that resulted in harmful child-rearing practices. He recommended transferring autistic children from their homes to a special therapeutic facility which would replace autistic acts with more acceptable conduct. Behaviorists, such as Ferster (1961), have attributed autism to parents' providing inappropriate consequences for children's actions. The behaviorists' attempted cure is to substitute more desirable reinforcement methods for the unconstructive ones.

Not all children diagnosed as autistic exhibit the same behavior. Thus, there have been efforts to define subgroups of the autistic. As one attempt, Wing (1983) divided autism into three major types in terms of individuals' social problems—the aloof, the passive, and the active-but-odd. Although the aloof can tolerate being around other people, they still desire and need to be by themselves a good deal. The passive more easily take part in group activities but fail to understand social meanings and relations. The active-but-odd engage in extended monologues and asked endless, repetitive questions. "People find interacting with this group rather unpleasant because they feel compelled to reply but soon learn that the more they respond, the more the initial demands are repeated" (Schopler & Mesibov, 1986, p. 6). However, such typologies as Wing's, while of some practical use, have not proven entirely satisfactory, so the efforts to delineate types of autism continue.

The following theory, chosen to illustrate attempts at explaining the cause of autism, is a variety of evolutionary psychology that has its roots in Charles Darwin's conception of how living organisms—plants, animals, and people—acquire characteristics that permit their genetic lineages to survive.

Title: Mindblindness Theory, as formulated by Simon Baron-Cohen (1995), a lecturer in psychopathology at England's Cambridge University.

Key tenets: As a foundation for his theory, Baron-Cohen accepts Darwin's proposal that the characteristics exhibited by all living organisms are the result of those organisms' attempts to survive in the particular environments they inhabit. The architecture of these characteristics derives from the pattern of genes that members of each generation inherit from their parents. When environmental conditions change (climate turns colder, traditional food sources become scarce, water sources dry up, predators arrive, new diseases are introduced), those organisms whose combination of genes is best suited to producing characteristics that cope well with the particular environmental change are the ones that survive and pass on their fortuitous genetic composition to their offspring.

Baron-Cohen speculates that among a certain class of hominids in the far-distant past, the brain—as the central interpretation-and-action-control center for humans and animals—was impelled by environmental changes to increase in size and complexity. The most dramatic advance in brain development occurred during the Pleistocene epoch around 2 million years ago, when humans lived as hunters-gatherers, and also during the several hundred million years prior to Pleistocene times. Those eras established "which set of environments and conditions defined the adaptive problems the mind was shaped to cope with: Pleistocene conditions, rather than modern conditions" (Cosmides, Tooby, & Barkow, 1992, p. 5).

> The increase in brain size is likely to have had many causes, but one key factor upon which many theorists agree is the need for greater "social intelligence"— shorthand for the ability to process information about the behavior of others and to react adaptively to their behavior. It is likely that there was a need for greater social intelligence because the vast majority of non-human primate species are social animals, living in groups that range from as few as two individuals to as many as 200. . . . If you are living in a group of 200, making sense of the social behavior is staggeringly complex. One needs a powerful device—or set of devices—to make sense of actions, rapidly, in order to survive and prosper. (Baron-Cohen, 1995, pp. 13-14)

The acquired set of devices equipped people with the ability to estimate what others were thinking—in short, the ability to *read* others' *minds* in the sense of drawing useful inferences about other people's thoughts, ideas, beliefs, desires, intents, plans, understandings, puzzlements, conflicts, agreements, disagreements, emotions (pleasure, pain, anger), and more. According to Baron-Cohen, such inferences are constructed from people's ability to (a) understand the contents of their own minds by dint of introspection and (b) interpret clues from other people's behavior that suggest similar contents of others' minds. The clues include others' choice of words, voice inflections, gestures, eye movements, smiles, smirks, frowns, postures, and the like. He labels this mind-reading talent *folk psychology*—a genetically determined capacity common throughout humankind.

A further proposition in Baron-Cohen's theory is that the brain—and its invisible product, the mind—are organized in the form of modules, with each module consisting of a special pattern of brain cells equipped to perform a distinguishable mental function. As key components of his theory, Baron-Cohen postulates four mechanisms necessary for normal social intercourse. First is the *intentionality detector* (ID), the mental module that equips the child to recognize that people display *desires* and *goals* in the acts they perform. This detector appears in early infancy, between birth and 9 months of age. Second is the *eye-direction detector* (EDD), the ability to watch another person's eyes and estimate what those eyes are looking at. The EDD typically arises shortly after or simultaneously with the ID. Thus, the social understanding of the infant during the first 9 months is limited to identifying, at a primitive level, people's desires and goals and recognizing where their eyes are looking. The third module is the *shared-attention mechanism* (SAM), the ability to understand that another person is attending to the same thing you are attending to. SAM is a triadic function, establishing a relationship in the child's mind that links the child, another person, and the object they are both seeing or hearing. This preparatory skill for "reading" another person's mind normally appears between 9 and 18 months of age. The last of the four modules, a *theory-of-mind mechanism* (ToMM), completes the child's mindreading development. The ToMM performs two functions. First is that of representing *epistemic states*, meaning the types of knowledge that people can have in mind as intended by such terms as *ideas, beliefs, thoughts, emotions, speculations, doubts,* and the like. In addition to the ToMM module's capacity to conceive that people have such things in mind, the ToMM also performs the function of tying all those things together in the form of a theory. As a result of this second function, a child can interpret other people's actions as proceeding from *perceptions* (seeing, hearing, smelling, touching, feeling) to *beliefs* (knowing, suspecting, estimating, supposing, doubting) to *actions* (saying, hitting, laughing, writing) and to *reactions* (guilt, dismay, joy, sadness) (Baron-Cohen, 1995, p. 54). In effect, the theory assumes that a child's social behavior is crucially influenced by this ability to estimate what other people are thinking.

Baron-Cohen now uses his model to explain what has gone wrong in the autistic child's brain circuitry, and thereby in the child's mindreading ability. From an extended series of experiments with normal, mentally retarded, and autistic children, he concludes that the development of the autistic brain has proceeded adequately for the first two hypothesized modules, the *attention* and *eye-direction detection* mechanisms, but has gone amiss for the third and fourth, the *shared-attention* and *theory-of-mind* mechanisms. As a result, the autistic child is *mindblinded*, unable to estimate what other people are thinking, with disastrous consequences for the child's social behavior.

Principal variables: In Baron-Cohen's model, the most important immediate causal factor in autism is the damage to the *shared-attention* and *theory-of-mind* mechanisms in the child's brain. The underlying cause of this damage is faulty neural circuitry in the brain that is apparently the result of a disordered pattern of genes in the DNA inherited from the autistic child's parents. Or perhaps damage to the genetic structure occurred in some other manner.

Although flawed brain circuitry is the chief factor in autism, environmental influences can also affect how the malady manifests itself. A variety of treatments—pharmacological, childcare, educational, behavioral—can be effective in ameliorating the disorder. It is also the case that the symptoms of autism can diminish with advancing age, so possibly the needed brain circuitry for assembling a normal theory-of-mind mechanism is slow to develop in some people rather than incapable of developing.

Differences among cultures: Three ways that cultures may differ in their perceptions of autism are in (a) the incidence of autism, (b) estimated causes of the disorder, and (c) the social status ascribed to people who exhibit the autism syndrome.

Incidence. Baron-Cohen states that autism has been found in every country and on every social-class level in which it has been looked for, and that it occurs in between 4 and 15 children per 10,000. However, Sanua's (1984) review of the professional literature has suggested that infantile autism appears more often in Western civilizations and countries of high technology in which the nuclear family, in contrast to the extended family, dominates. He concludes that reports of autism among infants have been rare among black and Hispanic families in the United States, as well as infrequent in Latin America, Africa, and India, but high in westernized families in Japan.

A 1994 survey of 5-year-olds in Yokohama, Japan, placed the incidence of autism at 21.1 per 10,000 children. Among those diagnosed as autistic, half had intelligence quotients above 70 (Honda, Shimizu, Misumi, & Niimi, 1996). A 1998 study in Norway of children aged 3-14 placed the frequency at 5 per 10,000 in contrast to earlier reports of higher rates of the disorder (Sponheim & Skjeldal, 1998). The screening of 1,300 mentally handicapped children in five African countries revealed 30 with some autistic-like behavior; 9 of them fit Western criteria for autism. In terms of sex and social backgrounds, the ratios of children in the African sample were comparable to the ratios in European and North American groups (Lotter, 1978). A survey of children aged 3-15 in a Welsh health district suggested a growing incidence of autism over past decades. However, it was unclear whether this trend, reported in a number of other nations as well, was due to an actual increase in autistic children or to inconsistency in the methods used in different cultures for detecting and reporting the malady (Webb, Lobo, Hervas, & Scourfield, 1997).

In summary, the true similarities and differences across cultures in the prevalence of autism is unclear as a result of at least three factors—(a) autism has been a labeled disorder for little more than 50 years, so information about autism has not been communicated equally well in all cultures, (b) the stigmata of the disorder can differ somewhat from one victim to another, and (c) the methods and thoroughness of gathering data about autism have not been the same from one society to another. As a result, reports of the incidence of the disorder not only vary across cultures, but the confidence to be placed in the accuracy of such reports varies as well.

Causes. As noted earlier, theorists have proposed a variety of causes of autism over the decades since Kanner's first speculations in the 1940s. However, by the late 1990s in advanced industrialized societies—and particularly in Europe and North America—most research supported Baron-Cohen's proposal that faulty genetic inheritance is the primary cause of the condition.

Although several questions remain unanswered, it is clear that genetic mechanisms make a very important contribution to the etiology of autism [and] the mode of transmission is complex. Factors accounting for this complexity include the possibility that a large number of genes are involved, that variable expressivity may exist and lead to different manifestations of the gene, and that it is a heterogeneous disorder with several different genetic mechanisms. (Szatmari & Mahoney, 1993, p. 39)

But it is also true that the way the flawed genetic structure manifests itself in behavior is significantly influenced by a child's social contexts—the attitudes and modes of treatment of the people with whom the child daily interacts.

However, in a variety of traditional cultures not strongly affected by Western science and medicine, people continue to believe that the symptoms of autism are the result of spirit possession. Spirits are held responsible for the social detachment and disconnected communicative behavior of the affected individuals. For example, Ellenberger (1968) reported the belief in West Africa in the *Nit-ku-bon* type child, one who is supposed to be possessed by a spirit or to be the reincarnation of an ancestor, and whose behavior would fit the Western description of early autism.

Social status. The term *social status* in the present context refers to the level of respect or admiration accorded a type of individual. In Western industrialized societies, children displaying autistic symptoms are typically low in social status, often the objects of sympathy but not of respect or admiration. Among the autistic, ones that are aggressive (attacking other people) or self-destructive (such as hitting their heads against the wall) are less socially acceptable than the passive, retiring types. However, cultures that attribute autistic-like behavior to possession by spirits can elevate individuals who exhibit such behavior to a respected position reserved for enchanted members of society. Such is the case of individuals classed as *Nit-ku-bon* in West Africa, where an infant who would be diagnosed as autistic in Western cultures is considered a "marvelous child" (Ellenberger, 1968).

Cross-cultural encounters: Conflicts can arise when immigrants from a culture that subscribes to a spirit-possession explanation of autistic symptoms enter a culture that locates the cause of autism in faulty functions of the brain that can sometimes be rectified with such chemical substances as secretin or olanzapine. If the immigrants assume that their affected child's soul is the reincarnation of a revered ancestor's soul, they can be expected to refuse medical treatment for the child.

Another form of encounter may result in disappointment for parents from a third-world society if they enter a Western European or North American nation with the expectation that technologically advanced Western medical practice will provide a sure cure for their autistic child's condition. They will learn that Western medicine offers no sure cures, only the possibility of improving some of the symptoms in some of the children who suffer the malady.

Practical applications: In the standard psychological literature a substantial portion of the 5,500 journal articles and books about autism suggest ways to help autistic children. The varied forms that those ways may assume are illustrated in the following three examples and demonstrates the limited success that is usually achieved in efforts to ameliorate the effects of autism.

First, two communication deficiencies typically displayed by autistic children are their inability to expand on conversation or to use mental-state terms (such as *believes, feels, thinks, wants, plans, intends)* in their speech. Baron-Cohen and his associates attempted to teach 30 autistic children (aged 4-13) how to pass tests that assess children's ability to understand people's mental states. Although the children did learn to pass tasks concerned with understanding emotions and beliefs, there was no discernible affect of this training on the subjects' shortcomings in expanding on their conversation or on their including references to mental states in those conversations (Hadwin, Baron-Cohen, Howlin, & Hill, 1997).

Thirty-seven autistic children between ages 2 and 7 were administered the substance fluoxetine for a treatment period extending an average of 21 months. Researchers who monitored the subjects' language, cognitive, emotional, and social behavior concluded that 30% made excellent improvement in all four areas of behavior and were able to enter mainstream classrooms, another 30% improved but were still identifiably autistic, and the remaining 40% showed no benefit from fluoxetine (DeLong, Teague, & Kamran, 1998).

Three problems commonly associated with autism are inattentiveness (off-task behavior), touch aversion, and withdrawal. Twenty-two autistic preschoolers (mean age 4.5 years) who displayed these symptoms were divided into two treatment groups. One group of 11 received touch therapy while each of the other 11 sat on a volunteer's lap and engaged in a game. Subjects in the touch-therapy group were rubbed on the head, neck, arms, hands, torso, legs, and feet by volunteers.

> Results show that touch aversion and off-task behavior decreased in both groups. Orienting to irrelevant sounds and stereotypic behaviors decreased in both groups, but significantly more in the touch therapy group. (Field, Lasko, Mundy, & Henteleff, 1997, p. 333)

SUMMARY

Throughout this chapter, *learning* has been defined as "the process of acquiring knowledge and new behaviors as a result of encounters with the environment," with culture regarded as an important component of environments. One way to summarize the place that culture has been assigned in the chapter's theories is to identify in each theory the aspects of environments that should be considered cultural and those that should not. To prepare for this analysis, the term *cultural* is defined as "any feature (belief, behavior, object) that is prevalent throughout a general culture (national, regional) or subculture (ethnic, social-class, religious, age-related, or the like)." The term *noncultural* refers to "any feature that is quite rare/unique/idiosyncratic within a culture."

The following examples are intended to support the proposition that all four of the steps in the learning process are predominantly cultural in their content.

First, consider the mixture of cultural and noncultural sources in Eleanor Gibson's theory that recognizes three types of attention—captured/involuntary, self-directed-voluntary, and other-directed. In the captured/involuntary type, people notice aspects of the environment that stand out because they are different from what the person has witnessed in the past. Many cultural elements that serve as "attention grabbers" for young children are not salient for older members of the society who have often "seen that before." In effect, the more experience individuals have had within a particular culture, the less likely elements of that culture will capture their attention. However, among young and old alike, their attention can be attracted by elements of other cultures that are foreign to their experience, such as a strange hairdo, language, or kind of food imported from abroad.

Whereas unfamiliar cultural elements are the relevant objects of captured/involuntary attention, the opposite tends to be true of the self-directed-voluntary type. In this case, attention is directed by the person's goal or need, so he or she seeks out objects that are expected to satisfy the need; those objects will usually be cultural, that is, modes of need fulfillment well known in the society.

In like manner, the other-directed type of attention—which in essence is instruction—focuses chiefly on cultural material, because most teaching is designed to socialize the young by equipping them with the beliefs and behaviors that typify the culture in which they are raised.

Next, consider the mix of cultural and noncultural aspects of the Gibsons' theory of perception. An essential component of their model is the concept *affordances,* which can be defined as "features of the environment that people interpret as opportunities for achieving—or at least for pursuing—their goals." Judgments about which affordances are suitable and which are not suitable can have either a cultural or an idiosyncratic origin. When judgments reflect standards held widely within a group, they are cultural. When judgments derive from standards unique to one or two individuals, they are noncultural. So most appraisals of affordances are culturally based.

Now to the conception of modeling that is a key element of Bandura's social-cognition theory. It seems apparent that the overwhelming majority of models of behavior that people imitate are cultural, in that those models reflect values widely held throughout the society, or at least values held within one of the society's subcultures. Far less often, individuals will copy a person who does not typify either the general culture or a subculture. Because such a model is exceptional, the modeling is deemed idiosyncratic/noncultural.

Skinner's theory about the place of consequences in the learning process implies that culture plays the dominant role in determining the consequences that individuals will attempt to apply in an effort to guide other people's future behavior. Observations of daily life in any group suggest that each culture includes shared beliefs about which consequences are appropriate under which conditions, and which consequences are not. These beliefs are adopted by members of the society who (a) consider such standards to be effective for modifying people's behavior and/or (b) fear the aversive sanctions that the culture's majority will apply if they fail to abide by those standards.

Finally, consider the mixture of cultural and noncultural influences in Baron-Cohen's theory of autism. According to Baron-Cohen, the dominant cause of autism is biological, that is, noncultural. The disorder is basically the result of an aberration in the victim's genetic structure. However, cultural factors that can operate as minor influences on the severity of the disorder are the attitudes toward and treatment of the autistic child among the people with whom the child daily interacts. Such attitudes and treatment methods are usually fashioned by the culture.

4

Attitudes, Emotions, and Values

This chapter's twofold purpose is:

- To illustrate aspects of culture that can be revealed through the windows of theories about three realms of phenomena that have been studied extensively by psychologists, by anthropologists, and by sociologists—the realms of *attitudes, emotions*, and *values*.
- To show how theories focusing on the same general phenomenon can be on different levels of specificity.

The chapter's contents are organized around four theories. Attitudes are represented by a composite model of the development of prejudice. The realm of affect is portrayed through Michael Lewis's general emotion-socialization theory and Catherine Sanders' model of grief as a specific emotion. The development of values is viewed from the vantage point of Lawrence Kohlberg's moral-reasoning proposal.

PREJUDICE AND DISCRIMINATION

Attitudes can be defined as underlying propensities to act either positively or negatively toward people, institutions, or events. Thus, attitudes can be seen as expectations that guide behavior.

Prejudice is one kind of attitude, a kind that consists of making factually incorrect, negative, predisposing judgments of other people. The word *discrimination* refers to action based on such judgments.

The process of adopting a prejudice can be seen as consisting of three phases:

1. attributing characteristics—which usually are undesirable traits—to a class of people (such as the Irish, blacks, women, homosexuals, Hindus, dwarfs, the deaf, the homeless, the rich, the unschooled, and more),

2. identifying a particular person as belonging in that class or in a combination of classes, and
3. attributing to that person the supposed undesirable characteristics of the class without learning whether such traits are true of that individual.

Numerous theories have been proposed to account for how prejudice develops and is sustained. Some authors center their explanations on psychological features of the individual as a prejudiced person or as a victim of prejudice. Other writers explain prejudice as the consequence of societal conditions—of economic, social, political, or cultural factors that are said to produce a prejudiced populous. Still other theorists fault both the individual and the societal perspectives; they propose, instead, a multi-factor model that envisions prejudice as resulting from interactions among multiple types of personalities and multiple types of societies.

The version described in the following paragraphs is a scheme formed from the proposals of several such theorists.

Title: A Composite Theory of Prejudice that draws principally on proposals by Mark Snyder and Peter Miene of the University of Minnesota and by Irwin Katz of the City University of New York.

Key tenets: The term *prejudice* cannot properly be used in the singular. Rather, the term should be used in the plural, because individuals do not maintain a general dislike and distrust for all groups of people. Instead, they hold negative attitudes toward selected others. In short, people exhibit diverse *prejudices*.

One way of viewing prejudices is in terms of the hierarchical stratification of societies. In their structure, societies can be perceived as socially stratified, with each member of the society occupying a particular position on various scales of privilege, respect, opportunity, authority, power, achievement, and reward. The hierarchies are often highly correlated, so that people who are accorded the greatest respect also frequently enjoy a high level of privilege, power, and reward, and vice versa. Furthermore, a distinction can be drawn between people's *ascribed* and *earned* status. Prejudice is involved when a person's location in a structure is ascribed on the basis of that individual's membership in a group, such as a group defined by ethnicity, socioeconomic status, gender, religious affiliation, citizenship, age, or the like. Thus, by simply being a Hindu from India, a resident of Great Britain can be relegated to a position lower in the social-status hierarchy than is a Protestant from Wales. In contrast, prejudice is not the deciding factor in hierarchies based entirely on an individual's talent, achievement, character, or contributions to society. It is the case, however, that the opportunity to develop and display talent or contributions may be affected by prejudice. For instance, a girl's achievement and social status are curtailed in cultures that deny females the same educational experiences available to males. And societies that offer preferential job opportunities to a given ethnic or religious group limit the ability of members of other groups to reach their potential.

Three interlinked processes can be identified as contributing to the development and maintenance of prejudices. First is the *limited-capacity* proposal which holds that humans are limited in the amount of information they can manage, so the burden of processing incoming stimuli is lessened if an individual can develop a restricted set of categories into which impressions can be placed. These categories are stereotypes "that can be construed as serving the function of *cognitive economy* by helping their holders to reduce information to a manageable size, thereby lending a sense of predictability to the social world" (Snyder & Miene, 1994, p. 36). Consequently, when we meet a stranger, we find it is easier to place the stranger in one or more established categories (female, short in stature, dark complexioned, Moslem garbed, speaks French) than to withhold judgment until we become well acquainted with the person and can achieve a more precise, complex understanding of her personal attributes.

A second factor that contributes to prejudice is the *ego defense* process, a psychological device which helps people feel secure and good about themselves by characterizing others in ways that make those others seem less threatening. Labeling all Scots or Jews as stingy and money-grubbing or all Irish as drunken brawlers can render seemingly successful Scots, Jews, and Irishmen reprehensible and deserving censure.

Third is the *cultural-fit* process. As children grow up, they learn by direct observation and by formal and informal instruction a cluster of stereotyped beliefs about their own and other cultural groups. These stereotypes serve the socialization function of providing the values and norms that guide a person's behavior and interpretation of experience. People who live by the standards of one's own culture are viewed as more acceptable—as good and proper folks— than those who live by other standards. Associated with the cultural-fit process is a *group-solidarity* function that encourages individuals to support the policies and members of their own group and to resist and challenge the policies and members of opposing groups.

Prejudices can vary in how deeply an individual feels warranted in maintaining a negative image of certain kinds of other people. For instance, one Chinese may feel thoroughly comfortable in believing that all Japanese are devious and untrustworthy, whereas a second Chinese may harbor mixed feelings about the Japanese. Those mixed feelings may assume at least two forms of ambivalence. Form 1 involves attributing both positive and negative characteristics to the target group (in this case, perhaps admiring Japanese people's putative diligence and self-discipline, but disapproving of their supposed cruelty and intolerance). Form 2 consists of ascribing negative attributes to the target group in general, but making an exception for some of the group's members who are seen as displaying virtues untypical of the group. Either of these forms can produce psychological conflict for the person who holds such opinions (Katz, 1981).

In summary, as children progress through adolescence into adulthood, their daily experiences encourage them to adopt stereotypical images of people who are seen as members of various social groupings. Those stereotypes persist whenever they accommodate the child's limited perceptual capacities, help defend the child's ego, and fit the child into a cultural niche that offers standards for guiding life's social decisions. Furthermore, if an image a person holds exhibits conflicting positive and negative attributes, that person can be expected to experience a measure of psychological distress.

Principal variables: Prejudices can vary in numerous ways, including (a) the types of people on which they focus, (b) the intensity of feeling, (c) the extent that groups, other than one's own, are seen as threats to one's welfare, and (d) the degree to which prejudices are institutionalized.

Types of people that are frequently the target of prejudice are females, members of selected ethnic categories, citizens of particular nations, the lower-social-class poor, members of certain religious bodies, and adherents of various political and philosophical persuasions. Landrine, Klonoff, Alcaraz, Scott, and Wilkens, (1995) have offered a *multiple-jeopardy hypothesis* which proposes that the people who may be harmed most by prejudicial attitudes are those who are identified with more than one of these victim types. Therefore, in the United States we might expect economically poor Indian women—because of their low status in terms of social class, ethnicity, and gender—to suffer more damaging social discrimination than other people who are not burdened with all three sources of prejudice (such other people as higher-class Indian men, lower-class white men, and middle-class white women).

Prejudices can be mild, moderate, or intense. The more intense a prejudice, the more resistant it is to efforts at reducing or dispelling it. Higher levels of intensity can be expected for prejudices that (a) most adequately simplify the processing of stimuli from the environment, (b) enhance one's ego and self-concept, and (c) serve to defend one's cultural values against the threat of different values espoused by other cultures.

Prejudices can vary in the extent to which they are institutionalized. The term *institutionalized* refers to how much a discriminatory practice is formally adopted in a society. The greatest degree of institutionalization occurs when a practice takes the form of written law. A lesser degree of institutionalization exists when the practice is not cast as a written law but is widely endorsed informally by members of the society. The lowest level of institutionalization obtains when a practice does not take the form of written law nor does it enjoy universal support but, rather, it remains controversial—sanctioned by some people and opposed by others.

Differences among cultures: Prejudice and discrimination are so widespread that there is little need to offer a host of examples of how prejudicial attitudes may differ from one culture to another. Thus, the following few instances are included merely to illustrate typical kinds of people who can be the subject of prejudice and discrimination, different levels of prejudice in different cultures, and the consequences that can be expected for individuals and their society as the result of those different levels. These examples, drawn from news reports over the years 1995-1998, involve prejudices relating to gender, ethnicity, and religious affiliation (Burdin & Thomas, 1995, 1996; Gutek & Thomas, 1997, 1998). The cases suggest how trends in discrimination practices as well as in antidiscrimination policies can affect people's educational opportunities and experiences.

Gender. Afghanistan's Kabul University reopened in March 1997 after having been closed for 6 months by the Taliban Islamic-fundamentalist militia. However, because more than half of the university's teaching staff before the shutdown had been women, the conduct of classes upon the school's reopening was seriously crippled by the militia's ban against women at the university as either students or teachers.

A French parliament report in 1997 criticized sexist portrayals of women in school textbooks. Definitions in children's dictionaries associated gentle, passive, and home-based qualities with females and assertive qualities with males.

That same year, in South Africa, Mamphela Aletta Ramphele, a physician and anthropologist, was installed as vice-chancellor of the University of Cape Town, the first black woman to hold that position in a South African university. In Japan, where only 10% of the nation's faculty members were women, Masako Niwa of Nara Women's University became the first woman president of a national university.

The U.S. Supreme Court ruled the Virginia Military Institute's all-male enrollment policy unconstitutional. This ended the all-male policy in the last public higher-education institution in the United States that had practiced gender discrimination.

Ethnicity. Four years after the former Yugoslav republic of Macedonia achieved independence, representatives of the nation's ethnic Albanians sought to establish an Albanian-language university. The plan was denounced by government authorities, who felt that Albanians were entitled only to primary and secondary education in their native language.

The South African government sought to reverse years of ethnic discrimination by committing itself to furnishing every child, regardless of racial background, with 10 years of schooling at government expense. Educational segregation was officially abolished, and improved training for black teachers was planned.

The number of Canada's aboriginal peoples—Indians and Inuits—enrolled in higher education increased fourfold between 1985 and 1995, owing largely to government financial aid and a growing number of academic programs designed for the nation's indigenous ethnic groups.

Religious affiliation. In 1997, educational authorities in France were criticized by Islamic leaders for not permitting women students to wear head scarves in the public schools. Officials claimed that displaying the traditional Islamic head coverings violated France's law banning religion in the schools, even though Catholic students were still allowed to wear crosses.

In Israel, military forces arrested a group of Islamic students at a college near Jerusalem on charges of anti-Israeli propaganda, and Israeli officials stopped granting entry permits to Palestinian students in an effort to discourage Palestinian nationalistic activism.

The Canadian Supreme Court ruled that the province of Ontario was not obligated to finance non-Catholic religious schools, even though the province had paid for Catholic schools for more than a century and could continue to do so.

Cross-cultural encounters: Three of the possible outcomes of interactions between cultural groups are (a) feelings of ambivalence, (b) intensification of prejudice, and (c) reduction of prejudice.

As an example of ambivalence, Katz and Hass (1988) studied the attitudes of white American college students toward black Americans and concluded that the whites held feelings of both friendliness and rejection toward black people. These conflicting emotions appeared to derive from two largely independent, core value orientations of American culture: (a) humanitarianism-egalitarianism, which fosters sympathy for blacks as a deprived group and (b) the Protestant work ethic "with its emphasis on self-reliance and self-discipline, which seems to generate critical perceptions of blacks" (Katz & Hass, 1988, p. 902).

Azoulay (1997) has proposed that a three-way form of ambivalence lies behind the unwillingness of white Jewish couples in the United States to adopt children who are products of interracial (white/black) parentage, even when the children are committed to the Jewish faith. In Azoulay's opinion, the intellectual and emotional strife suffered by such couples involves conflict among (a) their subscribing to liberal social attitudes that accord equal rights and respect to people of all ethnic origins, (b) their favoring the Jewish religion and its adherents, and (c) their prejudice against people of color.

Prejudice can be intensified when personal encounters confirm negative stereotypes of people or social groups other than one's own. To illustrate, the attempt of the United States government to force racial integration in public schools in the 1960s included a program of busing children to distant schools that would then be populated by students from a variety of neighborhoods. As a consequence, students who had never before mixed with ones from ethnic and social-class backgrounds unlike their own were now interacting on a daily basis with such agemates. When the characteristics of these new acquaintances were ones admired by the students of a different ethnic or social-class category, and when their relationships were amicable, then prejudicial stereotypes declined. But frequently the opposite occurred—personal contact confirmed negative stereotypes whenever the appearance and habits of an unfamiliar group seemed to match those stereotypes. In effect, whether the law-makers succeeded in reducing prejudice by means of forced direct social interaction depended on the quality of that interaction (Thomas, 1967).

Practical applications: The kinds of applications most often proposed are ones intended to combat prejudice and discrimination.

For instance, Hoffman (1987) has recommended an educational approach to prejudice reduction that "stresses the common humanity of all people and includes efforts to raise people's levels of empathy for outgroup members." The method involves participants' (a) admitting that everyone holds certain biased views of other people, (b) recognizing the nature of their own biases and those of others, and (c) suggesting rules for judging others that minimize bias and encourage impartiality. Hoffman's approach includes participants having direct face-to-face contact with people of other cultures and engaging in role-taking exercises that require participants to assume the roles of people from cultural backgrounds other than their own. "The combination of rule systems and empathy-enhancing moral education should expand the range of people to whom individuals can respond empathically, thus reducing familiarity-similarity bias" (Hoffman, 1987, pp. 69-70).

From the perspective of our composite theory of prejudice, the following are ways of attempting to reduce people's prejudices in relation to *cognitive economy, ego defense,* and *goodness of fit* between one's own worldview and that of one's culture.

Cognitive economy. The cognitive-economy hypothesis holds that people's limited capacity to keep in mind complex depictions of social relations causes them to adopt simplistic stereotypical beliefs about people they meet. But whenever their encounters with the world contradict their beliefs (meeting people whose behavior fails to conform to the stereotypes), their confidence in their mental map is shaken, resulting in a state of cognitive dissonance or intellectual disorder that they seek to resolve. One type of resolution consists of their discarding the stereotype and henceforth judging others on the basis of those others' individual characteristics rather than on their membership in a particular ethnic, gender, religious, or age group. One teaching method designed to stimulate such cognitive dissonance consists of confronting prejudiced individuals with inconsistencies among their values. As an example, in Katz and Hass's (1988, p. 903) study of attitudes of whites toward blacks in America, they proposed that whites' commitment to egalitarianism, which caused them to have "sympathy for blacks as a deprived group, suggests the usefulness of an educational strategy that strengthens the egalitarian outlook and spells out its relation to minority rights." In effect, ethnic prejudices are expected to decline as the result of educational programs that illustrate how a commitment to equal rights for all ethnic groups applies in daily life situations.

Ego defense. From the viewpoint of the ego-defense hypothesis, an appropriate way to reduce individuals' prejudices is to provide counseling and educational experiences that strengthen people's self confidence, thereby reducing the need for them to defend their egos by denigrating others on the basis of the others' membership in some selected social category. In support of this proposal, Ponterotto and Pedersen (1993, p. 90) cite research showing a strong correlation between high self-esteem and lower levels of prejudice. The evidence suggests that among ethnic groups, counseling sessions that build a sense of ethnic identity contribute to personal esteem. As a device for reducing prejudices, building self-esteem in a school setting can be most successful when combined with teaching techniques that (a) build a climate of respect and trust among members of a classroom of students, (b) permit the open expression of opinions, (c) encourage a spirit of inquiry into people's reasons for their attitudes, (d) foster respect for diverse viewpoints, and (e) promote objective, analytical thinking by openly identifying the strengths and weaknesses of different patterns of reasoning (Ponterotto & Pedersen, 1993, pp. 89-91).

Goodness of fit. A society's legal system—its laws and regulations—can be seen as a collection of cultural ideals that members of the society are expected to promote. Thus, an important task for adults is to direct children's attitudes and actions to match those ideals. The term *social progress,* in one of its meanings, refers to changes in a society's ideals that are reflected in laws and regulations relating to social discrimination. In the United States, such progress in the mid-19th century took the form of the emancipation of slaves; in 1918 of extending voting rights to women; in 1954 of desegregating schools; and in recent years of legislation aimed at providing people of all ethnicities, genders, religious commitments, and ages equal rights to occupational, educational, and social-intercourse opportunities. Therefore, with the passing of time, cultural ideals which the young are to adopt can change, so that habits of discrimination which were once acceptable may no longer be acceptable at a later time. Consequently, even though individuals' prejudices can be highly resistant to change, new laws and regulations aimed at reducing discrimination can establish a new cultural standard into which the young are expected to fit. Refusing to adopt those standards makes individuals subject to social sanctions. Therefore, one important way to reduce prejudices is to foster legislation designed to promote equal opportunities for all and to teach the young to abide by the legislation so they can deserve the title *good citizen.*

EMOTIONS: GENERAL

Among the many available theories of emotional development, a prominent issue that theorists address—either directly or by implication—is the question of whether (a) the emotions observed in one culture are universal throughout all cultures, and thus are characteristic of humankind, or (b) emotions vary from one culture to another and thus are culturally constructed. Scheff's (1983) review of cross-cultural studies of emotional behavior led him to observe that

> Most universalists believe that the seat of emotions is in the center of the body, in the viscera. . . . Like Darwin, they see emotions as biological, genetically determined reactions that are universal in the human species. Most of those who take the culture-specific approach, on the other hand, take the opposite position, that emotions occur in the mind and in the mind's reactions to the immediate environment, particularly the social environment. . . . According to the [currently popular] cultural-specific perspective, there is only one type of physical arousal, and this one type plays a role in all emotions. [So] the differences among the various emotions experienced—grief, fear, anger, shame, and so on—is not physiological but is caused by differences of *interpretation* of the same bodily arousal. In a context interpreted by self and/or others as one of danger. . . then autonomic arousal occurs and is usually interpreted as the feeling of fear. (Scheff, 1983, p. 335)

Scheff concludes that the evidence for the universality position is at least as strong as—"and probably stronger than"—the evidence for cultural specificity. What may be the case is that such emotional responses as crying, smiling, startle, and disgust are fundamental and universal, whereas other more specific emotional displays may depend on culture. In effect, cultural traditions may determine the particular occasions on which expressing different feelings is socially acceptable; hence, the culture governs the form those displays assume.

The following theory is one that recognizes both biological and social influences but actually emphasizes the cultural-specific position.

Title: Emotional Socialization Theory, as proposed by Michael Lewis.

Key tenets: Emotions are most usefully defined in terms of elicitors, receptors, states, expressions, and experiences. *Elicitors* are events that stimulate emotional *receptors*, which are relatively specific locations or pathways in the central nervous system that activate changes in a person's physiological and/or mental states. *Emotional states* are the patterns of change in somatic and/or neuronal activity that accompany the activation of receptors. *Emotional expressions* are the potentially observable surface changes in a person's face, body, voice, and activity that accompany emotional states. *Emotional experiences* are people's conscious or unconscious interpretation of their perceived states and expressions (Lewis & Michalson, 1982, p. 182). A typical emotional event begins with stimuli impacting on a receptor, which sets off both a state change and emotional expression, then culminates in an emotional experience. However, this sequence is sometimes altered.

In contrast to biological theories of emotional development, socialization theory does not contend that the above five features of emotions are so thoroughly grounded in the biological composition of humans that the five appear in the same form in all cultures. Instead, while socialization theory "does not deny the importance of organismic functions, . . . it stresses the equally important role of socialization in learning and emotional development" (Lewis & Saarni, 1985, p. 2).

Principal variables: The two major sets of variables for analyzing emotional development are: (1) a culture's dominant beliefs about what constitutes appropriate emotional behavior, and (2) the socialization techniques (learning activities) employed for teaching the young how to respond properly to emotion-eliciting events. Each of these categories is composed of several components.

Appropriate behavior. Three variables important for understanding a culture's conception of acceptable emotional behavior are people's shared beliefs about (a) the kinds of emotional *expressions* and (b) *experiences* (interpretations) that should be evoked by (c) different types of *environmental stimuli* (elicitors).

Teaching emotional behavior. The emotional behaviors children and youths come to display are determined by both direct and indirect sources of influence. Two direct sources are *instrumental learning* and *didactic teaching.* Two indirect sources are *identification* and *imitation.*

Instrumental learning consists of a child discovering by direct encounters with daily-life incidents what consequences accompany different kinds of emotional expression that the child may exhibit in emotion-eliciting circumstances. In other words, children learn which kinds of expression—crying, laughing, complaining, smiling, attacking, running away—serve as instruments for producing desired, rewarding consequences and which kinds produce unpleasant, punishing consequences. Children who become successfully socialized are those who adopt the eliciter-expression combinations that are approved and rewarded by their culture's socializing agents (parents, guardians, teachers, athletic coaches, police officers, and the like) and who abandon the combinations disapproved and punished by such agents.

Didactic teaching involves a socializing agent instructing the child about what expressions to display under various emotion-rousing conditions. The coach of a baseball team of American ten-year-olds warns the players, "When you strike out, you don't throw your bat and stomp away grumbling; and you don't start weeping when the team loses." The mother of a 16-year-old Australian girl says, "If the other girls don't invite you to the party, don't frown and pout; just smile and act as if you don't care." Agents not only instruct the young in which ways of expressing feelings are most acceptable, but they frequently suggest how the young should experience an emotionally charged event. "It wasn't your fault, so you have no reason to feel bad" or "You did it on purpose; you ought to be ashamed."

Identification is the psychological process of persons extending their own sense of self to embrace characteristics of things in the environment—such things as people, animals, objects (works of art, endangered plant species), or institutions (schools, clubs, fraternal organizations, governments, religions, philosophical traditions). The extent of a child's identification with a *thing* is reflected in the quality and degree of emotion the child feels when learning of what has happened to that thing.   The identification is strong if the child feels highly elated upon learning of the thing's successes and feels deeply depressed upon learning of the thing's defeats.   If the child experiences no emotion upon learning the fate of the thing, then the child has established no identification with it.   Identification is usually not accomplished by conscious intent but, rather, takes place automatically, operating at a subconscious level.   Thus, the child can acquire elicitor-expression combinations by identifying with someone who displays those patterns of emotional response.

Intimately linked to identification is the process of imitation in which children and youth intentionally model their emotional behavior after that of individuals they admire.   By seeing which consequences accompany the ways other people react to emotion-evoking events, children can vicariously learn the forms of emotional expression approved and disapproved in their culture.

Differences among cultures: Five important ways in which cultures differ in the socialization of emotions are in (a) how to express emotions, (b) when to express them, (c) how a person learns to manage or control emotions, (d) how emotions are labeled, and (e) how they are interpreted (Lewis & Michalson, 1982, p. 191).

The clearest evidence that culture influences emotional development is found in emotional expression and experience (interpretation).   People discover from their society which expressions of fear, grief, joy, guilt, or embarrassment are considered most appropriate on different eliciting occasions.   Children learn that "how people feel in a particular situation is not only supposed to be 'natural,' given the situation, but it is also socially expected, or even socially required" (Schieffelin, 1985, p. 169).   In the culture of the Kaluli tribe of Papua New Guinea:

> A man's temper, or 'tendency to get angry,' is a major feature by which Kaluli judge his character and assess the degree to which he is a force to be reckoned with.   It represents the vigor with which he will stand up for or pursue his interest vis-à-vis others, and the likelihood that he will retaliate for wrong or injury.   Anger is an affect that is both feared and admired.   The vigor or personal energy a person is expected to have is broadly exemplified in an emotional style I have characterized as volatile . . . expressively passionate. . . .   Rage, grief, dismay, embarrassment, fear, and compassion may be openly and often dramatically expressed. (Schieffelin, 1985, p. 173)

In contrast, on another island of the Indonesian archipelago, Java, life among the Javanese calls for quite the opposite expression of emotion—hiding anger and dismay behind a facade of calm composure and equanimity that minimizes interpersonal conflict (Geertz, 1976).   However, the cultural ideal does not always determine practice.   For instance, the dominant culture of the island of Bali teaches that one should not cry during mourning, but in practice the Balinese weep as much as members of other cultures (Scheff, 1983).

A study by Harris (1989) of Dutch, English, and Nepalese children showed that in all three countries children between ages 5 and 14 followed a highly similar pattern of development in recognizing various emotions. The younger children were adept at identifying emotions that could be revealed by distinctive facial or posture cues—*fear, happiness, sadness, anger,* and *shyness.* Then, beyond age 7, children could also cite situations that evoked emotions which had no obvious expressive display—*pride, jealousy, gratitude, worry, relief, guilt,* and *excitement.* However, the Nepalese participants differed from their European agemates in the life situations described as elicitors of various emotions. Specifically, the themes reflected in the examples offered by children in the remote Nepalese village featured

> the burdens and anxieties of agricultural labor . . . ; the pleasures associated with certain special foods or treats in an otherwise bland diet of rice or maize and lentils . . . ; [and] the proximity of serious illness, poverty, and death. . . . By comparison, the European children . . . inhabited a more protected world of toys, pets, and school. (Harris, 1989, p. 84)

From their society, children also learn how they should experience or interpret their feelings. Less clear is the process of how a given culture determines which kinds of events should generate which emotions. And least apparent is how—or even if—patterns of culture affect neural receptors and emotional states (Lewis & Saarni, 1985, pp. 3-10).

In every society, the *how* and *when* to express feelings is taught by example, instruction, and the administration of reward and punishment from the time of infancy. Not only may the approved elicitor-expression linkages vary from one society to another, but the linkages may differ from one age period to another. For example, among the Kipsigis people of Kenya's western highlands, infants who cry from physical or emotional distress are immediately comforted by their mothers.

> The idea of leaving a baby to cry in order not to "spoil" it would be seen as bizarre, and the American practices of letting babies or toddlers cry for long periods at night in order to break them of the habit of getting up was strongly disapproved by Kipsigis observers. (Harkness & Super, 1995, pp. 25-26)

However, by later childhood, crying is highly condemned by the Kipsigis, especially at the time of circumcision for boys and clitoridectomy for girls (puberty rites of passage). At that period of life, crying children bring disgrace on themselves and their family.

Cultures also vary in the labels they attach to emotions. The feelings associated with what seem to be equivalent terms in different languages can actually vary from one culture to another. Such is the case with the emotional state and the interpretation allied with the English-language label *love* as compared with the ostensibly equivalent French *amour,* German *Liebe,* and

Indonesian *cinta*. These terms may not all imply exactly the same emotional experience in different cultures. Even within a single society, such labels as *love, fear, joy, guilt,* and *distrust* are not conceived precisely the same way by all members of the society, because each person has constructed his or her emotional state and interpretation from a different set of instrumental-learning, didactic-instruction, identification, and modeling events.

Variations are found as well in the sorts of events that are expected to elicit different emotions. Among American Indians, Apaches are considered "by nature" a people who like to laugh, particularly at people finding themselves in an embarrassing or ridiculous position. Outburst of laughter are rarely restrained unless there is the risk of hurting someone's feelings or there are strangers around (Goodwin, 1942/1969, p. 556).

Cultures are sometimes characterized by the dominance of certain emotions. An example is the prominent place of shame (*haka'ika*) or embarrassment in the Marquesas Island culture of the Southeastern Pacific. All sorts of situations that would not cause shame in other cultures will bring on shame or "stage fright" in the Marquesas as well as in a variety of other Polynesian societies. Furthermore, the social function of shame can vary with the stage of life.

> Shame emerges in childhood, for Marquesans, out of a less valued and less differentiated "fear" (*ha'ameta'u*). The "shame" of the young may paralyze action when they are subjected to disapproval. With adults, "shame" is expected to function more as a guidepost to situations to be minimized or avoided. (Kirkpatrick, 1985 p. 110)

Differences in the socialization of girls and boys can account for differences in how females and males experience emotion-laden events. Furthermore, those differences can vary across cultures. To illustrate, in a study conducted in India and in England, preschool and early-primary-school children in the two countries listened to a series of stories in which a central character feigned an emotion. The task of the children was to identify whether the expressed emotion was real or only appeared genuine. The Indian preschool girls proved more adept than either the English girls or the Indian and English boys at distinguishing between real and feigned emotion. In way of explanation, the authors suggested that girls in India are more often restricted to the home setting than are boys so that girls experience many more situations in which children are expected to show appropriate behavior toward adults.

> A greater emphasis is placed on deference and decorum in the socialization of girls than of boys. . . . [Because] the ability to conceal inappropriate emotion from significant others (i.e., to "be polite") is culturally valued, then it is not surprising that girls achieve this understanding at an earlier age than boys, given the pressure on them to conform. (Joshi & MacLean, 1994, p. 1380)

In both the Indian and English samples, the children's justifications for their answers led the authors to conclude that it was not a heightened sense of empathy that motivated children's close attention to adults' expressed emotion but, rather, the driving force was their desire to avoid "being smacked or scolded by adults, with the Indian children making many more references than the English children to physical punishment" (Joshi & MacLean, 1994, p. 1380). As might be expected, the ability to differentiate between real and feigned affect increased with age among both Indian and English girls and boys.

Cross-cultural encounters: Misunderstandings can result from the fact that a label identifying a widely recognized emotional state within one culture may not be easily translated into the language of another culture and thus may not be comprehended by members of the other culture. An example is the emotional condition commonly expressed with a single word in certain Pacific Island cultures but not adequately conveyed by any term in English-speaking societies. That word is *musu* in the Samoan Islands and *nguch* in the Ifaluk Atoll (Gerber, 1985; Lutz, 1985; Thomas, 1987). The emotional quality of *musu* or *nguch* can only be approximated among English-language speakers by an admixture of such terms as *bored, irritable, not up to it, kind of sick, distressed, fed up, and dissatisfied.* In islanders' tradition, feeling *musu* is an acceptable reason for getting up late in the morning, being absent from school or work, or avoiding routine responsibilities. In an islander's home culture

> One's musu is a sufficient explanation; it is never questioned by others or justified by the person who experiences it. The self-attribution of musu serves, then, as a mechanism by which a person can avoid a burdensome situation while at the same time not having to admit to the existence of unacceptable feelings. (Gerber, 1985, p. 129)

However, problems arise when islanders move into other societies where pleading *musu* or *nguch* is of no avail—societies in which people are responsible for meeting their obligations despite feeling irritable and out of sorts.

Misunderstandings also arise when a given event that would acceptably evoke laughter in one culture would not be considered a proper source of humor in another. Likewise, expressions of grief regarded as suitable in one society may not be appropriate in another, so that unintentional injury to feelings and condemnation of improper behavior can occur when people behave in a manner appropriate to their cultural origins but inappropriate in their present cultural context.

An important cause of cross-cultural misunderstanding of emotion is that the rationale linking emotions to behavior in one society may be either incomprehensible or unacceptable in a different one. During research in the Samoan Islands, Eleanor Gerber was puzzled by Samoan informants telling her that fathers severely beat their children in a spirit of love (*alofa*). The explanation she received was that

Fathers and children are closely identified, and the behavior of children reflects almost directly on the reputation of the parents. . . . Because of this close identification, fathers stand to be shamed if their children misbehave. They must teach them right from wrong, but children, especially young children, learn only with the incentive of pain. Concerned fathers, who worry about their children's capacity to shame them and wish to make their children good people, therefore beat them. (Gerber, 1985, p. 131)

Practical applications: A learning activity known as *emotional-experiences exchange* is intended to increase people's understanding of the approved forms of emotion in different cultures. In a multicultural counseling group or classroom of students, the activity consists of participants sharing their understanding of how different kinds of emotional behavior are viewed within a culture about which they have intimate knowledge. The activity is directed by a leader— usually a counselor or classroom teacher—who poses a sequence of questions that participants take turns answering in relation to a given culture, which is usually the culture in which the participant was reared. The activity assumes the form of an interview. In one variation of the procedure, the questions center on a particular emotion (such as joy, fear, anger, sadness, disgust, disappointment) or a resultant behavior (weeping, laughing, ridiculing, running away, striking out, or the like). Here is an example of a question sequence focusing on weeping—a sequence suitable for other emotional behaviors as well.

> In your culture, when is it considered all right to cry? I mean, under what conditions is crying acceptable?
> Are there times when it's all right for children to cry but not for adults? If so, at what age does this expectation change and why?
> Are the expectations or rules about crying the same for males and females? If not, how are they different, and why?
> On what occasions would it be considered wrong to cry, and why? What happens to people if they cry on inappropriate occasions?

In another variation of the approach, the series of questions focuses on a particular kind of event—a dramatic performance in a theater, the funeral of a grandparent, a soccer game, a pupil making an error while giving an oral report before the class, a chess match, accidentally smashing one's finger in a car door, a classmate making a derogatory remark about one's ethnic group, or a valedictorian including a "dirty joke" in his graduation speech. The following is such a sequence in which the focal event is a religious service.

> Within your culture, in what kinds of religious service do people participate?
> During the service, how are people supposed to act?
> What emotions are they supposed to feel during the service?
> What would be a wrong way to act, and why?
> What are some wrong kinds of emotion to feel or display?

EMOTIONS: GRIEF

Various theories have been proposed to explain the sense of loss and despair known as grief. Here are three examples.

The first is a medical model, depicting grief as a disease that is a "debilitating condition, accompanied by pain, anguish, and increased morbidity; it is associated with a consistent etiology (real, threatened, or even fantasized object loss); and it fulfills all of the criteria of a discrete syndrome, with relatively predictable symptomatology and course" (Averill & Nunley, 1993, p. 85). For instance, in Tahitian culture, reactions to the loss of a loved one or friend have traditionally been viewed as symptoms of illness or fatigue.

A second type is a social-constructionist model, which asserts that the basic physiological and psychological concomitants of grief are universal throughout humankind. However, the events that warrant grief, the way people respond to those events, and the process of recovering from grief are very much determined by the culture—by the values and practices of a society. Thus, grief is pictured as a normal emotion, with significant differences to be expected from one culture to another in the ways an emotion is represented in thought and behavior (Averill & Nunley, 1993).

A third perspective is *cognitive-experiential self-theory* (CEST) that postulates two human conceptual systems: (a) the rational (conscious, socially prescribed rules for drawing inferences and citing evidence) and (b) the experiential (subconscious, intuitive, quick, imagery oriented, emotional, self-evidently valid). Epstein's view of the likely conflict between the two systems enables him to account for people's puzzlement at their reactions to death.

> A person, in his or her conscious, rational system may believe that he or she should be deeply distressed following the death of a sibling. In the experiential system, however, the death may be perceived as the defeat of a rival and evoke feelings of victory among with those of regret. In such a case, the person is apt to be surprised by the inappropriate feelings that he or she experiences. (Epstein, 1993, p. 115)

The theory described in the following paragraphs is one that assumes an underlying psycho-biological base common to all humans, but provides as well for the influence of cultural and individual factors that affect the grief people experience at the death of someone they especially value.

Title: An Integrative Theory of Grief and Bereavement, as conceived by Catherine M. Sanders, a clinical psychologist in Charlotte, North Carolina.

Key tenets: Sanders distinguishes among the concepts *bereavement, grief,* and *mourning.* Bereavement is the experiential state one endures after a loss—the feelings and changed conditions that the loss produces. *Grief* is the reaction a person experiences while in the state of bereavement, including such reactions as anger, guilt, anxiety, fear, despair, sadness, physical complaints, and illness.

Mourning refers to the behavior a particular culture identifies as appropriate following a death.

Principal variables: Sanders' model of the grief and bereavement process can be cast as four stages (Figure 4-1). First is the death of a valued person. Second is the initial impact of the event on an aggrieved individual, with the nature of the impact influenced by both external and internal factors. Third is the series of bereavement phases. Fourth is the outcome of the bereavement process.

Figure 4-1

An Integrative Theory of Bereavement

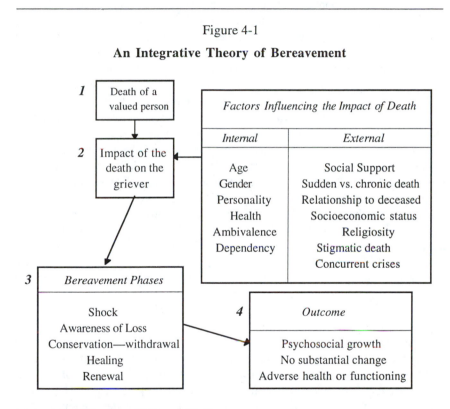

Adapted from Sanders, 1989, pp. 37-41.

As shown in Figure 4-1, the effect of a death on the person who suffers the loss is seen by Sanders as a product of a variety of factors, both within the person and within the surrounding environment.

Internal factors. The model's six internal variables include age, gender, personality, health status, ambivalent feelings toward the deceased, and the extent of the griever's dependence on the deceased.

In respect to age, it is apparent that the effect of a loved one's death on the living will differ if the griever is 2 years old rather than 14, 21, 48, or 89. The griever's gender may also affect the impact of loss, particularly if cultural tradition holds different expectations for mourning by males than by females.

Sanders has identified four personality types she considers important in individuals' success in coping with grief. First is the *disturbed* type—people who have few internal resources for gaining relief from distress. "They rarely learn to profit from their life experiences. When this [type] suffers a severe loss, the result is one of long-lasting desolation" (Sanders, 1989, p. 128). Next are the *depressed* personalities—those people whose lives have been marked by multiple family loses or strained interpersonal relationships. Their resulting tenuous hold on security renders them dependent on others. When an important friend or family member is lost, their dormant negative self-concept comes to the fore, accompanied by panic and rage. Third is the *denial* type—people who need strong defenses to cope with crises, so their way of dealing with death is to keep a "stiff upper lip", refuse to admit human weakness, and divert attention from their loss by intensifying their activity at work, in social service, in sports, or in the church. Last is the *normal-grief* type—individuals with high ego strength, confidence, emotional control, and little confusion or indulgence in unreality.

The conditions of grievers' health obviously affects their reaction to death. Physical or mental disorders reduce the chances of individuals constructively weathering bereavement.

People who had harbored ambivalent feelings toward the deceased can be tormented by the memory of such discordant love/hate emotions and thus find it difficult to resolve their grief. The problem of ambivalence is particularly acute when a loved one dies after a long illness that seriously disrupted the griever's life, and the griever then feels guilty about having resented the deceased and perhaps having wished the sick one dead.

Those who had been highly dependent—financially, socially, or emotion-ally—on the deceased will often suffer a longer period of mourning and have more difficulty dispelling their grief than do ones who were less dependent.

External factors. In Sanders' theory, the foregoing internal conditions interact with seven influences from the environment to determine the impact of the loss on the griever. The seven include mourners' social support, relationship to the deceased, socioeconomic status, the religious context, sudden versus chronic death, stigmatic death, and other crises in the grievers' lives.

Social support consists of the kind and amount of aid furnished the mourner by other individuals and agencies. Social support is strongly influenced by culture, since the type of support and the conditions under which it is provided are typically defined by tradition.

The term *chronic death* usually means the demise of a person who has been seriously ill for an extended period of time, so death comes as no surprise. Indeed, such death is sometimes considered a blessing, as it releases the loved one from pain and travail. *Sudden death*—by accident, violence, or an abrupt fatal disease—catches grievers unprepared, making their bereavement particularly difficult, especially if the deceased was a young person who, as is often proposed, was robbed of a fair chance to live a full life.

The relationship between the deceased and the bereaved affects the extent and handling of grief. An elderly spouse can be expected to react differently to the loss than does a parent of a school-age child. An adult son who has lived for years a great distance from his parents is likely to be less distraught by his father's or mother's death than a son who lived nearby and was his parent's frequent companion and support.

The financial status of mourners can influence their ability to recover from the death of someone on whom they depended. A widow left with no financial resources and incapable to taking a job undergoes greater stress than does one whose husband left her with a comfortable income.

In every society, certain sources of death carry greater stigma than do other sources. Whether the bereaved are burdened with shame and guilt depends to a considerable degree on a culture's moral values. Death by suicide, murder, drug overdose, AIDS (acquired immune deficiency syndrome), or drunk driving is often considered an embarrassment in North American culture. A person who suffers a fatal heart attack in the midst of an adulterous amour can also disgrace family members and add to the difficulty of resolving their grief.

Finally, other crises in grievers' lives at the time of the death usually intensify the difficulty of recovering from the loss. Crises can be of many sorts—family members quarreling over the property of the departed, the illness of a valued friend, the mourner's own poor health, creditors badgering the griever for the payment of debts, an unmarried teenage daughter's pregnancy, and more.

The bereavement process. A death's initial impact, which results from the confluence of the multiple internal and external causes, establishes the platform for a bereavement process that Sanders divides into five phases—shock, awareness of loss, withdrawal, healing (the turning point), and renewal.

The term *shock* refers to the trauma a person experiences at the death of a valued friend and is characterized by disbelief, confusion, restlessness, feelings of unreality, frequent regression to immature ways of behaving, a sense of helplessness, and intense physical alarm "that is governed by the sympathetic part of the autonomic nervous system, causing physical changes that . . . if allowed to continue over a period of time, could inhibit the body's immune system, which, in turn, would reduce the capacity to resist infection and disease" (Sanders, 1989, p. 49).

After the funeral, when friends and family have resumed their normal lives, the second phase—*awareness of loss*—typically appears, marked by separation anxiety, conflicts over how to continue one's life, acting out emotional expectations (weeping, physical ailments), and prolonged stress that is often accompanied by oversensitivity, denial of the death, fear of death, and disturbing dreams.

The third phase is characterized by withdrawal from the company of others, despair, diminished social support as other people go about their own business, and the sense of helplessness that occurs when events seem uncontrollable. Symptoms of this phase include weakness, fatigue, a need for more sleep, and a diminished immune system. The mourner avoids other people, obsessively reviewing the loss over and over in the "ruminating and unfocused concentration" that Sanders calls *grief work* that brings the mourner to a final acknowledgment that "old conditions are no longer attainable. The deceased is gone, and life will never be as it once was" (Sanders, 1989, p. 81). This realization prepares the griever for the next period.

Sanders' fourth phase, labeled *the turning point*, involves grievers' intellectually and emotionally accepting the loss and adopting a new worldview that matches their new reality. The process consists of assuming control of their life, rebuilding their self-concept, and relinquishing the role they performed in relationship to the deceased—the role of spouse, parent, daughter, son, lover, companion. With this advance in controlling their lives, mourners' physical ailments abate, energy recovers, sleep is restored, and the immune system improves. Grievances against the deceased are forgiven, guilt diminished, the pain of loss forgotten, the search for new meanings in life advances, and hope is restored.

The final phase of *renewal* consists of the mourner gaining a new self-awareness, accepting responsibility to act, and learning to live without the departed.

How successfully mourners progress through the five stages depends both on the complex of internal and external mediators that determined the impact of the death and on the sorts of support and nurturance the individual receives throughout the bereavement process. The form and amount of nurturance can vary from one culture to another, and different individuals can be expected to advance through the phases at different rates and along different pathways. What works well for one person may not work for another.

The outcome of bereavement. Sanders has proposed three principal results of the bereavement process, which she labels *psychological growth, no substantial change,* and *adverse change in health or functioning.* In practice, each of these reactions can assume a multitude of subtypes and combinations that represent individual people's final response to the death of someone important in their life.

The most constructive reaction is psychological growth achieved by letting go of the deceased, forming new and satisfying relationships, adopting a new positive self-concept, and enthusiastically entering life's mainstream.

Far less constructive is the maintenance of old habits, with the griever pretending to live as if the deceased were just away for a while.

Least desirable is the failure to invest the energy needed to build a new life. Instead, the mourner sinks into despair, seclusion, sickness, or into death itself. Sanders's proposal that this is a self-imposed outcome "is based on the theoretical notion that each individual has control over personal destiny and can choose either health and integration or disease and disintegration" (Sanders, 1989, p. 17).

With the Sanders model now in mind, we consider forms of mourning and grief in various societies.

Differences among cultures: Grief, as the reactions a person experiences from the loss of a friend or relative, can vary from one person to another within the same culture. Mourning, as the culturally defined acts customarily performed after a death, can vary from one society to another. Thus, in comparing cultures, our focus is not on the idiosyncratic grief of individuals but, rather, on the actions that cultures expect following a death.

> Americans mourn in a way quite different from those who mourn in Greece or India. For most individuals in our [American] culture, mourning is on a small scale, private, and personal. It is usually over too soon for bereaved persons to realize the full impact of the loss. Nevertheless, general rules are usually followed. Most often, there is a visitation period before the funeral and a short graveside service before the burial. The funeral itself is usually stylized and brief. On the other hand, prominent figures require more outward signs of mourning such as large military displays or, at least, flags flown at half-mast. (Sanders, 1989, p. 10)

Multiple mourning traditions. In matters of death, any complex society can include religious cultures whose traditions differ. Sometimes the traditions exist in parallel. Other times one dominates, or else the traditions merge to comprise a syncretic mode of mourning.

Parallel customs found in multicultural societies can be illustrated with Catholic, Jewish, and Muslim patterns of mourning. For Catholics, the body of the deceased is displayed, the priest conducting the funeral wears black vestments to symbolize death, incense is burned to honor the flesh that soon will turn to dust, and the somber Latin funeral hymn *Dies Irae* will be played. Traditional Jews do not put the body on display nor have it cremated, but bury the dead within 24 hours, if possible, without embalming, and in a plain wooden coffin. Survivors may cut their clothing with a razor to symbolize the rending of life that death has caused. For the first week thereafter, men do not shave, survivors do not wash their whole bodies, and the family receives visitors while sitting on the floor or on low stools to signify their pain. Formal mourning may continue for a month, or for most of a year if the departed one was a parent. Muslims mourn in a mosque, not a funeral home. Within hours of death, the male members of the community walk in a procession to the gravesite, and the body is buried after a close friend of the departed climbs into the grave to read instructions intended to prepare the deceased to meet Allah. Women later visit the grave during a 40-day mourning period (Woodward, 1997).

Syncretic mourning practice is illustrated in Jamaica where Jewish and Hindu rituals not only feature traditional Jewish and Hindu customs but incorporate such African death rites as "nine night—a ceremony of passage, where people meet to give comfort and support to the relatives of the deceased and to wish the departed a safe journey to life's next stage" (Burrell, 1996, p. 1). Another widely adopted element of African origin is the belief that the spirit of the dead can do harm.

Changing conditions within a society can affect the popularity of modes of mourning. In China, expensive, lavish funerals and burials that use up land needed for other purposes have been disapproved by the government in recent times. In Beijing, families have been encouraged to cremate the deceased and scatter the ashes in the sea ("Reforming Funeral and Interment Methods," 1997).

Sometimes a widespread cultural custom will unexpectedly be breached and inspire observers to try to rationalize the deviation.

> The astonishing response to the death of Diana, Princess of Wales—[marked by] the invention of quite un-British rituals (the sea of flowers, the trees and lamp-posts ringed with candles, the home-made icons and teddy bears, the outpouring of doggerel verse)—has defied explanation by any commentators on the nation's psychology. In terms of vernacular ritual, it is closest to the attempts to grieve those killed in a national disaster. . . . [I believe that] the people chose this occasion to make a point, simply and childishly perhaps, that they were deeply saddened and let themselves go with the spontaneity of children. And they will doubtless become British again very soon, demonstrating all the old qualities of the "grit of the breed." Being un-British is a very British thing to do, now and again. (Weightman, 1997, p. 6)

Form and function. Two noteworthy aspects of grief and mourning in cross-cultural comparisons are *form* and *function*. Form means the outward appearance of mourning. Function refers to what the mourning acts accomplish—or are intended to accomplish—for the mourner, the observers, or the society in general. Relieving mourners of their grief is the function emphasized in Sanders's theory. Whereas the resolution of grief is likely an aim of mourning in all cultures, mourning may also be expected to perform additional functions as well. In way of illustration, the following examples of practices demonstrate such additional functions as (a) maintaining tradition while, at the same time, implying that the social system is unjust (Crete), (b) reinforcing the society's status structure by a public display of the status hierarchy (Tonga), and (c) attempting posthumous "face saving" or "ego enhancement" (Japan).

Herzfeld (1993) reports that the typical form of mourning in villages on the island of Crete consist of (a) grievers lamenting at a wake immediately following the death and (b) close relatives of the deceased engaging in extended poetic wailing during the march to the graveyard. At the wake, relatives and friends gather around the bed on which the deceased is laid out, while women bewail the loss and men tell tales of the deceased's life.

Only close kinswomen would sob and from time to time break into fits of lamenting, but even they interrupted these dramatic outbursts quite suddenly to remark, in more "normal" voices altered only by increasing hoarseness, on some incident in the dead person's life. This sudden switching between raucous lament and relatively calm recollection . . . is especially common at the funerals of old people and suggests that the villagers recognize a need for conventional outpourings of grief even when inner feelings may not fully correspond to those outpourings. (Herzfeld, 1993, p. 246)

Such behavior can be interpreted as displaying Cretan culture's respect for the deceased in a fashion that releases the living ones from their dependence on the departed.   Even for those who do not deeply feel the loss, it is necessary for social-acceptance purposes to exhibit the traditional appearance of mourning.

At the Cretan funeral of a 90-year-old man of low social status, the task of publicly mourning the death fell on the shoulders of a teenage daughter, a child from the man's second marriage to a ineffectual lower-class woman. In the girl's sing-song lament as the funeral party trudged to the graveyard, she bemoaned being left an orphan "in a world hostile to women without fathers or brothers to defend their reputations and chastity," which is a serious social disadvantage in a heavily male-dominated culture that insists on female sexual purity (Herzfeld, 1993, p. 247). The girl also made clear her intent to take responsibility for the future of her younger sister and her ailing mother, a role typically expected of a male. Herzfeld estimates that the functions served by such a lament included the girl's showing that she could perform the customary mourning rite, however inexpertly, and thereby win a measure of community approval for taking on what was traditionally a male burden. At the same time,

not only [was she issuing a general criticism of Cretan social structure by] categorically protesting her lot as a woman, she was also protesting, and rejecting, the categorical definition of herself as a woman limited by her gender. Nobody could deny that she had tried to act like a mature woman. Her very solecisms highlighted her determination to act appropriately and so helped to deflect the fatalistic self-image that lies in wait for any young woman in circumstances comparable to hers. (Herzfeld, 1993, p. 251)

In the Polynesian culture of Tonga, the verbal expression of grief assumes two poetic forms. One is *tangi* (to cry), consisting of stylized, rhythmic weeping that includes improvised or preset texts explaining why people are sorry the deceased has departed. The other is *laulau* (from *tangilaulau*—to lament), eulogies that are more thoughtful poetic expressions of what the mourner feels in his or her heart. Tongan society is dramatically stratified, with people's status constantly in the fore of social relations. Within such a culture, death and its associated funeral rituals form "an individual's most important *rite de passage*; a funeral records for all to see, and to pass on through the oral tradition, how the individual was related to others, what his or her dignity and rank were, and how much and by whom he or she was beloved" (Keppler, 1993, p. 476)

> At funerals one can see how the various elements of society fit together, and especially how hierarchical principles of status and rank pervade life and death. Funerals can also make statements of political reality, indicate the elevation of certain lineages over others, and suggest what elements of the stratified social system the family wishes to bring to the attention of the public. (Keppler, 1993, p. 476)

Thus, Tongan mourning traditions not only are intended to help resolve personal grief but also to serve educational and political functions by instructing the observers in the nature of the Tongan social system and by delineating the version of hierarchical relationships that the relatives of the deceased wish to impress on the community.

In Japan, the popularity and respect that the deceased enjoyed during his or her lifetime is, upon the person's death, often assumed to be reflected in the number of people attending the funeral. This expectation has led to the creation of the funeral-guest rental industry that provides mourners who openly grieve at the interment. The implied function of such a practice is that of posthumous face saving or ego enhancement for both the deceased and the remaining family members (Sallot, 1996).

Cross-cultural encounters: One increasingly common type of encounter involves modifications in societies' mourning practices that accompany other sorts of widescale social change, as illustrated in Korea, Russia, Germany, and the United States.

Particularly since the early 1980s, Korean burial patterns have become simpler and more secular, shown by a shift toward cremations held in mortuaries rather than burials out of homes. Emotional displays of mourning have diminished, and social support for the bereaved has been transferring from the family and neighborhood to urban friendship networks and professional services. Song (1996) attributes these trends to increased urbanization, industrialization, and the infusion of Western culture, including Christianity. Such changes can result in a measure of distress for older people who consider the innovations insulting to the deceased and an impediment to resolving grief in a customary manner.

In Russia, after seven decades of antireligious Soviet rule, precommunist religious burial and mourning elements continue to appear, particularly in village funerals. Although a priest would not be in attendance, the grave would still be marked with a cross. And prior to the burial, the spouse of the deceased is likely to display her or his distress by lying on the coffin ("Dying in the Countryside," 1998).

Downey (1998) sketched the following vignette to dramatize the secularization of funerals in present-day Germany.

Family and friends have assembled in a chapel on cemetery grounds. They hear not a hymn but a piece of classical music. Then a man rises and walks to the podium. He is dressed not in an ecclesiastical robe, but in a business suit, and his first words are not "In the name of the Father and of the Son and of the Holy Ghost," but "We are assembled to remember a life which has come to an end." He reads poetry, perhaps German classics, or something folksy. He may set forth Marxist ideals, although that occurs less and less often these days. He recalls the life of the deceased. More secular music follows as the family makes its way to the grave. (Downey, 1998, p. 358)

In effect, German funerals are increasingly conducted without clergy, scriptures, prayer, or religious music. The absence of Christian mourning practices might be expected in East Germany, where communist ideology discouraged religious belief over the four decades prior to Germany's unification in 1990. However, the trend toward secular funerals seems less likely in West Germany, with its solid Christian tradition. By the mid-1990s, 1 funeral in 10 in the West was secular, and in large cities the number was nearly one in four.

A similar move toward the secularization of mourning has occurred in the United States, as reflected in a rapid increase in cremating rather than burying the dead. By the mid-1990s, about 22% of corpses were cremated. Increased population mobility in America, which separates members of the extended family, has been partially credited with the higher percentages of cremation in states that experience heavy immigration from other parts of the nation. Nearly 54% of the dead are cremated in Nevada, 53% in Washington, and 40% in Arizona, California, Colorado, and Florida (Alger, 1996).

Such trends often disturb members of the older generation whose expressions of grief and respect for the departed are anchored in religious traditions that the young dismiss. Consequently, cross-cultural difficulties related to grief and mourning increasingly take the form of cross-generational differences within the same society.

Practical applications: Sanders draws on several established approaches to psychotherapy in suggesting how counselors can help mourners recover from their grief. Each approach is linked to one or more of her phases of the bereavement process. In the first two phases—shock, awareness of loss—grievers profit from the understanding and support provided by client-centered therapy and from the transference feature of psychoanalysis. Client-centered counseling provides the mourner with genuine acceptance, nonpossessive warmth, and authentic empathy, whereas transference allows the mourner to regard the therapist as a substitute for the deceased and thereby work through unresolved feelings of guilt and shame that are barriers to resolving the grief.

A humanistic-existential approach is recommended for phase three—conservation/withdrawal—by focusing the mourners' attention on self-awareness and on striving toward purpose in life and establishing new relationships with others.

Gestalt and behavior therapy are suited to the fourth and fifth phases—healing and renewal. The Gestalt approach shifts mourners' attention from the past to the present and future, challenging them to move from depending on others to depending on themselves. Behavior therapy focuses on new ways of acting, on eliminating maladaptive ways, and on strengthening existing desirable behaviors (Sanders, 1989, pp. 226-228).

Two issues that warrant further investigation concern (a) whether the grief process in all cultures fits Sanders' model and (b) how suitable her recommended counseling approaches may be in different cultures.

MORAL VALUES

Values are people's convictions about the desirability, propriety, or goodness of something. The "something" may be a person, an object, a place, an event, an idea, a kind of behavior, or the like.   Statements of value tell whether something is good or bad, well done or poorly done, suitable or unsuitable.

Values can be categorized into different classes. For instance, there are *aesthetic values* that involve judgments offered from an artistic viewpoint. Aesthetic values, when applied to a flower garden, a poem, a painting, or a dance performance, are reflected in such phrases as "beautifully arranged," or "nicely turned metaphor," or "uninspired, reflecting no creativity whatever." Another class is that of *functional values*. These focus on how efficiently something operates or on how well its parts coordinate. People are applying functional values when they complain about an erratic washing machine or about government inefficiency. *Economic values* concern now much profit or loss an investment yields. *Prudential values* guide an individual's social relations and use of time and energy so as to produce the greatest personal benefits. A girl finds it prudential not to tell her teacher that the teacher's breath smells sour, and a husband finds it prudential to bring his wife a gift when he has arrived late for their evening at the theater. *Moral values* are convictions people hold about proper ways to behave toward other humans. Many people extend their moral values to include ways of acting toward supernatural beings (gods, spirits of ancestors), animals, and the natural environment. Moral values are the focus of our concern in this chapter.

Over the centuries, many dozens of theories have been offered to explain how moral values develop. Some theories are embedded in such religious traditions as Judaism, Christianity, Islam, Buddhism, and Shinto.   Others theories are secular proposals rather than components of religious persuasions (Thomas, 1997). Conceptions of how people acquire their moral values come in many forms. Among the secular models, the one that has drawn the greatest attention over the past three decades is a version devised to reveal stages through which people's moral reasoning evolves.

Title: The Psychology of Moral Development, as formulated by a Harvard University professor, Lawrence Kohlberg.

Key tenets: The essence of morality is found in the concept of justice, with such morality represented on different levels. The lowest level of justice is self-centered hedonism— "Rules are absolute and inviolate, so obey the rules to avoid punishment." The highest level is even-handed justice, with everyone enjoying negotiated equal rights based on the sanctity of human life as the core value.

People's moral reasoning at any given time is determined by the present state of their cognitive structures. Each time someone encounters a moral incident, that individual's cognitive structures fashion the meaning that he or she will assign to—or derive from—the incident. Cognitive structures, in effect, serve as mental lenses that cast life's experiences in particular configurations. Because one person's structures differ in some degree from another's, the interpretation that one person places on a moral episode is expected to differ somewhat from the interpretation that another assigns to the same episode.

During the years of childhood, cognitive structures change with advancing age. Human development naturally progresses from the lowest level in early childhood toward the highest level over the years of later childhood and youth. But how far up the hierarchy of levels a person advances and how fast depend on a combination of that individual's genetic inheritance and environmental encounters. In effect, the composition of a person's mental templates at any time of life is the product of transactions between that individual's genetic code and daily experiences. The genetic timing system establishes the period in life that a given structure can be activated; then experience in the world fashions the exact way the structure evolves.

In sum, the development of moral reasoning consists of a sequence of changes in a person's cognitive structures (the interpretive mechanisms of the mind) and in the contents of the mind (memories, beliefs) that have been forged by the operation of those structures.

Kohlberg labeled his theory a "rational reconstruction of the ontogenesis of justice reasoning" and not, as people have often assumed, a complete depiction of moral development.

> I have always tried to be clear that my states are stages of justice reasoning, not of emotions, aspirations, or action. Our data base has been a set of hypothetical dilemmas posing conflicts between the rights or claims of different persons in dilemma situations. (Kohlberg, 1984, p. 224)

The dilemmas are nine brief life-like moral episodes described in the form of anecdotes. People who hear the anecdotes are asked to tell how the characters in the episodes should have behaved and to support their recommendation with a line of reasoning.

Kohlberg postulated six stages in the evolution of moral reasoning from early childhood into adult life. The following brief glimpse of the stages in their mid-1980s version suggests several of their distinguishing characteristics. The presentation advances from the earliest levels, indicative of the thinking processes of young children, to the higher levels, which can be achieved by individuals who are intellectually more mature (Kohlberg, 1984, pp. 621–639). Kohlberg linked his scheme to Piaget's stages of logical reasoning by contending that the growing child had to reach a suitable level of logical thought before being able to advance to a comparable stage of moral reasoning. For example, Kohlberg proposed that an individual must be capable of Piaget's concrete-operational thought in order to adopt Kohlberg's Stage 2 (individualistic, instrumental morality) approach to moral judgments. An older child needed to command Piaget's full formal-operations thought processes before reaching Kohlberg's Stage 4 (social-system morality) (Kegan, 1982, p. 86).

Stage 1: Heteronomous Morality. Kohlberg refers to the perspective at this initial stage as *moral realism* in which a person assumes that moral judgments are so self-evident that no justification is needed beyond simply stating the rule that has been broken. Failing to tell the truth or using an object that belongs to someone else is absolutely wrong and automatically warrants punishment. There are no such things as extenuating circumstances, such as people's intentions or their knowledge of right from wrong. This stage represents Piaget's heteronomous justice—absolute obedience to authority and the letter of the law.

Stage 2: Individualistic, Instrumental Morality. At this second level, the person recognizes that different people can have different points of view toward a moral incident. "Since each person's primary aim is to pursue his or her own interests, the perspective is pragmatic—to maximize satisfaction of one's needs and desires while minimizing negative consequences to the self" (Kohlberg, 1984, p. 626). Thus, the participants in a moral incident seek to negotiate a deal with each other as the instrument for coordinating their efforts for mutual benefit. No general moral principles guide their action, so that each case is handled separately. However, such a pragmatic approach "fails to provide a means for deciding among conflicting claims, ordering or setting priorities on conflicting needs and interests" (Kohlberg, 1984, p. 626).

Stage 3: Impersonally Normative Morality. The notion of justice advances beyond the individual-interest level to a conception of shared moral norms that guide everyone's moral behavior, regardless of the particular situations or particular people involved. In contrast to Stage 1, where rules are handed down by authority, the shared norms at Stage 3 are the result of general agreement about what constitutes suitable social behavior. Individuals operating from a Stage 3 perspective are concerned with playing their social role in a positive, constructive manner, with good motives instead of bad motives as evidence of one's general personal morality. The guide to action is provided by the Golden

Rule—do unto others as you would have others do unto you. People at Stage 3 are especially concerned with maintaining mutual trust and social approval.

Stage 4: Social System Morality. People at this level look beyond informal, commonly agreed-upon rules for individuals' interactions and now encompass the entire social system in their purview of moral behavior. "The pursuit of individual interests is considered legitimate only when it is consistent with the maintenance of the sociomoral system as a whole. . . . A social structure that includes formal institutions and social roles serves to mediate conflicting claims and promote the common good" (Kohlberg, 1984, p. 631). This perspective recognizes a societal, legal, or religious system that has developed codified rules and practices for adjudicating moral conflicts. In some settings, the laws may be ones representing an overarching philosophical or religious conviction rooted in the individual's conscience, a conviction that can be in conflict with the society's dominant legal system. In summary, moral judgments at Stage 4 are founded on legal or religious institutions and belief systems.

Stage 5: Human-Rights and Social-Welfare Morality. In contrast to accepting the rules of a society as they are already constituted, Kohlberg posits at Stage 5 a perception of morality that people would rationally build into a social system to promote universal values and rights. This prior-to-society viewpoint asks what rules would guide a society that fosters equality, equity, and general welfare for all. Upon answering this question, people are then obligated to make moral choices in keeping with those rules, even when their choices conflict with the society's present codes. Stage 5 provides a concern for the protection of the rights of the minority that cannot be derived from the social system perspective of Stage 4, since "social institutions, rules, or laws are evaluated by reference to their long-term consequences for the welfare of each person or group in the society" (Kohlberg, 1984, p. 634).

Stage 6: Morality of Universalizable, Reversible, and Prescriptive General Ethical Principles. Kohlberg describes this stage as *the moral point of view* that "all human beings should take toward one another as free and equal autonomous persons" (Kohlberg, 1984, p. 636). Such morality is universalizable in being applicable at all times and in all places among all peoples. It is reversible, in that the plaintiff and defendant in a moral incident could exchange places and the decision for resolving the issue would not be affected—a kind of "moral musical chairs" or second-order application of the Golden Rule. Each person understands and respects the point of view of every other person. "General principles are distinct from either rules or rights, first, in being positive *pre*scriptions rather than negative *pro*scriptions (don't kill, don't steal or cheat)" (Kohlberg, 1984, p. 636). One general principle can be that of respect for human personality or dignity. Another can be benevolence or universal compassion and care. Or moral decisions can derive from a cluster of principles—maximum quality of life for everyone, maximum individual liberty in relation to like liberty for others, and the equitable distribution of goods and services. (Summarized from Kohlberg, 1984, pp. 621–639)

Empirical studies of moral reasoning in a variety of societies have confirmed that people do indeed apply the perspectives of the first five stages in their responses to hypothetical moral dilemmas. However, there remains a question about whether Stage 6 might perhaps be an ideal condition never actually achieved in practice (Colby, Kohlberg, Gibbs, & Lieberman, 1983, p. 5).

Principal variables: Kohlberg proposed that (a) four chief causal factors interact to determine (b) the resulting outcome variable, which is how far up the six-stage hierarchy a person will progress and when he or she will arrive at each stage.

The first causal factor, and the one with the greatest genetic component, is the individual's *level of logical reasoning* as identified in Piaget's basic mental-growth stages. The second variable, a personal factor that probably has both genetic and environmental elements, is the individual's desire or *motivation*, sometimes referred to as the person's needs. The remaining two factors are cultural: (a) opportunities to learn *social roles* and (b) the *form of justice* in the social institutions with which the person is familiar.

In regard to roles, Kohlberg agreed with many social psychologists that children become socialized by learning to take the roles displayed by people around them. As children interact with others, they imagine themselves in the others' shoes and see life from others' perspectives. This ability increases with advancing age as children increasingly abandon a completely egocentric mode of perceiving life and become more adept at adopting other people's viewpoints. Thus, mature moral judgment "is based on sympathy for others, as well as on the notion that the moral judge must adopt the perspective of the 'impartial spec- tator' or the 'generalized other' " (Kohlberg, 1971, p. 190). How well children learn to assume others' roles depends to a great extent on the conditions of their social environment. Some environments encourage role-taking and thus hasten children's advance up the moral judgment ladder. Other environments limit opportunities to learn role-taking and thus slow children's progress in moral reasoning and may prevent them from ever reaching Stages 4 or 5.

Kohlberg's fourth variable that contributes to growth in moral judgment is the justice structure of the social groups or institutions with which the child interacts—the family, the school, the church, and the local and national govern- ments. At all stages of moral growth, the individual has some sort of concern for the welfare of other people. But only at Stage 5 is this concern based on what Kohlberg regarded as principles of true justice, those of *equality* and *reciprocity*. The principle of equality holds that we "treat every man's claim equally, regardless of the man" (Kohlberg, 1967, p. 169). The principle of reciprocity means equality of exchange—"punishment for something bad, reward for something good, and contractual exchange" or fulfilling one's bargain. In each society the groups or institutions with which the growing child is intimately involved vary in their justice structures. A family dominated by an autocratic father differs from a family in which children are encouraged to make decisions, to take responsibility, and to be rewarded in accordance with how they carry out their self-imposed commitments. A dictatorial government that allows no voicing of contrary opinions differs from a multiparty democracy that permits freedom of expression. Kohlberg proposed that people who participate in social groups that operate on a high level of equality and reciprocity will advance to higher levels of moral judgment than will individuals whose main participation is in groups that display less equality and reciprocity.

Although Kohlberg's attention focused chiefly on group trends rather than on individual differences, it can be assumed that the variations among people in moral reasoning result from the differences among them in the four causal factors described above. A child whose genetic endowment leads to slower than average mental development, who lacks the will to abide by societal rules, who has few opportunities to adopt social roles, and who is raised in an autocratic social setting will exhibit a lower level of moral judgment than a child whose native endowment, motivation, and social environment are quite the opposite.

Differences among cultures: More than 50 studies conducted in widely diverse societies have inspected likenesses and differences among cultures from the viewpoint of Kohlberg's six-stage scheme (Snarey, 1985). Kohlberg interpreted these cross-cultural results to mean that in virtually all groups there are people on different levels of the stage hierarchy, but the dominant moral stage of one society can be different from the dominant stage of another. For instance, research on the levels of moral reasoning of boys ages 10, 13, and 16 in Mexico, Turkey, and the United States showed that a larger percentage of Mexican and U.S. boys were at higher stages than were Turkish boys at each age level (Kohlberg & Kramer, 1969, p. 104). Furthermore, differences have been identified not only between nations but also between socioeconomic classes.

> In four different cultures, middle-class children were found to be more advanced in moral judgment than matched lower-class children. This was not because the middle-class children heavily favored a certain type of thought which corresponded to the prevailing middle-class pattern. Instead, the working-class children seemed to move through the same sequences, but the middle-class children seemed to move faster and farther. (Kohlberg, 1971, p. 190)

Investigations aimed at discovering whether all of Kohlberg's stages appear in all cultures have suggested that Stages 2, 3, and 4 are universal, but Stages 1 and 5 may not be generally found in every society. Eckensberger and Zimba (1997) have noted that Stage 5 was rarely encountered in the United States, Bahamas, Tibet, and Turkey but appeared in Israel's Kibbutzim, in Germany, India (middle and upper classes), Poland, and China, with the transition phase between Stages 4 and 5 often found in Taiwanese protocols. Studies in several developing countries reveal no more than weak evidence for the principled reasoning of Stage 5.

A study of Hong Kong Chinese responses to Rest's *Defining Issues Test* (a group-administered version of Kohlberg's moral dilemmas) led Ma and Cheung to observe that Chinese subjects' Confucian background significantly affected the moral viewpoints reflected in their test scores.

> The major theme of [Kohlberg's] Stage 3 concerns affection, conformity, and loyalty within a primary group such as the family. This theme is often emphasized in Chinese traditions, norms, and child-rearing practices and is therefore quite acceptable and familiar to Chinese. On the other hand, the emphasis on the institutionalized social law in Stage 4 and the law-making perspective in Stage 5 may be at odds with the Chinese affective collectivistic perspective and therefore appears to be a bit abstract and less familiar to the Chinese. In other words, Chinese tend to construe the characteristics of Stages 4 and 5 as more similar than those of Stages 3 and 4. (Ma & Cheung, 1996, p. 703)

An extensive collection of investigations in a broad variety of cultures supports the proposal that few, in any, moral values are universal, that is, are embraced as desirable in all societies. Moral values, instead of being universal, are relative to the history and present conditions of a given culture. For example, Verhoef and Michel's (1997) study of value commitments in sub-Saharan Africa led them to conclude that, despite considerable ethnic differences in social structure and belief systems of African peoples, within those variations of belief is an understanding that

> moral processes are primarily concerned with the maintenance of *good* relationships with others as opposed to the maintenance of justice and individual rights What is right is what connects people together; what separates people is wrong. . . . [Thus,] all Africans, regardless of ethnic group, place a high value on harmonious human relations which link people together in a collective existence through an interconnected web. (Verhoef & Michel, 1997, p. 395, 397)

In effect, equal-handed justice as based on a contractual agreement among members of a society is not the overriding principle on which traditional African moral decisions are founded. Instead, according to Verhoef and Michel, morality in African cultures is judged on the basis of such interacting aims and conditions as (Verhoef & Michel, 1997, pp. 389-404):

- Do not fracture community cohesion by failing to fulfill social obligations.
- Moral decisions must take into account the intention behind each act, the seriousness of the consequences of the act, and the social status of the people involved with the act.
- In regard to people's social status, (a) the rights and privileges of older people take precedence over the rights and privileges of younger ones, (b)

the rights and privileges of closer kinfolk take precedence over the rights and privileges of people whose relationship is more distant, and (c) people with good moral reputations deserve greater consideration in moral decisions than ones with poor reputations.

- The solving of serious moral conflicts should not be negotiated between individuals but, rather, the entire community or a representative group should participate in the negotiation process.

Cross-cultural encounters: Two noteworthy types of encounter are (a) ones focusing on the definition of morality itself and (b) ones leading to conflicts between individuals or groups because of their different levels on Kohlberg's moral-stage hierarchy.

Definitions of morality. A variety of critics have contested Kohlberg's assertion that even-handed justice should be the exclusive—or even the dominant—value upon which to base moral decisions. For example, morality for millions of Jews, Christians, Moslems, and Hindus is defined as obedience to the dictates of a Supreme Being or Cosmic Soul. Therefore, reasoning about a case of sexual intercourse between two males could differ markedly if based on Kohlberg's scheme than if based on the injunction against homosexual behavior attributed to God in the Jewish Torah (the early portion of the Old Testament in the Christian Bible). As another example, Carol Gilligan (1982), one of Kohlberg's colleagues at Harvard, has contended that *compassionate caring* and a sense of *responsibility* rather than *even-handed justice* is the dominant value on which females usually base their moral judgments. Thus, a 12-year-old boy from an abusive home background, arrested for vandalizing a neighbor's home, might well be treated differently by a judge who adopts an even-handed justice viewpoint than by one who favors compassionate caring. However, surveys of studies comparing male and female responses to Kohlberg's moral dilemmas have usually found no significant differences between the sexes in their stages of moral reasoning on Kohlberg's even-handed-justice hierarchy (Walker, 1984; Eckensberger & Zimba, 1997).

Interstage conflicts. A problem frequently met in schools that draw their students from different cultural backgrounds is that the dominant basis for moral judgments (the stage in Kohlberg's system) can differ between the school's practices and the preferences of individual students. As methods of dealing with this problem, educators have at least two contradictory ways of teaching moral values: *values indoctrination* and *values clarification.* Indoctrination involves teaching students a single set of moral principles and insisting that these are the only correct, acceptable bases for moral behavior. Indoctrination tactics can range from commanding belief through threats of punishment to employing gentle persuasion. On the other hand, values clarification consists of instructors presenting alternative moral principles, then encouraging the learners to weigh the virtues and limitations of the various options and to draw their own conclusions about which values they prefer as guides for their own actions and for judging other people's behavior (Raths, Harmin, & Simon, 1964). These two approaches to values education are logically allied with contrasting levels of Kohlberg's moral-development hierarchy. Indoctrination is in keeping with Kohlberg's Stage 1 of heteronomous morality, whereas values clarification is commensurate with Stage 5—human-rights and social-welfare morality.

Difficulties can arise when a school's values-education approach conflicts with the conception of values that students learned at home, at church, or at a different school. For instance, when youths who are accustomed to indoctrination find themselves in a values-clarification program, they may feel insecure by having doubt cast on authority-prescribed rules for value decisions. In contrast, students trained in values clarification can feel constrained and oppressed when confronted with an indoctrination approach.

Practical applications: Two ways Kohlberg applied his theory have been in (a) a recommended *values-raising* mode of instruction and (b) the establishment of a *just community* within a school.

Values-raising instruction. In Kohlberg's opinion, the goal of moral education is not to inculcate a particular set of values that are dominant or at least common within a given society. Instead, the goal is to stimulate a child's advance through the stages that he considered valid for all cultures. The teacher's expectation for where the child or youth should be in moral growth at a particular time is governed by the teacher's recognition of the level of a child's cognitive development (per Piaget) and of the opportunities the child enjoys to adopt roles in social groups. This expectation is also influenced by the sorts of justice found in the groups in which the child participates and by the child's motivation. That is, will it seem worthwhile to the child to think at a higher moral level than her or his present level?

The methodology the teacher adopts consists of posing moral problems for the students and having various ones give their arguments to support their decisions. In this process, some students may argue from a higher stage than others. The resulting conflict of arguments is intended to produce a feeling of disequilibrium in young people who are approaching the threshold of a new stage, so that the basis for their thinking begins to change and they are hoisted to a new level.

A just community. Kohlberg used the term *just community* to identify the practice of using the daily moral dilemmas faced in school as the subject of students' study of moral decision making. The just-community approach was tried out in an alternative school that operated under the aegis of a larger, "regular" high school. The 60 or so students enrolled in the alternative school were ones who had difficulty meeting the academic and social behavior standards of the regular high school. Kohlberg's staff guided the faculty and students in establishing a system of democratic governance in which students and teachers would "overcome their reliance on traditional authority patterns" and "learn to democratically share the responsibility for decision making" (Hersh, Miller, &

Fielding, 1980, p. 151). Events during the school day that involved stealing, missing classes, using drugs, and the like became issues discussed, with students and faculty members having an equal voice in how to resolve the issues. The program was judged to have been a moderate success.

SUMMARY

As explained earlier, one purpose of this chapter has been to illustrate the concept *levels of theory specificity*. To clarify that concept, the following summary assumes the form of three outlines, with one outline for each of the realms from which the chapter's four theories were drawn—the realms of attitudes, emotions, and values. Each outline opens with a general definition of the phenomenon of interest, then displays at various levels of specificity some of the topics that can become the objects of separate theories. In the outlines, each number signifies a different category of theory.

From their inspection of the outlines, readers will recognize that:

- These outlines are far from complete. Hundreds more topics could be added under *attitudes* and dozens under *emotions* and *values*. Thus, the outlines represent no more than segments of much more extensive possibilities.
- The levels of specificity could be cast in patterns different from the ones illustrated here. Other equally useful versions of the outlines are possible.

In keeping with the central theme of this book, every theory would be expected to serve as a window for revealing different aspects of culture than those aspects exposed by other models.

Where this chapter's four theories would be located in the three outlines has been indicated by our printing the four models' categories in bold-face type.

Attitudes: Attitudes can be defined as underlying propensities to act either positively or negatively toward people, institutions, or events.

Therefore, different theories can focus on the development of attitudes about:

1. People, institutions, or events in general
   1.1 People in general (A Composite Theory of Prejudice)
   1.1.1 Ethnic groups in general
   1.1.1.1 Native Americans (American Indians)
   1.1.1.2 European Americans
   1.1.1.3 Hispanic Americans
   1.1.1.4 African Americans
   1.1.1.5 Asian Americans
   1.1.2 Religious groups in general
   1.1.2.1 Fundamentalist Christians
   1.1.2.2 Roman Catholics
   1.1.2.3 Muslims

1.1.2.4 Buddhists
1.1.3 Gender groups in general
    1.1.3.1 Females in general
        1.1.3.1.1 Infant females
        1.1.3.1.2 Girl children (ages 2-12)
        1.1.3.1.3 Adolescent girls (ages 12-20)
        1.1.3.1.4 Young adult women (ages 21-40)
        1.1.3.1.5 Middle-aged women (ages 41-60)
        1.1.3.1.6 Elderly women (ages 61+)
    1.1.3.2 Males in general
        1.1.3.1.+ (Same age categories as for females)
1.2 Institutions in general
    1.2.1 Nations/Governments in general
        1.2.1.1 The United States in general
            1.2.1.1.1 Foreign policy
            1.2.1.1.2 Form of governance
            1.2.1.1.3 Socioeconomic development
        1.2.1.2 Ireland in general (Same specific topics as for the U.S.)
        1.2.1.3 France in general (Same specific topics as for the U.S.)
        1.2.1.4 Britain in general(Same specific topics as for the U.S.)
1.3 Events
    1.3.1 Holidays in general
        1.3.1.1 Christmas
        1.3.1.2 Independence Day
            1.2.1.2.1 U.S. July 4
            1.2.1.2.2 Indonesian August 17
    1.3.2 Wars in general
        1.2.2.1 U.S. Revolutionary War
            1.2.2.1.1 From a U.S. perspective
            1.2.2.1.2 From a British perspective
        1.2.2.2 World War II
            1.2.2.2.1 From a U.S. perspective
            1.2.2.2.2 From a German perspective
            1.2.2.2.3 From a Japanese perspective
            1.2.2.2.4 From a Chinese perspective

Emotions: Emotions can be defined in terms of elicitors, receptors, states, expressions, and experiences. *Elicitors* are events that stimulate emotional *receptors*, which are relatively specific locations or pathways in the central nervous system that activate changes in a person's physiological and/or mental states. *Emotional states* are the patterns of change in somatic and/or neuronal activity that accompany the activation of receptors. *Emotional expressions* are the potentially observable surface changes in a person's face, body, voice, and activity that accompany emotional states. *Emotional experiences* are people's conscious or unconscious interpretation of their perceived states and expressions (Lewis & Michalson, 1982, p. 182).

Different theories of the development of emotions can focus on each of the following aspects of emotions or on a combination of two or more of the aspects: elicitors, receptors, states, expressions, experiences. The following brief outline accommodates theories that address (a) all five of the aspects and (b) a combination of eliciting conditions, states, and expressions. Other outlines can be constructed that treat either a single aspect or various combinations of two to four of the aspects.

1. Theories that address the development of *all five* aspects of emotion:
   1.1 Emotions in general (Emotional Socialization Theory)
   - 1.1.1 Depression
   - 1.1.2 Envy
   - 1.1.3 Fear
   - 1.1.4 Grief
   - 1.1.5 Guilt
   - 1.1.6 Hate
   - 1.1.7 Joy, elation
   - 1.1.8 Love, affection
   - 1.1.9 Sadness
   - 1.1.10 Shame
2. Theories that address the development of a combination of three aspects— *elicitors, states,* and *expressions*:
   2.1 Emotions in general
   - 2.1.1 Depression
   - 2.1.2 Envy
   - 2.1.3 Fear
   - **2.1.4 Grief (Sanders's Theory of Grief and Bereavement)**
   - 2.1.5 Guilt
   - 2.1.6 Hate
   - 2.1.7 Joy, elation
   - 2.1.8 Love, affection
   - 2.1.9 Sadness
   - 2.1.10 Shame

Values: Values can be defined as people's convictions about the desirability, propriety, or goodness of something. The "something" may be a person, an object, a place, an event, an idea, a kind of behavior, or the like. Statements of value tell whether something is good or bad, well done or poorly done, suitable or unsuitable.

Theories of human values development can focus on either people's *expressed beliefs* about values, on their *actions* (behavior) in value-relevant situations, or on *both* expressed beliefs and behavior.

1. Theories of the development of *beliefs* about values can concern:
    1.1 Values in general
        1.1.1 Artistic, aesthetic values
            1.1.1.1 Architecture
            1.1.1.2 Drama
            1.1.1.3 Graphic arts, painting, drawing
            1.1.1.4 Literature
            1.1.1.5 Music
        1.1.2 Economic values
        1.1.3 Moral values(Kohlberg's Moral Reasoning Theory)
        1.1.4 Political values
        1.1.5 Religious values
2. Theories of the development of *behavior* in value-relevant situations:
    1.1.1 Artistic, aesthetic values
        1.1.1.1 Architecture
        1.1.1.2 Drama
        1.1.1.3 Graphic arts, painting, drawing
        1.1.1.4 Literature
        1.1.1.5 Music
    1.1.2 Economic values
    1.1.3 Moral values
    1.1.4 Political values
    1.1.5 Religious values

Finally, it is useful to recognize that theories at different levels of specificity are characterized by different advantages and limitations. Theories at the most widely encompassing levels, such as ones focusing on *values in general,* have the advantage of furnishing principles applicable to many kinds of values—aesthetic, political, religious, prudential, and more. However, in attempting to accommodate such diverse kinds, theories at that general level fail to explain the precise conditions that account for the differences between one subrealm of value and another. For example, although the aesthetic criteria for distinguishing architectural quality from musical quality can share certain elements in common, those criteria should not be identical in all respects. But separate theories for architecture and for music can include elements unique to each of those artistic forms, thereby explaining more precisely why people's judgments of architecture can develop somewhat differently than their judgments of music.

Part II

Structural Features of Theories

The nine models described in Part II are presented from two perspectives toward analyzing theories: (a) the configurations of variables that are believed to explain human development and (b) the types of interactions among variables that account for development.

5

Development Configurations

Each theory in this book has its particular structure—its special components and their postulated relationships. However, in the chapters of Part I, the configuration that development assumes from one year to the next is not the characteristic that is featured. Instead, the emphasis in those chapters is on psychological processes and products (cognition, learning, attitudes, emotions, values). The purpose of the present chapter is to direct attention to how components of theories can be patterned differently in five illustrative theories and to suggest how such patterning may vary across cultures. The components that distinguish one scheme's pattern from another are found in the theories' key tenets and principal variables.

In accounting for how and why people grow up as they do, virtually all modern-day theorists conceive of development as resulting, not from one sort of causal influence (component) acting alone, but rather from the interaction of two or more sources of influence. The pair of components most frequently mentioned are heredity and environment. In typical usage, *heredity* refers to determinants of development that reside in the genetic structure which each individual has acquired from the sperm and ovum furnished by the parents at the time of conception. *Environment* refers to influences in a person's surroundings that affect his or her development. Culture, in the sense of shared beliefs and practices, can be seen as a highly important feature of the environment.

Theorists also often credit the individual person with being an important factor in development, on the grounds that each person brings influential motives, capacities, abilities, and a physical appearance to daily encounters with environments. Although these attributes or components are assumed to be grounded in genetic structures, they are not unalterably set by heredity. Instead, they obviously are affected by environments and assume a unique pattern in each person. The attributes then serve as forces in themselves, helping formulate each personality.

Two other sorts of influence that some theorists include are supernatural forces and chance. *Supernatural forces* can be of various types—gods, spirits of departed ancestors, configurations of celestial bodies (as in astrology), combinations of symbols (as in numerology), animals or plants with mystic powers, and more. When we cite *chance* or *fate* or *the breaks* as a cause, we are actually admitting our ignorance about what has produced a developmental outcome.

In theorists' causal attributions, the features that distinguish one model from another are (a) the sources of influence (that is, the postulated principal variables or causal components) and (b) the manner in which those sources are conceived to interact. Chapter 5 focuses on the nature of components. Chapter 6 directs attention to patterns of interaction among components.

The five theories described in the following pages are Robert Havighurst's set of developmental tasks, Bruce Biddle's role theory, a Kelley and Weiner version of attribution theory, Raymond Eve's interpretation of social-exchange theory, and a sociohistorical life-course model proposed by Glen H. Elder, Jr.

In Havighurst's life-stages model, development is portrayed as a succession of tasks that children are obliged to master. In Biddle's theory, development takes the form of changing roles children assume as they grow up. The structure of development in attribution theory is the patterning of characteristics that people cite as causes of behavior. Eve's rendition of social-exchange theory casts development in terms of the changes that occur in people's beliefs about the obligations they incur when they receive favors from others. Elder's life-course model emphasizes the influence of the surrounding society on individuals' lives at successive periods of their development.

The summary at the end of the chapter compares the five theories in regard to (a) their definitions of development, (b) their components of cause (inputs) and effect (outputs or products), and (c) what constitutes satisfactory development.

LIFE-STAGES THEORIES

The label *life-stages theories* is applied to conceptions of development that divide the human life span into a series of periods that are typically defined by age. The central assumption underlying these conceptions is that the people who fit into a given age period share certain characteristics that are different in kind or quantity from the characteristics shared by people at other stages. Thus, children within a stage called *infancy* are alike in identifiable ways and, in those same ways, are unlike people at other stages of life—*later childhood, adolescence, middle age,* and such.

A great many life-stage theories exist, including commonsense notions found among members of the general public *(naive* or *folk psychologies)* and schemes devised by scholars *(formal* or *scientific theories).* Formal theories differ from each other in four principal ways: (a) in the aspects of development on which they focus, (b) in the number and sizes of stages they include, (c) in the labels they attach to the stages, and (d) in the kinds of markers or indicators used to distinguish one stage from another.

In regard to aspects, some theories encompass many facets of human development, whereas others center attention on only a single feature or perhaps a limited few. One broadly inclusive proposal is a scheme created by Arnold Gesell, a Yale University medical doctor and child-development authority. He described stages of growth for:

1. Motor characteristics (bodily activity, the development of eye and hand coordination)
2. Personal hygiene (eating, sleeping, elimination, bathing, dressing, health, somatic complaints, tensional outlets)
3. Emotional expression (affective attitudes, assertion, anger, crying, and related behaviors)
4. Fears and dreams
5. Self-concept and sexual behavior
6. Interpersonal relations
7. Play and pastimes (general interests, reading, music, television)
8. School life (adjustment to school, classroom demeanor, progress in school studies)
9. Ethical sense (blaming and alibiing; responsiveness to direction, punishment, praise, and reasoning; sense of good, bad, truth, and property)
10. Philosophic outlook (time, space, language and thought, death, deity) (Gesell, Ilg, Ames, & Bullis, 1977, p. 58)

An example of a narrow-scope theory is a psychosocial model offered by Erik Erikson, a Harvard University professor and psychoanalyst. Erikson's proposal focuses on the ways individuals resolve conflicts between opposing psychological tendencies (*psychosocial crises*) that are faced at successive age levels. The following list identifies the pairs of opposing dispositions and the ages at which the dispositions demand the greatest attention (Erikson, 1959, p. 166).

Stage	Psychosocial Crisis	Age Range
1	trust vs. mistrust	0-1
2	autonomy vs. shame and doubt	2-3
3	initiative vs. guilt	3-6
4	industry vs. inferiority	7-12 or so
5	identity vs. identity diffusion	12-18 or so
6	intimacy vs. isolation	the 20s
7	generativity vs. isolation	late 20s to 50s
8	integrity vs. despair	50s and beyond

Other stage theories address different aspects of growth. Piaget's (1950) model focuses on intellectual skills, Freud's (1938) on psychosexual characteristics, and Kohlberg's (1984) on moral reasoning.

The number of stages into which the life span is divided can differ from one theory to another and even from one version of a scholar's model to a later version. Gesell & Ilg (1949) divided the period from birth to age 10 into 10 single-year stages. Erikson, as noted above, recognized eight stages between birth and death. One variation of Piaget's scheme identifies four major stages over the first two decades of life, whereas other variations portray mental development as consisting of three main periods, with each involving two or more substages.

Labels for stages often vary from one scheme to another. Furthermore, some authors avoid the word *stage* entirely, preferring to identify their proposed development segments as *periods, levels, ages,* or *gradients.*

Theorists often differ over the types of indicators they consider most appro-priate for distinguishing one stage from another. The evidence used by Gesell was in the form of physical measurements, observations of social behavior, and children's habits as reported by parents, with these data organized according to children's ages. Piaget's stages were based on children's answers to reasoning problems posed in interviews, with the answers clustered by types of reasoning children displayed. Kohlberg's stages were founded on the judgments adolescents offered about moral dilemmas described in anecdotes, with each respondent assigned to a stage marked by a particular kind of reasoning offered in support of the youth's decisions.

The example selected for illustrating the way culture can be viewed through the lens of a stage theory is one that evolved in the United States during the progressive-education movement of the 1930s and 1940s.

Title: Developmental Task Theory, as popularized by Robert J. Havighurst of the University of Chicago.

Key tenets: According to this model, the life span can usefully be divided into a sequence of periods, with each period characterized by tasks that an individual is expected to accomplish in order to become a reasonably happy and competent person.

> A developmental task is a task which arises at or about a certain period in the life of the individual, successful achievement of which leads to his [or her] happi-ness and to success with later tasks, while failure leads to unhappiness in the individual, disapproval by society, and difficulty with later tasks. (Havighurst, 1953, p. 2)

Havighurst divided the length of life into six stages: (a) infancy and early childhood (birth through age 5), (b) middle childhood (ages 6 though 12), (c) adolescence (ages 13 through 17), (d) early adulthood (ages 18 through 30), (e) middle age (ages 31 through 54), and (f) later maturity (ages 55 and beyond).

Tasks at each stage arise from one or more of three sources: (a) the biological structure and function of the individual, (b) the particular culture in which the person is reared, and (c) personal values and aspirations of the individual. Tasks that arise mainly from the biological nature of humans will be found in all societies, with their form essentially the same in all cultures. Tasks that derive from the unique cultural patterns of a given society will either exist in different forms in different societies or else will be found in some cultures but not in others. A task like learning to walk, which depends primarily on genetically determined growth factors, is essentially the same in all societies and arises at about the same time in each child's life. However, the task of selecting and preparing for an occupation is a complex one in highly industrialized societies that are characterized by much specialization and division of labor; while in nonindustrialized societies in which nearly everyone is a farmer or hunter or fisher, the task of choosing a vocation is simpler and achieved at a younger age than in industrialized settings. The tasks of learning to read and write, which are so important in highly literate cultures, do not even exist in preliterate ones.

Consequently, lists of developmental tasks will not be the same in all cultures, and the items in the lists identifying tasks will be determined to some degree by the personal value systems of the people who prepare them. Havighurst admitted that his tasks ware "based on American democratic values seen from a middle-class point of view, with some attempt at pointing out the variations for lower-class and upper-class Americans" (1953, p. 26).

A version of the theory that offers a more complex patterning of tasks than does Havighurst's is a scheme devised by Tryon and Lilienthal (1950) covering the first two decades or so of life. That 20- or 25-year range is divided into five stages: (I) infancy (birth to age 1 or 2), (II) early childhood (ages 2-3 to 5-7), (III) late childhood (ages 5-7 to pubescence), (IV) early adolescence (pubescence to puberty), and (V) late adolescence (puberty to early maturity). The theory addresses the 10 aspects of development that are listed down the left column of Table 5-1. The nature of tasks at successive development periods is illustrated with examples from two of the periods—early childhood and late adolescence.

Principal variables: Significant variables are primarily the particular theorist's interpretation, for each stage of development, about cultural expectations regarding: (a) physical attributes (appearance, skills), (b) knowledge and reasoning skills, (c) social-interaction skills, (d) values (moral, economic, aesthetic), and (e) perceptions of one's self (self-efficacy, self-concept).

Differences among cultures: Of particular interest are the variations across cultures in (a) the number and sizes of stages included and (b) the characteristics of a given task in different cultures.

Number and sizes of stages. An example of disagreement about stages between social-class levels within the same society is the criticism aimed at the use of such schemes as Tryon and Lilienthal's model for understanding the development of inner-city black youths in the United States.

Table 5-1

Developmental Tasks of Early Childhood and Late Adolescence

Aspect of Life: People face the tasks of . . .	Early Childhood (2-3 to 5-7 years)	Late Adolescence (puberty to early maturity)
I—Achieving appropriate dependence-independence pattern	Develop initial self-awareness	Establish adult form of self-concept
II—Giving and receiving affection	Develop initial sense of affection	Build mutual affection with potential spouse
III—Relating to changing social groups	Interact with agemates, adjust to family social expectations	Adopt adult social values
IV—Developing a conscience	Take directions, obey adult authority, use conscience as a guide	Resolve moral dilemmas
V—Finding one's psycho-socio-biological sex role	Identify with male and female adult roles	Explore future mate possibilities, choose vocation, adopt citizen role
VI-VII—Adjusting to a changing body	Adapt to changing musculature, adopt sex modesty	Learn appropriate outlets for sex drives, control a "new" adolescent body
VIII—Understanding the physical world	Meet adult expectations for acting in physical environments	Learn realistic ways of studying and controlling the physical world
IX—Developing conceptual abilities	Improve one's use of symbol systems	Reach one's highest potential in reasoning
X—Relating one's self to the cosmos	Begin to sense one's place in the cosmos	Formulate a secure belief and value system

(Source: "Developmental Tasks: The Concept and Its Importance" in *Fostering Mental Health in Our Schools* by C. Tryon & J. Lilienthal. Alexandria, VA: Association for Supervision and Curriculum Development. Copyright © 1950 ASCD. Reprinted by permission. All rights reserved.)

African American adolescents, particularly those who grow up in some economically deprived, high-risk neighborhoods, may follow developmental paths that are based on ideologies, role expectations, behavioral practices, and "rites of passage" that are contextually different from those reported in studies of white suburban middle-class teens. (Burton, Obeidallah, & Allison, 1996, p. 396)

In studies of contemporary American society, adolescence is typically portrayed as a period of transition between childhood and early adulthood. Following the onset of puberty, teenagers are pictured as gaining skill in abstract reasoning, acquiring a more complex notion of self, establishing stronger ties with peers, developing greater autonomy from their family, beginning to analyze social issues, and speculating about their future. Adolescents' activities, as guided by their mentors (parents, teachers, club leaders, pastors), are designed to prepare youths for adulthood but not to accord them actual adult status until ages 18, 21, or beyond. However, critics have contended that such a conception of adolescence, while valid for middle- and upper-class American youth, is not accurate for youths living in economically disadvantaged contexts where "many teens move from childhood to adulthood without distinctly experiencing the intermediate stage of adolescence" (Burton et al., 1996, p. 398). If the markers of adult status include giving birth or fathering a child, becoming economically independent, and autonomously choosing one's own companions and social activities, then many inner-city African American teenagers qualify as adults. Their life course does not include a transitional stage of adolescence. In a study of disadvantaged urban youths, researchers found that teens frequently had born children and become self-supportive through traditional employment, government grants (such as Aid to Families of Dependent Children), or such illegal activities as burglary and drug dealing (Burton et al., 1996, p. 400).

Variations in task characteristics. The attributes of a particular task can differ markedly from one culture to another. For example, consider the task of "finding one's psycho- socio-biological sex role." Table 5-2 summarizes the characteristics of this role for females as reflected in laws and customs of two societies—Iran and the United States. The table identifies the behaviors that girls and women are expected to adopt if they are to fit their societies' cultural norms (Calligan, 1992; "No Crime for Love," 1991; "Status of Women in Iran," 1998).

A further contrast in task characteristics is found in the psycho-socio-biological sex role for the period of late adolescence when youths in American society are involved in selecting and preparing for a vocation. Not only can the nature of this task vary across cultures, but the age level at which the task is typically required can differ as well. In such hunter-gatherer cultures as in the Miyanmin society of New Guinea, the selection of an occupation involves few options and is determined early in the child's life. Nearly all boys become hunters; girls become gatherers and householders. In Great Britain, choosing and preparing for an occupation comes in late adolescence or early adulthood, is often abetted by vocational counseling services, and involves selecting from among hundreds of options. Furthermore, the array of options in a society can change as the decades advance, with the change far slower in some cultures than in others. Among the

Table 5-2
Female Sex-Role Norms in Iran and the USA

Iran†	*USA**
—*Dress.* Women must cover hair and body except for hands and face. No cosmetics permitted. Violating the dress code can result in punishment ranging from verbal reprimand to a fine, 74 strokes of the lash, or a prison term of one month to a year.	Unrestricted garb and cosmetics allowed.
—*Marriage.* Legal age is 9 years, but at any age females must have the permission of their father or grandfather. Women may not marry anyone but a Muslim. Men may marry whomever they wish. A man can have four permanent wives and an unlimited number of temporary wives. Temporary marriage is a "contract for sexual services for a predetermined payment to the woman." Temporary marriages are for a specific time period, ranging from 1 hour to 99 years.	Legal age without parental permission is usually 18. After that age, women can marry whomever they please without seeking their family's permission. Although marriage to two or more spouses at the same time is illegal, violations are rarely prosecuted.
—*Divorce.* Men can divorce whenever they please. Women can divorce if they prove the marriage violated one of 12 rules.	Women and men have equal rights to divorce.
—*Adultery, homosexuality.* Punishment for either men or women adulterers includes stoning or flogging, usually to the death. Lesbians receive 100 lashes. If caught four times, they are put to death.	Laws against adultery and homosexual behavior are rarely enforced except in cases involving an adult and a minor. Relationships between *consenting adults* are usually accepted as lawful.
—*Segregation.* Women must sit in the rear seats on buses and enter public buildings through a separate entrance.	Women have the same public rights as men, even to join organizations formerly restricted to men.
—*Employment.* Married women may hold a job only with the written permission of their husbands.	Women need not seek their husbands' permission to hold a job.
—*Education.* Females cannot have male teachers. Married women cannot attend public secondary schools.	Females can have either men or women teachers and can attend any school for which they qualify.

†Iranian features based on Islamic religious law and Iranian civil code.
*USA features based on national laws or on laws of typical states.

Miyanmins, the occupations of hunting and gathering are age-old, much the same today as in centuries past. Among the British, a host of occupations that require skill in programming or operating computers have existed for no more than a decade or two (Morren, 1986).

Cross-cultural encounters: A key precept of Havighurst's theory is that failure with a task during its assigned critical period causes difficulties in performing later tasks related to the one that was failed. Failure in learning to talk, for example, will prevent children from learning to read and write and from understanding many concepts normal to people at later stages of growth (Havighurst, 1953, p. 3). Such *inadequate preparation* as a cause for problems in mastering tasks is particularly serious for individuals who enter a culture other than their original one, because the new tasks they face require the prior successful completion of preceding tasks that differed from ones those individuals experienced in their home cultures.

Consider, for instance, the task of adopting the role of *citizen* for a 21-year-old who immigrates to Australia from Albania and seeks to obtain citizenship. Australians are obligated to vote in all public elections. To perform this duty well, they are expected to understand the voting system, the ballot issues, and the backgrounds of candidates for office so as to learn of the candidates' policies and their past performance. Among youths who have grown up in Australia, preparation for this task has been provided (a) in school studies focusing on civic matters and the political process and (b) in newspapers and television newscasts. However, the Albanian newcomer has come from a society in which there have been no truly open elections nor choices among competing political convictions. Thus, the Albanian can expect to have more trouble with accomplishing the citizen task than will newcomers from societies with political systems more like that of Australia—such as Canada, the United Kingdom, France, and Germany. In this case, the Albanian will have "failed" by having lacked the opportunity to prepare for the Australian version of *citizen*.

Practical applications: Developmental-task theory is helpful for identifying which aspects of life pose problems for intercultural encounters. This use of the theory is founded on the dual assumption that (a) cultures can be more alike in some aspects of human development than in others and (b) problems in cross-cultural relations are most likely to occur with those aspects in which the two cultures differ most. Applying the approach involves interviewing informants who are intimately acquainted with a given culture and are capable of describing for that culture the typical characteristics of the tasks listed in Table 5-1, along with those tasks' age placement. Such information is compiled for different cultures, and a comparison is drawn to determine in which tasks (and the tasks' age placement) two cultures are most alike and in which tasks they are most dissimilar. The results of the comparison permits predictions about the kinds of tasks that are likely to cause the greatest difficulty for someone seeking to adjust to a new cultural setting.

ACCUMULATING ROLES

Title: Role Theory, as described by Bruce J. Biddle, a professor of social behavior on the Columbia campus of the University of Missouri.

Key tenets: As children advance from infancy through childhood, then into adolescence and adulthood, they learn to perform an increasing variety of culturally defined social roles. A social role consists of a set of behaviors, underlying attitudes, and types of knowledge that define a person's social position, with the term *social position* referring to "an identity that designates a commonly recognized set of persons" (Biddle, 1979, p. 5). Sets of persons who occupy recognized social positions are designated by such titles as physician, tenant farmer, housewife, grandmother, 6-year-old schoolgirl, juvenile delinquent, football fan, and the like. People within each set are expected to act in ways that the particular culture has come to anticipate for that set. Thus, in this sense, *role* can be defined as a particular cluster of expectations held for the behavior of people in a given social position.

From a role-theory perspective, a sketch of an individual's identity or personality can consist of enumerating social positions the person fills.

Marcia is the 16-year-old daughter of Merton Jensen (a landscape architect) and Claudine Jensen (a housewife) and the granddaughter of Thor Jensen, a member of the city council. Marcia is also the elder sister of Linda (age 7) and of brother Melville (age 4). At Eastside High School, Marcia is a junior, the lead clarinetist in the school band, a member of the Academic Honor Society, an alto in the girls' chorus, and a setter on the varsity volleyball team. On Sundays she sings in the Baptist Church choir. Occasionally she earns spending money by baby-sitting for neighbors. This year she obtained her license to drive a car, but she doesn't yet own a car so she must borrow her parents' van when she attends sessions of the Square Dance Club.

People who share the same culture typically agree in their expectations of how individuals within a particular role will behave. Those behaviors, and the attitudes underlying them, are not intuitively known by the young but, rather, must be learned from observing others and from direct training. Therefore, how one is expected to look and act as a college tennis player in North America or as a hunter of game on an African savanna is not "naturally known" but must be learned. With rare exception (such as the newborn's role as a passive recipient of adult care), all role behavior must be learned through such mechanisms of socialization as receiving formal instruction, having direct trial-and-error experiences, observing others' behavior, and receiving rewards and punishment. In short, "Persons must be taught roles and may find either joy or sorrow in the performance thereof" (Biddle, 1979, p. 8).

The expectations commonly held for how people in a given social position should think and act can be considered the *culture* of that role.

Most role behaviors are contextually bound, in that what is considered appropriate behavior is influenced by the social setting in which it occurs. The actions that make Marcia a good square dancer are somewhat different from those that make her an honor student or an obedient daughter. A young man can be expected to act differently during the Sunday church communion service than during the Saturday afternoon picnic or while playing point guard on the church basketball team. Consequently, judgments of the adequacy of role performance depend on how well the behavior fits a particular setting.

Some roles are assigned to a person by circumstances beyond the individual's control. Such is true with gender, age, and the family into which one is born, the family that establishes the individual's initial position in the culture's social-class system. Other roles are earned by dint of individuals' formal and informal education and diligence, thus rendering the positions more under their own control. Still other roles are acquired by a combination of circumstances and personal ability or striving—as when a college art student "fortunately" is placed with a dormitory roommate whose father is president of a greeting-card company, and through this social tie the art student is subsequently hired by the company.

From a role-theory perspective, human development is seen as the changes occurring in a person's social positions with the passing of time. Hence, the process of development from birth to adulthood consists of children adopting new roles that are expected in their culture for successive age levels and of abandoning roles identified with earlier age periods. As the years advance, an expanding range of role expectations is imposed on children, requiring them to learn a growing diversity of social-position behaviors and the conditions under which each set of actions is considered appropriate within their culture. Therefore, as children develop, they adopt a growing variety of parts to play, an extended vision of roles that other people fill, and an increasingly sophisticated set of criteria for judging the quality of performance of their own and others' roles. Furthermore, during the process of growing up, children's impressions of how well they are living up to the role expectations of the important people in their lives function as the building materials for children's self-concepts. "Who I am" becomes a reflection of "how well I fulfill the expectations held for my roles" (Biddle, 1979, p. 7).

Within a culture, the expectations serve as criteria for judging how satisfactorily a person performs in his or her social positions. Most people perform different roles at different levels of authenticity or skill. Therefore, Marcia might be judged a fine clarinetist, a moderately good setter on the volleyball team, but an erratic chauffeur.

Principal variables: An understanding of roles within a given culture derives from recognizing (a) each role's label or title; (b) the beliefs, appearance, and behaviors commonly expected for that role; (c) how the role is acquired; (d) the criteria used for judging the quality of people's role performance; and (e) consequences that can result from good versus poor performance.

Differences among cultures: Cultures can differ from each other in one or more of our five principal variables. Perhaps the most influential differences appear in variable (b)—a role's expected beliefs, appearance, and behaviors.

Variations in cultural beliefs about the proper way to perform the role of pupil have been demonstrated in a host of investigations. Such beliefs determine how adults treat children in defining the role of *student.* A study by Farver, Kim, and Lee (1995) demonstrated how role-forming influences may operate early in a child's school career. The researchers' compared Korean American with Anglo American preschool children, their nursery-school teachers' instructional techniques, and their mothers' attitudes about how the young should conduct themselves.

> The Anglo American teachers provided an environment that was conducive to independent thinking, problem solving, and active involvement in learning. Children had many opportunities for social interaction and play, and children were often involved in collaborative activities with teachers. Moreover, mothers' beliefs about the educational benefits of play for children were congruent with the play-oriented curriculum in the preschool settings.
>
> In the Korean American preschool, teachers organized their classrooms and lessons to encourage the development of academic skills, task perseverance, and passive involvement in learning. Children's social interaction and play were limited to periodic outdoor activity. Teachers and children rarely initiated or participated in collaborative play.
>
> The findings supported our prediction that the Anglo American children and their teachers would engage in more social interaction than Koran-American children and their teachers. Unlike Anglo American children, Korean American children view teachers as authority figures who are to be respected and shown deference. This attitude is fostered early in young Korean children, and they are taught to listen to their teachers' instruction without question. (Farver, Kim, & Lee, 1995, p. 1097)

The physical appearance associated with a role is not the same in all cultures. In hot desert regions of the Middle East, men dress in flowing white robes, and in West Java men wear skirt-like sarongs, whereas in many areas of the world robes and skirts are regarded as proper only for females.

Role expectations can also change with the passing of time. In North America a century ago, the attire considered proper for females was a dress or skirt. Today, American females are more often seen in pants than in dresses. In addition, occupations judged proper for North American and European women in the past were generally limited to those of housewife, nurse, teacher, secretary, store clerk, and—in agricultural societies—field worker. Today, women's options have expanded to nearly all vocations traditionally reserved for men.

The attire proper for people in certain occupations can also vary across cultures. Male university professors in much of Eastern Europe and the Far East are expected to wear a suit and tie. In some Western European institutions, lecturers continue to wear traditional black robes in the classroom. In North America during recent decades, male professors' apparel has ranged from coat and tie to shorts, T-shirts, and barefoot sandals.

The behaviors deemed suitable for occupations may differ from one culture to another. Journalists in Western Europe and North America are free to find fault with whoever they believe deserves criticism. However, journalists in such countries as Libya, Iraq, Iran, and Malaysia not only face public censure but may be jailed if they criticize their nation's political or religious leaders.

The prestige of occupations is not identical across societies. Medical doctors enjoy higher regard in the United States than in Russia, where physicians are mostly women. Acupuncturists are accorded greater prestige in China than in Great Britain, and the voodoo shaman is more respected in Haiti than in France.

Behaviors associated with roles can in some ways be consistent across cultures and ages, but in other ways they can vary. This point was illustrated in a comparison of Chinese children ages 8 through 12 with children in Western cultures. The investigation focused on the role acceptability of children's behavior in school settings (Chen, Rubin, & Li, 1995). The authors' survey of studies in Western societies suggested that children who were sociable (initiated friendly overtures) and were leaders (influenced their peers' activities) were not only warmly accepted by their peers but were judged by their teachers to be proficient in leadership and school achievement. In contrast, children who were aggressive and disruptive were rejected by peers, considered incompetent by their teachers, and judged to be maladjusted. Shy and retiring behavior was also seen as maladjustive and a cause for social rejection.

Among Chinese children, Chen and colleagues (1995) found the same disapproval of aggressive, disruptive behavior in middle childhood that was reported for Western societies. However, the literature covering role appropriateness of shy behavior suggested a significant cross-cultural difference.

> In Western cultures, social inhibition . . . is regarded as socially incompetent and immature. In this regard, social inhibition has been taken to reflect internal fearfulness and a lack of self-confidence. Unlike Western cultures, however, it has been argued that shy, sensitive, and inhibited behaviors in childhood are positively evaluated in Chinese culture. These behaviors are considered to reflect social maturity and understanding. Thus, it has been found that shyness-sensitivity is associated positively with peer acceptance in Chinese children. As such, whereas some social behaviors may have similar adaptive meanings in different cultures, others may have different meanings cross-culturally. (Chen et al. 1995, p. 513)

The authors' subsequent study of role acceptability in a sample of preadolescent children in the People's Republic of China confirmed such a view of children ages 8 to 11, but suggested that role expectation began to change by age 12 when shy, retiring behavior was deemed less appropriate and thus a reason for social rejection, especially for boys.

Cross-cultural encounters: Two noteworthy types of cross-cultural role encounters are those in which (a) people from one culture are confronted with unfamiliar roles in another culture or (b) the beliefs and behaviors appropriate for a given role in one culture differ from those associated with that same role in another culture.

Unfamiliar roles. When individuals move from one society to another, they often experience a conflict in typical role expectations that distinguish the two cultural settings.   Not everyone attempts to resolve the conflict in the same manner. This point can be illustrated with a study of immigrant families from India who settled in the United States (Patel, Power, & Bhavnagri, 1996).

As a background for their investigation, the researchers' summarized ethnographic accounts of immigrants from India which indicated that newcomers generally brought certain role characteristics compatible with American culture and other characteristics that were not.   On the one hand, the immigrants were usually achievement oriented, ambitious, materialistic, and intent on rising to advanced levels of the social structure. On the other hand, their Asian dedication to the collectivity (family, clan, Hindu religious community) motivated them to maintain such traditions, emphasizing the importance of the extended family, obedience to elders, established sex roles, arranged marriages, and the discouragement of autonomy in the young.

> Indian immigrants invest considerable effort and confront challenges in maintaining Indian cultural values and practices in the United States, especially in their adolescent children. Because their adolescents usually have considerable contact with peers from the larger U.S. culture, practices such as restrictions on social life and dating, arranged marriages, and the subjugation of adolescent wishes to parental authority often become sources of parent-adolescent tension. (Patel et al., 1996, p. 303)

This study focused on 100 Gujarati Hindu families that had teenage children. Most of the parents held university degrees and were engaged in professional or managerial occupations.   The results of the investigation illustrated "the limitations of drawing simplistic conclusions about the relations between parental attitudes and behavior in immigrant populations" (Patel et al., 1996, p. 311).   For instance, the most Americanized fathers were the ones who placed greatest emphasis on their teenage daughters abiding by traditional Indian manners, politeness, and deference to authority.   However, in the case of mothers, "in spite of their own values and beliefs, the longer mothers had been exposed to North American culture, the more they valued North American characteristics in their children" (Patel et al., 1996, p. 311).   In an effort to interpret the mothers' reactions, the authors suggested that:

> the socialization of females in traditional Indian culture places a greater emphasis on accommodation to new settings and to the needs of others than does the socialization of males. In traditional families, for example, much

socialization energy goes into preparing daughters to serve their future husbands and to help them adapt to life as a member of the husband's extended family. (Patel et al., 1996, p. 311)

Differing role characteristics. Years ago, at the end of my 3-year teaching assignment at Pajajaran University in West Java, the dean of the college of education scheduled an "evening of parting" to publicly recognize the valued service of the college's foreign professors before they returned to their homelands. When my turn came, the dean explained to the audience that I had often behaved in

> very strange ways that we find hard to understand. Although he has a car, each day he walks the five kilometers—mostly up hill—from his home to the university, wearing white running shoes. Sometimes, instead of lecturing, he puts the students in groups to work out problems on their own. And he is very blunt in his criticisms of what he considers weaknesses in master-degree theses. But when you get to know him, you find that he's a good person and means well.

It was thus that I learned the ways in which I had violated the Indonesian image of a proper college professor. In particular, my mode of evaluating theses had been ill-mannered (*kasar*) in contrast to the refined (*halus*) style of interpersonal relations of my Indonesian colleagues.

Practical applications: One approach to helping people who face cross-cultural role conflict consists of a three-phase program of recognition, training, and application. In the following description of the phases, the term *original culture* refers to the social tradition within which the person was reared, and the term *new culture* refers to a different milieu to which that person is now trying to adjust.

The first aspect of the recognition phase involves a counselor, teacher, or friend helping the person who faces the role conflict to recognize the likenesses and differences in cultural practices between the original and the new culture. The process of comparing and contrasting the two cultures focuses on which of the person's present behaviors are already suited to the new culture and which are ones that should be changed if the person is to meet the expectations of the new culture. The second aspect of the recognition phase consists of identifying the consequences that will likely result from the individual's continuing to perform the role in the manner of the original culture as compared to the consequences expected from adopting typical behaviors of the new society. This analysis of probable consequences is intended to influence the effort the person is willing to expend toward mastering the new role practices.

Phase two consists of role training designed to equip a person with the competencies needed for performing in the manner preferred in the new culture. Decisions about which training methods will be most successful depends on several variables, particularly on (a) the extent of difference between the elements of the role in the original culture and the elements in the new culture, (b) the developmental level (physical, intellectual, emotional, social) of the person who is attempting to adopt new role behaviors, and (c) the level of motivation the individual will dedicate to the task.

Sometimes the differences between the original culture and the new one are simple.   Other times the differences are extensive and complex.   A simple difference would be the change required when a person reared in a European tradition of eating with the use of knife, fork, and spoon attempts to adopt the East Asian practice of using chopsticks.   A complex difference would be found in the case of a native Italian seeking acceptance in Chinese culture by mastering spoken (*putonghua*) and written (*pinyin*) Chinese.   An important feature of a training program is the manner in which the instructor divides the content of a complex body of learning fare into a psychologically reasonable sequence of small segments to be mastered one at a time.

The influence of a learner's developmental level on the training methods employed becomes apparent when we consider the task of teaching a culture's spoken language to people from markedly different language backgrounds.   The methods of teaching, as well as the expectations for progress, will differ for 5-year-olds, for 15-year-olds or 55-year-olds.   The 5-year-olds will need to learn mainly by rote memorization, whereas the 15-year-olds can grasp principles of grammar, syntax, and word structure, then apply these principles in creating correct, novel utterances.   Furthermore, we can expect that 5-year-olds' pronunciation will more accurately reflect the pronunciation of people in the new culture than will 55-year-olds' speech whose original language habits will typically continue to tinge their utterances in the new language.

How successfully the role behavior of the new culture is adopted obviously depends heavily on the learner's level of motivation—on the amount of time and energy invested in acquiring new behaviors.   For instance, some people who enter an unfamiliar culture will work hard and long to master its language, whereas others make little or no attempt to learn the host culture's dialect.

The third phase, labeled *application*, concerns how adequately a person applies new cultural learnings outside the training context.   In effect, the training is judged successful to the degree that the individual displays the new role behaviors in the social encounters of everyday life that call for those behaviors.   Therefore, it is not enough that the learner perform satisfactorily in the classroom or during counseling sessions.   It is also necessary to display the new behaviors while shopping at the market, making deposits at the bank, meeting acquaintances at a public function, serving as a witness in court, and the like.   Hence, it is desirable to include in a training program provisions for monitoring learners' out-of-class behavior—an obligation that is difficult, and often impossible, to fulfill.

Finally, although in sketching the elements of a recognition/training/application program it is convenient to portray the three phases as sequential steps, actually putting the scheme into practice typically involves shuttling back and forth among the three phases during the role-learning process.

ATTRIBUTIONS

Attribution theory focuses on the causes that individuals propose when accounting for why people—including themselves—think and act as they do. In other words, attribution theory is concerned with explaining people's perceived causes of behavior. Hence, the question of interest becomes: To what do individuals attribute human thought and action, and how are their attribution conceptions organized?

However, it should be recognized that speaking of attribution theory in the singular is rather misleading, for there are multiple attribution models (Heider, 1958; Kelley, 1971; Shaver, 1975; Weiner, 1986).

Title: Commonsense Attribution Theory, with the following brief segments drawn chiefly from the writings of Harold Kelley (1967, 1971, 1992) and Bernard Weiner (1986) of the University of California at Los Angeles.

Key tenets: Everyone—scholar and lay person alike—holds beliefs about what causes people to think and act as they do.   Those beliefs can differ from one person to another, from one time to another in an individual's life, and from one culture to another.   The aim of attribution theory is to explain how people accumulate and refine their beliefs about the causes of human thought and action, in other words, about the factors in life that determine the outcome of events.

Principal variables: Two significant sets of variables involve the *structure* of causal attributions and the process for *verifying* an estimated cause.

Attributional structure. According to Weiner's (1986) analysis, any ascription of cause can be located at a position along each of three dimensions: (a) internal/external, (b) stable/labile, (c) controllable/uncontrollable .

Internal/external. The notion that cause can be attributed either to the person or to outside forces—or to some combination of the two—is at the heart of the theoretical issue known as *locus of control*, a reference to ascribing an incident primarily to an individual's own actions (*internal control*) or primarily to people and events outside that individual (*external control*).

In their attributions, people may locate the cause of an event in one or more of five sources. The first two causes are *internal* (within the person). The last three are *external* (outside the person).

1. the individual's genetic composition or inherited characteristics (level of "native intelligence," a genetically timed rate of physical development, particular facial features, and such)
2. the individual's lasting traits which have been acquired through a combination of genetic disposition and learning experiences (such traits as diligence, honesty, friendliness, forthrightness, aggressiveness, and conflict avoidance)
3. environmental forces (the influence of the physical and social setting)
4. supernatural powers (god, angels, spirits of dead ancestors)
5. chance (fate, luck, or "the breaks")

Stable/labile. Some characteristics of people and of the environment are seen as more lasting than others. People's aspects that are considered rather permanent are assigned trait labels that reflect stability—handsome, plain looking, dependable, irresponsible, intelligent, slow-witted. People's characteristics that may be expected to change from time to time or from one event to another are assigned terms that reflect lability—tired, disinterested, distracted, temporary exertion. Likewise, stability and lability can be ascribed to features of the environment. The word *weather* refers to a more changeable factor than *climate.* A school's attendance regulations are credited with greater stability than are the algebra teacher's moods.

Controllable/uncontrollable. Causal factors can also be seen as varying in the degree to which they are under a person's control.

> Mood, fatigue, and temporary effort . . . all are internal and unstable causes. Yet they are distinguishable in that effort is subject to volitional control—an individual can increase or decrease expenditure of effort. This is not typically true of mood or the onset of fatigue, which under most circumstances cannot be willed to change. The same distinction is found among the internal and stable causes. Socalled traits such as laziness, industriousness, and tolerance often are perceived as under volitional or optional control. This is not characteristic of other internal and stable causes of success and failure such as mathematical or artistic aptitude and physical coordination. (Weiner, 1986, p. 48)

Thus, we assume that any causal ascription can be located at a position along each of the three dimensions. To illustrate, imagine that we propose several causal factors that have apparently contributed to the outcome of an event (an interscholastic volleyball tournament), and we rate the performance of one high school girl, Jane, by locating her estimated position on each dimension. I begin by describing the girl and her achievement. In Table 5-3, I chart her position on each of the factors that we think might have contributed to her performance.

> Jane, 5-feet-11-inches tall, has played in varsity water polo tournaments the past 3 years. She is known as an excellent swimmer and shot blocker. However, her success in the present tournament has been inconsistent from one match to the next. She missed practice sessions all last week because of the flu. Her coach did not start her in the first game. Jane sat on the sidelines with her head down, apparently paying no attention to the progress of the game. When the coach did put Jane in the game, she appeared listless and stayed away from her teammates when they huddled together between quarters. But when the coach selected her as a starter in the second game, Jane was highly animated, cheered her teammates, blocked several opponents' shots, passed well, and made three goals.

On each of the three dimensions in Table 5-3, our hypothetical ratings are assumed to be along a 10-point scale.

Table 5-3

Causes of Jane's Performance on Three Dimensions

Assumed Causal Factors	*Dimensions of Cause*		
	Locus[a]	*Stability*[b]	*Controllability*[c]
Jane's height	1	1	10
Length of the pool	10	1	10
Water temperature	10	4	10
Jane's location in the pool	5	5	5
Jane's ability	1	4	5
Jane's effort	3	8	4
Coach's decisions	10	5	7
Teammates' behavior	10	5	7
Audience's cheers for Jane	10	5	6

[a] 1 = internal—within Jane; 10 = external —in Jane's environment
[b] 1 = stable; 10 = labile
[c] 1= controllable by Jane; 10 = uncontrollable by Jane

In summary, whenever people ascribe causes for achievements, they are estimating that success results from a combination of contributing causes that can differ from each other in those causes' locus of control, stability, and controllability.

Verification of causal ascriptions. The way people develop their causal attributions is from direct observation of events and from such vicarious experiences as reading books, listening to other people's description of events, watching television programs, receiving instruction, and the like.   As this learning process continues day after day and year after year, the developing child accumulates convictions about the locus, stability, and controllability of his or her causal attributions.   The learning process includes testing the accuracy of causal ascriptions by means of assessment criteria.   Kelley (1967, p. 197) has proposed that one's level of confidence in estimates of cause derives from the intuitive application of four criteria: distinctiveness, consistency over time, consistency over modality, and consensus.

1. Distinctiveness: The impression of cause is attributed to the thing that is being observed (person or object) if that impression occurs when the thing is present and does not occur in its absence.   (If the volleyball team wins only

when Jane is in the game, then much of the team's success is attributed to Jane and she is credited with a high degree of ability.)

2. Consistency over time: Each time the thing is present, the observer's impression must be the same or nearly so.   (The conviction that Jane is a significant cause of the team's fate is strengthened if, on successive occasions, the team wins when Jane plays but loses when she does not.)

3. Consistency over modality: The person's impression must be consistent even though his or her mode of interaction with the thing varies. (The conviction that Jane is a significant cause of the team's fate is strengthened if the person making the attribution not only witnesses games directly but also reads newspaper reports that are consistent with the attribution.)

4. Consensus: The thing's noticeable attributes are experienced the same way by all observers. (Faith in attributing the team's success to Jane is increased when many other fans also ascribe the team's achievement to Jane.)

To the extent that people's attributions fulfill all four criteria, they feel confident that they have an accurate picture of their external world and that their ascriptions of cause are warranted.

Differences among cultures: Two ways of looking at attributional differences across cultures are in terms of (a) locus of control and (b) conceptions of reality.

Locus of control. A considerable quantity of research has been conducted to discover if different cultural communities vary in the degree to which they locate cause in the person (internal locus of control) rather than in the environment (external locus of control).   Some investigators have predicted that non-Western peoples will assume a stronger external locus of control (so that individuals are thought to be more vulnerable to forces outside themselves) than Western peoples, because the non-Westerners may have less access than Westerners to power, material resources, and opportunities to improve their social positions. A further prediction has been that urban, high socioeconomic-status, ethnic-majority male members of society will exhibit higher internal locus of control than members who are rural, low socioeconomic-status, minority women.   In support of such predictions, Semin and Zwier (1997) cited reports that Swedish women and Polish students displayed more external locus of control than did Americans; and Fijian-Indians evidenced more internal control than did indigenous Fijians.   However, other studies have produced contrary results, thereby casting doubt on the universal applicability of such predictions. Although there may, indeed, be systematic differences across cultures in people's locus-of-control convictions,

> The research to date suggests an inconsistent pattern, and this appears to be due in large part of the absence of a theory relating culture to the conception of locus of control.   Given that there is no provision for cultural variation in this [ostensibly pan-cultural measure of attributional tendencies], the research

inevitably remains an accumulation of noncumulative correlational evidence. (Semin & Zwier, 1997, p. 56)

Some investigators have proposed that attributions of cause tend to differ between cultures that stress individualism and ones that stress the good of the group, with members of individualistic cultures tending to account for events by citing people's traits or dispositions as causes while members of group-centered cultures cite characteristics of the environment.

Conceptions of reality. The phrase *conceptions of reality* refers to people's beliefs about (a) what truly exists and (b) what connections or correlations obtain between things that exist. The correlations are typically interpreted in a causal fashion, with one of the things or phenomena believed to be the cause—at least partially—of the other phenomenon. The degree of correlation between the two entities reflects the extent of power that one entity is assumed to exert in determining the condition of the other. The two phenomena on which the following examples focus are *the human soul* and *drought.*

The soul. Questions about an entity called *the soul*—its nature and how it develops—have been debated in many cultures for untold centuries.

In Judeo-Christian-Islamic tradition, each human being consists of a body, a mind, and a soul. Whereas the body and mind disintegrate at the time of death, the invisible soul continues to exist, residing for eternity in one of three locations—heaven, hell, or a vaguely defined purgatory or limbo (Thomas, 1997b).

Buddhist doctrine teaches that each person's soul is a derivative of the Cosmic Soul that rules the universe. At the time of a person's earthly death, his or her soul is transported into a new body (human, animal, or inanimate object) for an additional sojourn on Earth. The process of the soul's inhabiting one body after another continues until the last person containing the particular soul lives such a morally pure life that the soul is permitted to reenter the Cosmic Soul for the remainder of eternity, and the cycle of earthly births and deaths comes to an end (Marek, 1988).

Adherents of the Shinto religion in Japan declare that the individual person's soul (*tama*) is intimately related to the souls of all other Japanese, past and present, so no one is "personified to the extent that he becomes easily distinguishable from his milieu; he is not individualized to the point where he might decide upon a course of life irrespective of others in his past, present, and future" (Spae, 1972, p. 30). At death, the soul can assume any of a number of forms, even appearing as a ghost, a monster, or a shining ball moving through the night air. The soul may become a *kami*—a spirit that can hover about to protect and bless the family of the person who has died.

In contrast to the foregoing religious perspectives, people who identify themselves as atheists, agnostics, or secular humanists typically deny the existence of *soul*. They find no convincing evidence for such an entity. Hence, they claim that *soul* is no more than a fiction created by people unwilling to accept the truth of their mortality—that someday they will expire and no longer exist in any form.

Drought.   An unexpected, long period of no rain can be explained differently in different cultures.   Whereas the existence of such a thing as *the soul* is a matter of debate, there is no debate about whether drought is real.   Tangible evidence is there for anyone to see.   But disagreement does arise over what causes drought.   In other words, what is it that correlates in a causal manner with a lack of rain?

The explanation in many cultures is that such disasters as drought, flood, hurricane, earthquake, and crop failure occur because supernatural forces—gods, spirits, unseen beings—are displeased with people's behavior and therefore vent their wrath in the form of catastrophes.   This supernatural-beings interpre-tation is offered by such diverse peoples as Zulus in South Africa, Haitians in the Caribbean, Pueblos in the Southwestern United States, and Okinawans in the Western Pacific.   Each of these cultures has favorite methods for placating the infuriated spirits and thereby ending the drought.   Zulus and Pueblos perform rain dances; Okinawans and adherents of Haitian voodoo may pray and reorganize their daily lives in ways that comply with the spirits' dicta.

However, instead of attributing drought to the ire of spirits from a shadow world, people who invest their faith in meteorological science ascribe drought to such palpable variables as atmospheric temperature and moisture content, barometric pressure, wind patterns, the chemical and electrical composition of clouds, and more.   Scientists' methods of affecting drought have included producing rain or snow by (a) seeding supercooled clouds with dry ice or with the smoke from burned silver iodide and lead iodide or (b) seeding warm clouds with sodium chloride, calcium chloride, or water spray (Battan, 1994).

Cross-cultural encounters: The concepts *soul* and *drought* can serve to illustrate consequences of contrasting cultural attributions.

People's contrary beliefs about *the soul* can lead to their regarding each other as irrational or at least peculiar.   The devoted Christian can be convinced that an atheist, who denies the existence of *soul*, is not only wrong but is in danger of a calamitous life after death.   The atheist can accuse the Christian of being stupid, or at least naive, to believe in *the soul* without substantial evidence of the soul's existence.

Disagreements between groups over the desirability of abortion as a birth-control technique can be seated in conflicting beliefs about *the soul.*   Numerous religious traditions hold that the essence of humanness is the soul.   That is, the soul is what distinguishes humans from animals.   Ending the life of a being that lacks a soul is permissible, but killing a being that has a soul is murder.   According to many Christian clerics, the soul is implanted in the unborn child at the time of conception, so that ending the life of an embryo at any stage of pregnancy is murder.   However, Islamic doctrine, according to a passage in a widely accepted version of the sacred Sunna, asserts that the soul enters the unborn child's body 120 days after conception.   Thus, not until after the fourth month of pregnancy is the fetus "human," so ending the pregnancy before that time would not be killing a human (Munzudi in Almunzri, 1977, p. 488). However, for people who do not believe in an entity called *the soul* and thus do not include the soul in their theory of development, judgments about the morality or desirability of abortion must be founded on other considerations.

Conflicting explanations of drought can also lead to people adopt negative opinions about each other. A traditional Pueblo can be confounded by an advocate of meteorology recommending that an exploding rocket containing lead iodide be fired into the clouds. In turn, a meteorologist can consider the Pueblo's dance a silly, futile, time-wasting device for luring rain from the skies.

Practical applications: One way to help people understand the bases of other folks' attributions involves a group-discussion approach that centers attention on three aspects of individuals' explanations of why events occur as they do. The three aspects are (a) underlying assumptions, (b) convincing evidence, and (c) line of logic.

An *assumption* in this context is a basic belief on which a person's explanation is built. The belief is usually considered to be self-evident, requiring no proof of its validity, particularly if the assumption is widely shared and therefore qualifies as a cultural "truth." People often are unaware of their assumptions. Here are four on which people might base their attributions of cause.

> Everyone has a soul.
> The world operates on the principle of justice, so people eventually receive their just deserts.
> With rare exception, the accounts of events described in newspapers or on television news programs are accurate.
> People are basically selfish; so when they must choose between fulfilling their own desires or aiding other people by sacrificing their own welfare, they act to fulfill their own desires.

The word *evidence* is used here to mean information or sources cited in support of a conclusion or a style of reasoning. The word *proof* is used to mean a person's decision that the evidence offered to support a conclusion is convincing. People's conflicts over the causes of an event often derive from their disagreeing about the sources of evidence that they find convincing. For instance, cultures can differ in the types of authority accepted as credible. Potentially competing authorities in the form of printed documents include the *United States Constitution,* the *Encyclopaedia Britannica,* the *World Almanac,* the Jewish Torah, the Christian Bible, the Islamic Qur'an, the *Analects of Confucius,* and the Hindu *Manu Smriti.* Cultures can also differ in the ways of obtaining evidence that they advocate. One way is to believe what a recognized authority says. Another way is to witness events directly ("I believe it when I see it."). A third way is to require that the presenter of the evidence describe precisely how the data were gathered, organized, and summarized.

The phrase *line of logic* refers to a pattern of reasoning adduced to arrive at a conclusion. Cultures can differ in the way ideas are marshaled for arriving at a convincing judgment.

The proposed group discussion involves participants from different cultural backgrounds—national, ethnic, religious, gender, and the like. The discussion designed to reveal the anatomy of people's causal attributions begins with the group leader describing and illustrating the meanings intended for *underlying assumptions, convincing evidence,* and *line of logic.* Next, the leader describes an incident, then asks different participants to explain why the events of the incident occurred. The explanation will usually include why the people in the episode acted as they did. The group members then compare different explanations in terms of their basic assumptions, their sources of evidence, and their lines of logic.

The incidents that serve as the focus of discussion can be presented in various forms—as episodes occurring within the group itself, as accounts described by group members from their own lives, as newspaper reports, as episodes from biographies, or as videotaped segments of movies or television documentaries.

SOCIAL RECIPROCITY

Social-exchange theory describes the principles governing transactions between individuals or groups, transactions that can contribute to the benefit or to the detriment of the participants. In classical economic-exchange theory, the nature of what is to be exchanged is specified in advance, so participants know what will be received for what is given. But in social-exchange theory, while it is assumed that when one person does a favor for another the recipient is then obligated to the giver, the nature of this obligation is usually not specified in advance. The resulting indeterminate nature of the exchange can be a source of misunderstanding and distress for giver and receiver. However, cultural traditions serve to reduce this uncertainty by informing people of the kinds of response on the part of recipients that are considered appropriate within the particular culture.

The version of the theory described in the following paragraphs focuses on how individuals' perceptions of exchange are likely to develop over the first two decades of life.

Title: Social-Exchange Theory, as interpreted by Raymond A. Eve of the University of Texas at Arlington.

Key tenets: People enter into new social relationships because they expect those relationships will provide rewards. They continue and extend such relationships to the degree that the associations are indeed rewarding.

An individual who benefits from another person's acts is obligated to reciprocate by furnishing benefits to that person in turn. For many common types of social interaction, proper exchange is dictated by cultural tradition in the form of expectations about fairness, expectations that assume the form of *exchange norms*. Such norms are adopted in a culture as devices for coercing the parties in a social transaction to abide by what is considered fair. Members of society impose social pressure to encourage people to comply with those norms. The extent to which people abide by exchange norms influences their status in the society's hierarchy of respect, prestige, and power. "When fairness does not occur [that is, when the norms are violated], the norms compel the party who fails to be fair to accept a degradation of status in the group as compensation for the imbalance" (Eve, 1986, p. 189).

Exchange norms are among the important learnings children are expected to acquire as they grow up. Consequently, one way to view human development over the first two decades of life is as a succession of advances in perceptions of what constitutes fairness of exchange.

In Eve's opinion, children typically progress through three stages of belief about exchange, stages inferred from the tactics the young employ in their social relations.

1. The youngest children will be most likely to rely on simple requests as a means for achieving their goals. This is largely due to the egocentric character of their developmental stage, which makes them unable to see why anything more would be required.
2. Children then enter a second stage where they . . . view all interaction as based on fraud or force. For example, children might begin by saying things such as, "If he doesn't give it to me, I'll hit him until he does." This should gradually change, as children mature, to "If he gives it to me, I'll do something nice for him," [thereby] becoming more positive in its thrust.
3. As children develop greater competence in social exchange, they pass into a third stage, where they begin to recognize the utility of bringing group pressure to bear on the method and outcomes of exchanges. This results in their greater likelihood of invoking norms as the reason why others should comply with their wishes. (Eve, 1986, p. 190)

Principal variables: The theory's two main classes of variables are causes and outcomes. Causes are the assumed determinants of two interlinked out-comes—(a) the perceptions of social exchanges that people acquire and (b) the resulting behavior that people display in social interactions.

In regard to causes, Eve observes that Piaget (1950) believed that the rate at which children's conceptions evolve is determined chiefly by children's biological growth schedule, that is, by the genetically set pace at which the neural system matures. In Eve's opinion, whereas the importance of such maturation deserves recognition, the evolution of children's understanding social exchange is more dependent on their daily experiences than on automatic internal maturation. I would suggest that those experiences are of three types:

1. direct social encounters (participating in exchanges),
2. vicarious interactions (seeing other people engage in exchanges, either by directly witnessing social encounters or by reading stories, viewing television programs, or hearing people describe incidents), and
3. being instructed about fairness of social intercourse, with the instruction either formal (as in a Sunday school lesson) or informal (as when a parent tells a child how to behave at a birthday party).

These three types are often interlinked. For example, a 5-year-old can learn from the direct experience of refusing to give another child a turn on the tricycle (resulting in the other child punching the rider and calling for the kindergarten teacher's help), with the event impelling the teacher to instruct the rider about the kindergarten culture's social-exchange expectations and of the consequences to be suffered for failing to abide by "the rules."

In brief, the immediate or proximate cause of children's social-exchange understanding is the interaction between their genetic maturation and daily experiences. In addition, a significant background variable—not mentioned in Eve's scheme—is the historical development of a culture's exchange norms that accounts for differences in social-exchange expectations across cultures.   In effect, for historical reasons, the guidelines for defining justice in exchanges can vary from one society to another. Consequently, what children in one society are taught about fair exchange may not be the same as what children in other societies are taught.

Differences among cultures: Exchanges can entail various kinds of items— material goods, opportunities, or such social-psychological benefits as pride for abiding by the dictates of one's conscience or public prestige for behaving in keeping with cultural ideals. Thus, social negotiations may involve exchanging diligent labor for a reputation as a hard worker, sexual favors for money, a cheerful disposition for invitations to parties, aiding the elderly for self-satisfaction, listening to a dull lecture for the goodwill of a teacher, and more.

The consequences of what is exchanged can vary from one society to another. Consider, for example, different consequences for how material property has been handled in American Indian cultures. Erikson's (1987, p. 378) observations revealed that among the Sioux of North Dakota an individual's distributing material possessions to other people earned that person prestige. "To the original Sioux, a 'hoarder' was the poorest kind of a man because, apparently, irrational anxiety caused him to mistrust the abundance of the [buffalo and deer] and the generosity of his fellow men" (Erikson, 1987, p. 451). In contrast, among the Yurok of Northern California prestige has been accorded those who amass property and keep it for their own use. The Yurok "owned real estate along the [Klamath] river, considered [such ownership] to be virtuous, which led to the storage of wealth and gave monetary value to every named item in their small world" (Erikson, 1987, pp. 446-447). Even more dramatic than the Sioux custom has been the potlatch practice among the Kwakiutl Indians of the Northwest Pacific Coast. Potlatch consists of a ceremonial distribution of one's accumulated property and gifts to affirm one's social status.

> Great feasts and generous hospitality accompanied the potlatch. . . . Important events such as marriages, births, deaths, and the initiations into secret societies were also occasions for potlaches; but trivial events were used just as often, because the main purpose of a potlatch was not the occasion itself but the valida-tion of claims to social rank. The potlatch was also used as a face-saving device by individuals who had suffered public embarrassment and as a means of compe-tition between rivals in social rank. ("Potlatch," 1994, p. 643)

Within present-day general North American culture, a combination of both amassing and dispersing property can enhance the social status of individuals who accumulate wealth, distribute a liberal portion in philanthropy, but keep a substantial sum for themselves. Such folks can be credited both with cleverness for accumulating wealth and with generosity for donating an abundant amount to worthy causes (Finn, 1998; Rogers, 1997).

A highly elaborate system of social exchange among groups of islands off the coast of Papua New Guinea involves food, shell necklaces, and armshells that are given away in order to earn of honor and fame for the givers. On occasion, a flotilla of canoes from one island sails to either a nearby or far-off island for the purpose of item exchange. In the case of food, it is not just a good reputation that one wins for generosity, but gifts of food also can obligate the receiver to reciprocate at a later time when the original giver is in need. Thus, the practice serves as a social-security investment.

> When a man or woman who has regularly fed a child grows old, the child in turn should care for this person—for instance, by giving daily food when the latter is ill. (Munn, 1986, p. 50)

Both the consumable (food) and nonconsumable (seashell ornaments) items perform a variety of exchange functions: (a) enhance the giver's reputation for generosity, (b) extend the individual's social relationships and fame beyond the local community, (c) increase the giver's political influence, and (d) acquire honor and political power for the giver's home community.

Cross-cultural encounters: Misunderstanding can result when people from different societies engage in social exchanges. The following two examples illustrate situations that can lead to misunderstanding. First,

> The Apache, when compared with the white, is extremely undemonstrative in expressing gratitude. The words for "thank you". . . are not often used. . . . The general feeling seems to be that gratitude is understood and need not be verbally indicated. It is shown rather by doing a return favor at some future time. (Goodwin, 1942/1969, p. 561)

Two results of incidents in which an Apache does not appear to appreciate a generous act are that: (a) in the opinion of the white, the Apache is socially diminished, and (b) the Apache is astonished by the reaction of the white who now emotionally distances himself from the seemingly ungrateful Indian.

The second example draws on my own experience while teaching in a university. It was the same experience that several of my colleagues reported. We found that an unusually large number of our Chinese and Japanese graduate students presented us with expressions of gratitude and gifts that we felt were far out of proportion to any value we had as their teachers. The gifts included such items as electronic calculators (which played tunes while calculating), Oriental art objects, neckties, fancy leather belts, culinary delicacies, and more. From our American perspective toward social exchange, the students' excellent performance in their studies was more than enough reward to us for whatever help we had been. Then, in reaction to the students' inordinate generosity, we felt obligated to offer an adequate response. By *adequate*, I mean a response that would be regarded as proper in their own culture. However, we never discovered what such a response would be, because if we asked outright what would be considered a suitable exchange in their culture, we imagined that the students would assure us that nothing was required.

Practical applications: An exercise that can be conducted to reveal differences across cultures in social-exchange expectations is an activity carried out in a group composed of people from various cultural backgrounds. The activity involves the group leader posing a series of incidents, then asking representatives from different cultural traditions to explain (a) types of response that would typically be considered appropriate and (b) types that would be regarded as inappropriate in the participants' home cultures. Here are three incidents that might serve as the focus of discussion.

Incident 1. A family living on a very small income suffered a fire that destroyed part of their home. They lacked the money to repair the damage. But a neighbor, who also had a very limited income, lent them money for the repairs. How should the family respond to their neighbor's act? In other words, should the family do anything in exchange?

What if it was not a neighbor but, rather, it was a bank that lent the money at a low rate of interest, say 2%? Should the family's response be different than to a neighbor? What if the interest rate was quite high, say 25%? Should the family's response to the bank be the same?

Incident 2. A 25-year-old man has begun dating a 25-year-old woman. On three occasions, when the young woman's family was going to a restaurant for dinner, they invited the young man along and paid for his dinner. How should the young man respond to the family's act?

What if it was a 12-year-old boy and a 12-year-old girl instead of two 25-year-olds? Should the boy's response be any different than the man's response?

Incident 3. Two girls, ages 15 and 16, were close friends. The 16-year-old had a driver's license and often used her parent's car to take her younger friend to parties, picnics, and movies. The 16-year-old also helped her friend with homework and arranged for the friend to be accepted as a member of a high school sorority that included the most popular girls in the school. Today, the 16-year-old asked her friend for a favor. It was to pretend that the 16-year-old was spending the night at the 15-year-old's house, just in case the 16-year-old's parents asked about it. The truth was that the 16-year-old planned to spend the night with her boyfriend. How should the 15-year-old respond to her friend's request?

If the two girls were age 21, should the response be any different? Or, what if they were ages 11 and 12?

THE SIGNIFICANCE OF SOCIETAL CIRCUMSTANCES

Lifespan or life-course models center attention on the question: How is a person's development influenced by the particular condition of the surrounding society at each juncture of the individual's lifespan? Thus, the theory described in the following paragraphs concerns the way development is configured for a biologically changing individual who interacts with social contexts that are sometimes stable and other times transitory.

Title: Sociohistorical Life-Course Theory, as proposed by Glen H. Elder, Jr., of the University of North Carolina.

Key tenets: The central propositions on which the theory is based focus on (a) societal stability and change and (b) the time and place in which an individual is located when social conditions are stable and when they are in flux.

Stability and change. Each child is born into, and raised within, a society that moves through phases of stability and change that can significantly influence the child's development (Elder, 1996; Elder, Modell, & Parke, 1993).

Time and place. Each person is located in a particular time and place in relation to a society's phases. *Time* refers to what is occurring in the society at different junctures in the person's development. In other words, *time* assumes the form of a life-stage principle which holds that "the influence of a historical event on the life course depends on the stage at which individuals experience the event" (Elder, 1996, p. 52).

Principal variables: Important factors that affect development are: (a) the biological and psychological condition of the person at a given period in her or his development, (b) features of the social environment that affect the individual at that period, and (c) the extent to which those factors are stable or are in transition.

Influential ways that societal factors can vary are in relation to:

public order and safety (peace vs. war, riots, civil disobedience, strikes, crime)

politics (system of governance—democratic, autocratic, socialistic) *economics* (prosperity vs. depression, capitalism vs. state socialism, job availability, credit availability, workforce productivity, income levels)

social-class structure (stability of classes, types and degrees of differences among classes, ease of mobility from one class to another)

ethnic composition (numbers and sizes of recognized ethnic divisions, extent of amicable vs. antagonistic relations among divisions, likenesses and differences among divisions [physical appearance, customs, usual roles in the society])

occupational structure (types and proportions of agricultural, industrial, and service occupations)

transportation media (horse and wagon, train, automobile, bus, airplane)

communication, information media (word of mouth, letters, books, newspapers, telephones, television, computer networks)

childrearing functionaries (nuclear biological-parents family, extended family, single-parent family, one biological parent plus one step-parent, foster family, social-service organization, school)

religious affiliation (numbers and sizes of religious denominations, similarities and differences of belief among denominations, extent of conflict among denominations)

health conditions and medical practices (prevalence of different diseases, availability of drugs and medical treatment)

The relationship between when children arrive in the world and the timing of societal eras is depicted in Figure 5-1 with four age cohorts—children born in 1940, in 1960, in 1980, and in 1995. Consider, first, the American children born in 1940 (Cohort One). Many would be raised during early childhood by their mothers and grandparents, because their fathers were away in the armed forces during World War II. For a substantial number of children, this early separation from their fathers would contribute to a difficult child-father relationship after the father returned home (Stolz, 1968). During the 1960s, members of Cohort One would be between ages 20 and 30, participating in the changed youth culture of that decade. For some youths—but certainly not all, and probably not the majority—this would mean rebelling against authorities, joining civil rights and antiwar demonstrations, using illicit drugs, and frequently changing sex partners. In the 1960s, Cohort One members would become the parents of Cohort Two children and often provide a different family context than they themselves had experienced as children during and after World War II. Unlike the Cohort One child, some Cohort Two children could more often see their family's and neighborhood's "normal way of life" as featuring marijuana and cocaine, casual sex, and rebellion against traditional authorities. Twenty years later, in the 1980s, members of Cohort One would be middle-aged, some of them now grandparents. But with the growing incidence of divorce, many would not be with their original conjugal partners. Members of Cohort

Figure 5-1

Relationship of Societal Conditions and Birth Cohorts

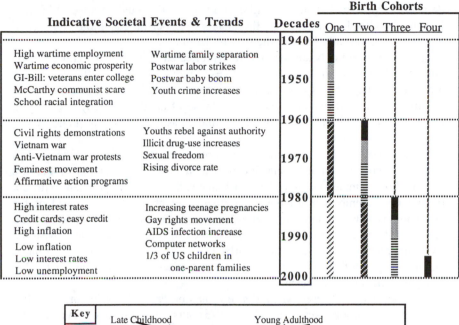

Indicative Societal Events & Trends		Decades	Birth Cohorts
			One Two Three Four
High wartime employment	Wartime family separation	1940	
Wartime economic prosperity	Postwar labor strikes		
GI-Bill: veterans enter college	Postwar baby boom	1950	
McCarthy communist scare	Youth crime increases		
School racial integration			
Civil rights demonstrations	Youths rebel against authority	1960	
Vietnam war	Illicit drug-use increases		
Anti-Vietnam war protests	Sexual freedom	1970	
Feminest movement	Rising divorce rate		
Affirmative action programs			
High interest rates	Increasing teenage pregnancies	1980	
Credit cards; easy credit	Gay rights movement		
High inflation	AIDS infection increase	1990	
Low inflation	Computer networks		
Low interest rates	1/3 of US children in		
Low unemployment	one-parent families	2000	

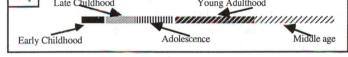

Key
Late Childhood   Young Adulthood

Early Childhood   Adolescence   Middle age

Two—now the parents of Cohort Three—would bring the attitudes acquired during their childhood to the task of child-rearing, including viewpoints from the growing feminist movement that asserted women's rights to pursue their own careers, either inside or outside of marriage. Cohort Three children would grow up at a time of easy financial credit, with many parents taking advantage of credit cards to indulge their own and their offsprings' desire for material goods in a spirit of, "We deserve to live well." During the middle and latter 1990s, financial interest rates were lower, credit not so easy, inflation low, and employment rates rather high. The United States labor market now differed significantly from that of the 1940s when manufacturing had been a dominant source of jobs in the United States. By the 1990s, many low-skill factory jobs had moved overseas to countries with low labor costs, so that jobs in the United States were increasingly in service and sales activities, with the better-paying jobs requiring specialized skills, such as those involving computers. In the realm of sexual behavior, children in Cohort Three would newly face choices posed by the popularizing of casual sexual intercourse in the mass-communication media (television, computer networks), the advance of the gay rights movement, and the growing incidence of AIDS (acquired immune deficiency syndrome). Finally, children born in 1995 would be affected in their late childhood and adolescence by the changes in societal conditions that would appear during the early years of the new millennium.

In summary, not only are societal trends reflected in the lives of children who constitute a given birth cohort, but the lives of individuals from different cohorts are linked in ways that also influence development, particularly when the values and lifestyles of one cohort conflict with those of another, thereby resulting in disagreements between parents and their children as well as among grandparents, parents, and the young.

Next, consider *place*, which in the present context refers to the child's combined geographical and social location at a given point in his or her life course. For example, one 5-year-old girl shares a two-room apartment with six other family members in a large city's ghetto neighborhood. The head of the household is an unwed mother—currently pregnant and on welfare—who had quit school in tenth grade to run away from home. In contrast, another 5-year-old lives in a nine-room house in the suburbs with her biological mother and father and a younger brother. Her father is employed as an accountant and her mother as a part-time real estate agent.

The coordination between a child's time and place exerts an important influence on the direction taken by the child's life course at any stage of development.

Differences among cultures: Perhaps the most enlightening contribution of life-course theory as a window on culture is its directing attention to the chronological dimension of culture. The theory accomplishes this by revealing (a) how the culture of a given society changes with the passing of time and (b) how the culture's effect on an individual depends on which stage of the life span the person is in at the time of the change. Therefore, from a life-course perspective, the phrase *differences among cultures* can mean differences across time periods within the same society as well as differences between one society and another.

Three interconnected ways that societal circumstances can affect developmental outcomes are in the values individuals adopt, the interests they express, and the abilities they develop. The following examples illustrate how such outcomes can vary both within a single society (cultural differences over time) and across societies (cultural differences by place).

Values. As proposed in Chapter 4, values are standards people use for distinguishing between good and bad, proper and improper, desirable and undesirable, well done and poorly done, and the like. A dramatic illustration of value changes over time is reflected in data on marriage and cohabitation during recent decades in the United States and Canada.

Since the 1960s, the incidence of marriage has declined and the incidence of unwed couples living together has risen in both the United States and Canada.

Between 1970 and the mid-1990s, the proportion of married adults in the United States. dropped from 72% to 61%, whereas the number of unmarried adults doubled. The number of never-married women in their late twenties and thirties tripled between 1970 and 1974 (Johnson, 1997, p. 434). In 1970, 75% of men and 69% of women were married. By 1994, the percentages had declined to 63% and 59% respectively. The number of marriages per 1000 people was 12.0 in 1940, 10.6 in 1970, and 8.9 in 1995 (Famighetti, 1996, pp. 382, 836). Households maintained by married couples decreased from 76% in 1960 to 67.6% in 1970, and to 55.5% in 1995. Households maintained by women with no husband present rose from 17.7% in 1960 to 24.4% in 1970, and to 33.5% in 1995 (Johnson, 1997, p. 838).

For Canada as a whole, the picture of marital conditions over recent decades was similar to that of the United States, but with the rate of change even more pronounced in Canada. While the crude marriage rate in the United States fell from 9.9 per 1,000 population in 1987 to 9.1 in 1994, Canada's dropped from 7.1 to 5.4 over the same period. Of particular significance in Canada was the distinction between the nation's two most notably different cultural regions— Francophone Quebec and the rest of the nation which traces its cultural roots to Britain. Over the final 25 years of the 20th century, marriage rates in Quebec declined far more rapidly than they did in other parts of Canada. The total first marriage rate for Quebec women (ages 15-49) in 1994 was only 373 per 1,000 compared with 608 per 1,000 for women in the rest of the nation. Pollard and Zheng (1998, p. 1) suggest that this "recent trend toward later and fewer marriages is not [just] a continuation of a long-term process. . . . [Marriage] as an institution is in crisis, particularly in Quebec." Part of the reason for the plunging marriage rates was the increase in couples cohabiting, that is, couples living together without being married. By 1996, 12% of Canadian unions were cohabitations, whereas in Quebec 24% involved cohabitation.

In seeking to account for such societal changes, Pollard and Zheng adopted Lesthaeghe's (1998) ideational theory to arrive at several likely factors working in concert—urbanization, industrialization, and a shift in the moral code toward greater tolerance and individual choice that led to changes in people's behavior.

> Until the late 1950s, Quebec continued to be characterized as a rural traditional society. Despite industrialization during World War II, the people retained a pre-industrial mentality. Growing conflict between the old guard and the more liberal younger population erupted, however, with the election of Jean Lesage and the Liberal party in 1960. The institutional, administrative, and ideological structures of Quebec were no longer compatible with the values of the population. . . . During the ["Quiet Revolution" of 1960 to 1966], the Quebec government modernized the political, economic, and educational infrastructure,

transforming the province from a religious, rural-based society to an urban industrial metropolis.

Despite the many institutional and political reforms of the Quiet Revolution, it was chiefly characterized by a "mental liberation, a development of critical attitude." Before the Revolution, Quebec society's values and attitudes toward women's roles and family formation were heavily influenced by the authority of existing institutions. With the rise in competing institutions, such as agencies for educational reform and feminist groups, the authority of traditional institutions weakened, and people grew increasingly independent of traditional forms of social control. (Pollard & Zheng, 1998, p. 6)

These value changes, reflected in rapidly shifting marriage and cohabitation rates, were accompanied by important consequences for children who, in growing numbers, would live in single-parent households or with a cohabiting couple who could easily change partners without the bother of getting a divorce.

Knowledge and skills. Like values, the knowledge and skills people need to survive and thrive can differ from one time to another within the same society and from one society to another during the same era. These points can be demonstrated in a comparison of the role of knowledge and skills in Taiwan and in Mongolia over the last half of the 20th century.

Immediately after World War II, Chinese Communists fought Chinese Nationalists in an effort to win complete political control of their nation. Their effort succeeded, and in December 1949 the defeated Nationalist forces fled to the nearby island of Taiwan to establish a separate government called the Republic of China in contrast to the Communists' People's Republic of China on the East Asian mainland. Over the subsequent 50 years, Taiwan society would pass through a rapid transition in economic structure, demographic distribution, educational progress, political control, and social problems that would require marked changes in what people needed to know and be able to do. For much of the population, the knowledge and skills appropriate in 1950 would no longer suffice in the 1990s.

When the Nationalist government—the Kuomintang—arrived in Taiwan, most of the island's people were engaged in agriculture, with much of the land held by the rich whose farms were worked by nonlanded peasants. Between 1949 and 1953, the government's land reform policies broke up large landholdings, distributed public lands, and altered the traditional landlord-tenant relationship that was a central feature of the island's social system. Consequently, the amount of land cultivated by owner-farmers increased from around 30% in 1948 to 60% in 1953. The new owners thus needed to acquire knowledge and skills related to operating their own ventures rather than simply working a landlord's fields.

The structure of the economy changed significantly over the last half of the century. Agriculture had dominated in the early 1950s, labor-intensive industry took the lead in the 1960s and 1970s, and high technology and service industries gained momentum in the 1980s and 1990s. In its early phases, Taiwan's economic development was built on low-cost but relatively well-trained and disciplined labor. By 1990 the economy was based on capital-intensive and knowledge-intensive industries, making Taiwan the world leader in producing microcomputers and computer parts (Copper, 1990, p. 38). The labor force necessarily followed these trends, so that people were continually obliged to acquire further knowledge and skills appropriate for their new employment opportunities (Table 5-4). Analysts concluded that between the 1950s and the 1990s Taiwan advanced from the status of an under-developed society to that of a mature industrial economy whose "per capita income in 1990 was just a bit under US$8,000, enough to place her in the World Bank's category of high-income countries" (Ranis, 1992, p. 1).

Table 5-4

Labor-Force Trends 1950-2000

Year	Percentagess of Workers in Principal Economic Sectors		
	Agriculture	Industry	Services
1952	52	22	26
1962	46	22	32
1972	33	32	35
1995	11	39	50

(Source: Copper, 1996, pp. 131-132. Copyright (c) 1996 by Westview Press. Reprinted by permission of Westview Press, a member of Perseus Books, L.L.C.)

Demographic changes over the half century included a reduction in the birth-rate from one of the world's highest in 1950 (4.66 per 1,000 population) to 3.27 in 1955, to 2.34 in 1980 (about the world average), and to 1.1 in the 1990s. Because of the influx of mainlanders in 1949 and the high birth rate in the early days, the island's population grew from 5.8 million in 1940 to 22 million by the end of the century, making Taiwan one of the most densely populated regions of the world, with the number of people per square kilometer twice that of Japan and five times that of mainland China (Copper, 1996, p. 8).

Urban living conditions also changed between 1950 and the late 1980s, as suggested in Winckler's observation that

For years Taipei [the capital city] was a mixture of traditional farmhouses, Japanese bungalows, and postwar lowrise apartments, strung along the river. Then in the 1970s, lowrise and highrise development remained about equal. By the 1980s, handsome highrises predominated, lined up near the airport. Farmhouses and bungalows became curiosities, and even lowrises began making way for more intensive development. (Winckler, 1988, p. 233)

Education has played a key role in the society's economic and social advances. In keeping with the traditional high respect for education in Chinese society, strong government and family efforts provided first-rate schooling, so that education over the years 1950-2000

> evoked social class change and mobility and has made the population more cosmopolitan. It has been the avenue of many new interactions and opportunities. It has also helped promote economic growth [and] a sense of national unity. . . . During the 1950s and 1960s, few [students who studied abroad] returned home after receiving their degrees. But this "brain drain" was reversed in the 1970s and 1980s as a result of Taiwan's prosperity and the job opportunities it created. . . . Currently, 70 percent of the members of the Cabinet had been educated abroad—with 60 percent holding PhD degrees. It has been described as the world's most educated Cabinet. (Copper, 1996, pp. 70, 73)

As for political control, Taiwan over the half-century shifted from a highly autocratic system—which permitted no political parties in opposition to the ruling Kuomintang—toward greater toleration of criticism, dissent, and free elections. In 1986, an opposition party (Democratic Progressive Party) was officially recognized so that the first two-party election could take place. In 1987, 40 years of martial law ended, and permission was granted for open political dissent that included public demonstrations. Thus, citizens faced a future in which they would need greater political sophistication than was required in the past if they were to participate constructively in the political process.

However, Taiwan's rapid social and economic progress was not without its problems. The environmental and social troubles that accompanied such development included widespread air and water pollution; noise; and rising rates of crime, drug use, divorce, suicide, ethnic and social-class conflict, and juvenile misbehavior that contributed to family disorder (Copper, 1996, pp. 77-78).

To summarize, a host of dramatic cultural changes in Taiwan over the last half of the 20th century placed heavy demands on people's ability to acquire the knowledge and skills necessary to adjust to the society's continuing transitions.

Next, consider Mongolia. Compared with social change in Taiwan, social change in Mongolia was far slower between 1950 and 1990, but accelerated radically in the early 1990s as the nation abruptly rejected the Soviet Union's version of state socialism. From 1921 until the end of the 1980s, Mongolia was a satellite of the Soviet Union, functioning under a communist government and a centrally planned economy that were replaced in 1992 by a new constitution featuring a democratic form of government and a potential market economy. These sudden changes caught the populace off guard, unprepared in knowledge, skills, and attitudes to cope easily with the demands of a political system that would accommodate multiple parties and the requirements of a capitalistic mode of producing and distributing goods and services. Previously, between one-third and one-half of the government's budget had been supplied by the now-dismantled Soviet Union. Mongolia's international debt was extremely high, and the low national income per capita sank even lower as the population continued to grow rapidly. Consequently, the 1990s resulted in painful consequences for the citizenry—price inflation, rising unemployment, shortages of basic goods, and food rationing ("Mongolia," 1994, p. 334).

Not only did the pace of change in Mongolia and Taiwan differ, but contrasting geographic, demographic, and technological conditions in the two nations called for different kinds of knowledge and skill within each population. Mongolia's territory was 67 times larger than Taiwan's (1.6 million square kilometers for Mongolia, 36 thousand for Taiwan), whereas the population of Taiwan at 21.6 million was nearly 10 times greater than that of Mongolia (2.4 million), so there were 587 persons per square kilometer in Taiwan compared with 1.5 in Mongolia (Calhoun, 1998, pp. 666, 719). Industry and high technology dominated Taiwan's economy by the close of the century. Although the government of Mongolia had earlier made great efforts to industrialize the country, the level of industrialization by the 1990s was nowhere near that of Taiwan. While agriculture in Taiwan focused chiefly on farming and fishing, in Mongolia 70% of agricultural production came from livestock—sheep, goats, cattle, horses, and camels. Thus, the need for knowledge regarding vocational preparation, birth control, urban crowding, and environmental pollution differed between the two cultures and from one era to another within the same culture.

In summary, from the perspective of Elder's life-course theory, the knowledge, skill, and attitude aspects of Mongolian and Taiwanese citizens' development would be significantly influenced by the conditions of the two cultures during each decade, 1950 to 2000, as those conditions interacted with the particular stage of life in which individuals found themselves at the time. In other words, a cultural condition during a given period would exert a different influence on one age cohort than it would on another, so that the same cultural change would affect children differently than it would adolescents, young adults, the middle-aged, or the elderly.

Cross-cultural encounters: The foregoing pair of differences among cultures—values and knowledge/skills—can serve to illustrate types of cross-cultural encounters from the perspective of life-course theory.

Values. In North America, the marked changes in values relating to marriage and family life between the mid-20th century and year 2000 produced inter-generational conflict between people who were adults at the time of World War II and their children and grandchildren who were born during later decades of the century. In the 1940s, the practice of couples living together outside the bonds of marriage was both uncommon and socially disapproved. This was no longer the case for the younger generations by the close of the century. Furthermore, divorce was far less frequent in the 1940s than in the 1990s, reflecting a change in values concerning parental and spousal responsibilities and regarding what people should be "willing to put up with" to keep a family intact. Members of the older generation observed their values about such matters rejected by the young, while research evidence accumulated to suggest that the life chances of children raised in single-parent and cohabiting households were less favorable than the chances of children reared in traditional family arrangements.   Reviews of the literature on family composition show that children in single-parent households, compared with those in two-parent families, (a) score lower on the average in measures of academic achievement and cognitive ability, (b) are more likely to drop out of high school and attain fewer years of education, (c) get lower-status jobs and earn less money in adulthood, (d) exhibit more behavior problems, and (e) more often give birth as a teenager or outside of marriage. Such outcomes have been found at least in the United States, Canada, England, Finland, and the Netherlands (Amato, 1995).

Skills and knowledge.   Intergenerational concerns over knowledge and skills could be expected in both Taiwan and Mongolia during the 1950-2000 half century.   In the past of both cultures, parents usually played an important role in preparing their offspring with job skills.   Taiwan's farmers taught the young agricultural practices. Mongolia's youth learned to ride horses and herd sheep by accompanying their elders to the fields.   But during the closing decades of the century, these methods of teaching occupational skills were less satisfactory.   In Taiwan, as the composition of the labor market changed from decade to decade, parents were no longer capable of furnishing vocational training.   In Mongolia, as change was slower over the 1950-1990 period, the vocational-education problem was not severe, but the 1990s produced a radically different social system that called for new sources of teaching both young and old the knowledge and skills required to cope with the new system.

Practical applications: People who furnish counseling services to troubled clients can profit from Elder's life-course by recognizing the importance of (a) identifying significant conditions in society that affect people's worldviews at the present stage of their life and (b) identifying ways that the differences in the viewpoints of different age cohorts may contribute to intergenerational conflict. Armed with this understanding, counselors are better prepared to help clients comprehend the conditions that influence both their own worldviews and the worldviews of acquaintances and family members who are at older and younger age stages. Counselors can also help clients identify the kinds of knowledge and skills people need as the job market changes and obliges workers to retrain in order to enter a new occupation.

SUMMARY

The term *development configurations* has been used throughout this chapter in reference to the patterning of theory components that are proposed as causes and effects of development.   In the following summary, the chapter's five theories are compared in terms of their (a) conceptions of development, (b) components of cause (inputs) and effect (outputs or products), and (c) how components change with the passing of time to effect satisfactory development.

Developmental Task Theory: Development consists of changes in the tasks individuals are expected to master at successive stages of life so as to fulfill their own needs and satisfy the expectations of their culture.

Components of cause and effect. Three components that determine how well people succeed with the tasks at each stage of growth are:

- the biological structure and function of the individual during that stage
- the expectations held within the culture regarding proper task performance during the individual's current period of life (expectations about which tasks are appropriate and how well they should be performed)
- individuals' personal values and aspirations

These three causal factors combine to produce the outcome component, which consists of the tasks people perform and the quality of their performance in terms of fulfilling both those individuals' needs and the culture's requirements.

Satisfactory development. Development is judged to be satisfactory when (a) the changes in individuals' physical and mental skills equip them to accomplish the tasks that the culture has set for their present growth stage and (b) those individuals value such tasks and aspire to master them.

Role Theory: Development is portrayed as a succession of culturally defined roles that individuals adopt as they advance from one period of life to another.

Components of cause and effect. Components that influence how adequately individuals perform in the roles they assume during successive periods of their lives include:

- cultural expectations about (a) which roles are appropriate for different age levels and (b) proper standards for judging the adequacy of role performance
- the circumstances that determine which roles people are free to choose and which roles they are obliged to play
- individuals' biologically determined physical and mental capabilities for per-forming the roles they attempt
- opportunities people have for acquiring the knowledge, skills, and attitudes for filling different roles

The outcome component resulting from this combination of causal conditions is the quality of people's performance in the roles they occupy.

Satisfactory development. Individuals are developing properly when (a) their accomplishment in the roles that their culture expects for their age level meets cultural standards of quality and (b) the individuals value their roles and are satisfied their performance in those roles.

Attribution Theory: Development assumes the form of increasingly complex explanations of the factors that cause events to occur as they do.

Components of cause and effect. Three components that combine to determine people's causal attributions are:

- the genetically timed maturation of the nervous system (especially brain circuitry) over first two decades of life that equips the growing child and adolescent to consider an increasingly greater complex of variables when arriving at conclusions about the causes behind events
- explanations of cause that are widespread in the culture and are taught to the young informally in the home and community and formally in the school and church
- individuals' personal experiences that influence them to make causal connections between events that seem to be correlated. That is, when two events appear to occur in sequence, the individual assumes that the first event causes the second rather than that the two events were just coincidental

The outcome component is the set of explanations—the attributions—that individuals offer to account for events that attract their attention.

Satisfactory development. Development is regarded as progressing satisfactorily when (a) members of the society regard the explanations proposed by a person to be reasonable ones for people of that person's age level and (b) when individuals themselves are content with the attributions they offer.

Social Exchange Theory: Development is characterized by an increase in individuals' understanding about what their culture expects them to give in return for what they receive.

Components of cause and effect.   Factors important in forming people's social-exchange practices include:

- the gradual maturation of the nervous system necessary for understanding the conditions that influence people's expectations about what should be returned for what has been received in social situations.
- cultural traditions regarding what constitutes proper social exchanges.
- formal and informal methods in the culture for teaching social-exchange traditions to the young.
- individuals' direct experiences with the consequences they enjoy or suffer from how they respond to what they have received from others.
- individuals' observations of the consequences other people experience from the ways they respond to how others treat them.

The product of the interaction of the foregoing components consists of (a) the set of social-exchange beliefs that individuals acquire and   (b) the individuals' responses to what they receive from others in social encounters.

Satisfactory development. Development is judged to be progressing satisfactorily when (a) a person's responses to the treatment by others match the culture's standards for what constitutes fair social exchange and (b) the person accepts those standards as proper and fair.

Sociohistorical Life Course Theory: Development consists of changes in people's knowledge, attitudes, and behavior as those changes have been affected by past and present sociohistorical events.

Components of cause and effect. Human development is conceived to be the result of transactions between two major components: (a) the culture and (b) the individual person. These two components advance in parallel with the passing of time. Each component is continually in transition, evolving from an earlier condition to a later condition. During their advance from one year to the next, the two components influence each other. Whereas the culture exerts a major influence on the individual's development, the typical individual exerts only a very minor influence on the culture. However, the cumulative influence of many individuals can alter the culture in major ways. The effect that the culture has on an individual's development depends on the stage of growth in which the individual is at the time. Thus, the state of the culture during a particular time will affect the development of a young child differently than it will affect the development of an adolescent, a young adult, or an elderly person.

The condition of each component at a particular time is both a cause and an effect. It is an *effect* (outcome or product) of the transactions between the culture and the individual that have occurred up to that moment. Furthermore, the condition of each component is a *causal factor* that influences the future development of both the person and the culture.

Satisfactory development. An individual's development is judged to be acceptable when (a) the person's beliefs and behavior match the dominant standards of desirability held within the culture at that time and (b) the person considers those standards fair.

6

Forms of Interaction

As suggested in Chapter 5, virtually all modern-day theorists conceive of development as resulting, not from just one cause or component, but from the interaction of two or more sources of influence. Whereas Chapter 5 focused on the nature of components, Chapter 6 inspects ways that components interact as depicted in (a) Thomas and Chess's dynamic interactionist model, (b) Bronfenbrenner's bioecological theory, (c) Freud's psychoanalysis, and (d) Hindu religious tradition in India.

To provide a framework within which the descriptions of the four theories can be interpreted, the chapter begins with a scheme for analyzing the forms of interaction that can be inferred in different theories. In the summary at the end of the chapter, that scheme is used for comparing the four theories' forms of interaction.

THE NATURE OF INTERACTIONS

The word *interaction,* as intended in this chapter, refers to the process by which an encounter between two or more components (variables) (a) alters one or more of the participating components and/or (b) generates new components that can henceforth engage in encounters. If an encounter among components neither alters any of them nor creates new components, then no interaction has taken place.

For convenience of discussion, the above two forms of interaction can be labeled *altering* and *generating.* An example from Chapter 5 of *an altering interaction* is Elder's proposal in his sociohistorical life-course model that the state of the culture at any point in history affects individual people's development, while at the same time people affect the condition of the culture.

An example from Chapter 2 of a *generative interaction* is D'Andrade's notion that the contents of the mind are socially constructed, so each new belief about what is real in the world is generated through people's engagements with their environments. The beliefs (mental constructions) resulting from engagements serve as new components in people's subsequent cultural encounters. Consequently, as the result of interactions with the culture, a girl becomes convinced that she has unusual musical talent, a man is persuaded that he is being persecuted, and church members envision a vengeful God. Each of these socially generated convictions becomes a component of the individuals' later person-and-culture engagements that influence their development.

Altering interactions can be either *unidirectional* or *reciprocal*. In unidirectional interactions, one component alters the other but remains itself unchanged. In reciprocal interactions, each component is changed by the engagement. However, in practice it is probably more useful to consider these two types as representing a continuum of influence rather than a dichotomy. Hence the question becomes: To what degree is each component affected by the encounter? For instance, as suggested in the analysis of Elder's theory in Chapter 5, the culture usually exerts great influence over the individual person's development, while the influence of most individuals (other than Einstein, Franklin Roosevelt, and the Beatles) on the general culture is so slight that it is imperceptible, seemingly an example of unidirectional interaction. The degree or strength of influence of one component on another can be called the influential component's *intensity.*

When viewed from the vantage point of frequency, interactions can be categorized as *singular, periodic,* or *continuous.* A singular interaction consists of a lone encounter between components, a periodic interaction consists of intermittent encounters of the same sort, and continuous interaction consists of an unbroken series of encounters over an extended period of time. Frequency combines with intensity to determine the amount of effect that an interaction exerts on a person's development. A singular encounter of high intensity (often referred to as a *critical incident,* such as a disabling accident, the death of a loved one, divorce, or an individual's receiving a large monetary inheritance) may have more dramatic consequences for a person's development than do periodic encounters of low intensity (such as a father's intermittently criticizing his daughter's choice of friends or a teacher's occasionally awarding a student an *A* on homework assignments).

The outcomes of interactions can assume the form of processes (such skills as creating, perceiving, recalling, judging) or products (memories of incidents, beliefs). Interactions can alter processes and products either by replacing them (*substitution*) or by adding to them (*cumulation*). In Piaget's theory (Chapter 2) of cognitive development, an example of substitution occurs in later childhood when formal operational thought can replace concrete operational thought in children's interpretations of events they witness in the physical world.

Likewise, in Kohlberg's model (Chapter 4), during early adolescence the increased maturation of the nervous system can prepare youths to replace individualistic, instrumental moral reasoning with impersonally normative reasoning as a result of their encounters with cultures in which impersonal normative reasoning is prominently displayed.

An example of cumulative outcomes, as envisioned in Bandura's social-cognition theory and Skinner's radical behaviorism (Chapter 3), is observed in the growing quantity of types of consequences—rewards and punishments—that people mentally compile over the years from their cultural experiences. When a new kind of consequence is learned, it becomes an added arrow in the individual's quiver of consequence options without eliminating any of the existing arrows.

Finally, in Chapter 5, culture was cited as a unitary component that singly affected development. However, for the purpose of analyzing interactions, it is useful to distinguish among different agents that serve as purveyors of culture—such agents as parents, teachers, religious leaders, peers, and mass communication media (books, magazines, movies, radio, TV, videos, the Internet).

With the foregoing scheme for analyzing interactions in mind, we turn now to the chapter's four theories and the aspects of culture that they may reveal.

BIOLOGY AND CULTURE

Title: A Dynamic Interactionist Model of Psychological Development, as described by Alexander Thomas and Stella Chess, professors of psychiatry at the New York University Medical Center.

Key tenets: Psychological development, "whether adaptive or pathological, is always simultaneously biological and cultural" (Thomas & Chess, 1980, p.19).

Humans exceed all other forms of life in their ability to adapt to, and thrive within, diverse environments. This adaptive capacity is primarily a result of a highly plastic brain that is not "hard wired" to react in specific ways to specific environmental conditions. Instead, the human brain is equipped to distinguish subtle differences among environmental stimuli and to learn multiple ways to respond to those stimuli. The newborn's biological inheritance furnishes the learning capacity for the neonate to begin immediately fashioning its development to suit the culture of its caregivers.

> With the first fondling, the first feeding, the first perception of the human face and human voice, the newborn responds to and integrates inputs from the environment which have both cultural and sensorimotor significance. In turn, the active responses of the infant influence the character of the caretaker's attitudes and handling. (Thomas & Chess, 1980, p. 40)

Because children bring different genetic potentials to their upbringing, and are reared in very different physical and cultural settings, they come to display quite individualistic personalities and patterns of growth. As a result, "there are many different pathways to optimal learning and effective social functioning" (Thomas & Chess, 1980, p. 21).

An important factor contributing to a person's development is *temperament*, which Thomas and Chess define as the *how* of behavior. Temperament or *behavioral style* is displayed in individuals' quickness versus slowness of movement, persistence versus distractibility, ease versus difficulty in approaching new situations, intensity of mood expression, level of anxiety, and more. For the purpose of diagnosing children's behavioral styles, the authors recommend rating individuals in nine categories: activity level, rhythmicity or regularity of biological functions, approach or withdrawal in novel situations, adaptability to new conditions, ease of sensory response to stimuli, reaction intensity, mood quality, distractibility, and persistence.

Three constellations of temperament attributes were identified in a New York City longitudinal study of 136 middle-class children (infancy to early adulthood). The "Easy Child" pattern exhibited by 40% of the sample was characterized by regularity of biological functions, a positive approach to new experiences, ready adaptability to change, and mild or moderately intense mood responses. The "Difficult Child" pattern, observed in 10% of the sample, featured irregularity of biological functions, negative withdrawal from new experience, poor adaptation to change, and frequent, intense, negative moods. The "Slow-To-Warm-Up Child" (15% of the sample) was marked by a combination of negative responses of mild intensity to new stimuli and slow adaptability after repeated encounters (Thomas & Chess, 1980, pp. 71-72).

Principal variables: Two main classes of variables contribute to understanding an individual's development from the viewpoint of the Thomas-Chess model: (a) a set of causal factors that interrelate to produce (b) the developmental outcome, which consists of the psychological condition and behavior patterns of the growing child or youth.

1. Causal variables whose interactions effect development include:
   a. The person's genetically designed biological inheritance.
   b. Postnatal events that affect the growing child's sensorimotor and central-nervous systems (and may result in such handicaps as mental retardation, blindness, deafness, lameness, dyslexia, attention-deficient disorder, and others).
   c. Motivation—the pursuit of beneficial social relations and task mastery.
   d. Temperament or behavioral style.
   e. Childrearing practices of caregivers, as embedded in cultural traditions.
   f. Experiences with environments beyond the home, as embedded in cultural traditions.

2. The outcome variable is the person's unique pattern of mental characteristics and overt behavior.

Differences among cultures: In dynamic interactionism, cultural influences on human development that warrant special attention concern motivation, child-rearing practices, cultural settings, developmental plasticity, and goodness of fit.

Motivation. The motivation for human action derives from two basic adaptive goals—the mastery of social relations and the mastery of tasks and skills. These two goals energize action at all stages of life, with the preferred techniques of social interaction and task mastery often varying from one culture to another. Some cultures focus greater attention on work skills, that is, on performing tasks. Others emphasize social relations. A comparison of child-rearing among New York City families and among families in Puerto Rico showed that the New Yorkers emphasized the importance of children's task performance and of interactions with their parents. In contrast, Puerto Rican families focused greater attention on children developing amicable social interactions with peers than on task performance, such as mastering school assignments (Thomas & Chess, 1980, pp. 55-56).

Childrearing practices. Methods of raising the young that are encouraged in one culture may not be acceptable—or at least not preferred—in other cultures. For instance, Western anthropologists' observations of parent-child interactions in the South Pacific island kingdom of Tonga led to the conclusion that, as noted in Chapter 1,

> The Tongan mother has not the slightest hesitation in herself picking up a stick or coconut switch and beating her child with a thwarted fury . . . [while] screaming and ranting all the time. . . . The beatings appear to be village-practice in enforcing discipline. . . . [This bullying and terrorism experienced in childhood] must be important factors in the formation and development of the typical Tongan adult personality. (Beaglehole & Beaglehole, 1941, p. 82)

Cultural settings. A cultural setting is the context within which particular childrearing practices are displayed. The type of setting often influences adults' socialization attempts, which can vary from one society to another. In Tonga

> Behavior that is acceptable within the family may be punished if visitors are present, or when away from home, and even within the family more strictures are placed on behavior on Sundays. Specific incidents of punishment . . . are motivated by very clear precepts in Tonga, particularly the importance of childrens' obedient and respectful behavior These precepts are seldom directly explained to children at the time of punishment. More often, the immediate reason for punishment is expressed through a series of questions directed at children as they are being hit. . . . This lack of explanation is balanced to some extent by the formal moral instruction (*akonaki*) and less formal advice (*fakahinohino*) children receive in contexts such as family religious meetings or social gatherings, in church, at school, and in the many speeches given at funerals, feasts, and other events. (Kapavalu, 1993, p. 6)

Developmental plasticity. Whereas such theorists as Piaget and Vygotsky focused chiefly on how children are similar in their advance from one developmental stage to another, Thomas and Chess have emphasized children's individuality—the different patterns of personality made possible by the extraordinary plasticity of the human brain. Such plasticity helps account for the remarkable differences in the approved developmental patterns observed across cultures. To illustrate, in Samoan culture precocity in intellectual endeavors and in displays of initiative is discouraged. Instead, performing at the average of one's age group is expected. Thus, bright children at school conform to social norms by not appearing to outstrip their peers and by assisting their less-gifted classmates in ways that teachers from a Western tradition may interpret as cheating (Thomas, 1987). In Australian Aboriginal societies that depend heavily on hunting as a way of life, boys are encouraged to hone their skills of spotting and stealthily approaching distant game. Moslem cultures have traditionally placed high value on aggressivity in males and on shy, retiring behavior in females. However, the recent feminist movement, particularly as it has evolved in North America and parts of Europe, has demonstrated that occupations and avocations requiring aggressivity and initiative can be pursued successfully by females, thereby leading to increased social approval of girls and women engaging in such activities.

Goodness of fit. The phrase *goodness of fit* refers to how closely individuals' biological constitution, temperament, and learning aptitude match the cultural standards of the society in which they are reared. To illustrate, the middle-class New York parents studied by Thomas and Chess demanded regularity of bedtime and sleep schedules of their preschool children, a requirement that was stressful for youngsters whose biological functions were irregular. However, because Puerto Rican working-class parents did not insist on consistent bedtimes, biologically irregular children in their culture did not develop sleep problems (Thomas & Chess, 1980, p. 85). There is also a chronological dimension to goodness of fit. Characteristics of a person that are well suited to personal/social adjustment at one period of growth may not be well suited to good adjustment at another period. The inordinately inquisitive boy may be punished for appearing disrespectful and unruly at age 7, but in early adulthood may be lauded for his inventiveness and ingenuity.

Cross-cultural encounters: A person's moving from one cultural setting to another can produce personal-social adjustment outcomes that are either negative or positive, or some combination of both.

Children raised in a culture that places great value on harmonious social relations (such as Fijian culture in the South Pacific and Javanese culture in the Indonesian archipelago) often have difficulty in school settings that give higher priority to task orientation (as in Finland, Germany, or Sweden). In school, "these children may be considered by their teachers to be disinterested, unwilling to learn, and inattentive" (Hertzig, Birch, Thomas, & Mendez, 1968, p. 46). If a teacher then treats those pupils as if such a negative portrayal is true, the pupils may well respond in a fashion that appears to match the teacher's belief that they are incorrigibly incompetent. In other words, the children may behave in ways that fulfill the teacher's prophecy.

A more positive outcome results when the attitudes children bring from their indigenous culture are valued in the settings they subsequently inhabit. The Confucian tradition under which Chinese and Japanese children are typically raised (a) places high value on academic performance and (b) holds the individual responsible for working industriously to succeed in school. Except for those individuals who suffer obvious mental or physical disabilities, substandard performance is not blamed on a child's inherited capacity or on such environmental factors as a teacher's prejudice or agemates who serve as poor models of behavior. Instead, the individual himself or herself is blamed for failing to try hard enough (Stevenson, Azuma, & Hakuta, 1986; Thomas, 1997, p. 238). Consequently, when children who are reared under Confucian cultural expectations enter schools and workplaces in societies like those of Australia or New Zealand, such individuals tend to perform at a high level of efficiency and thereby enjoy the rewards that task-oriented cultures accord high accomplishment, including the rewards of excellent school grades, public praise, scholarships, further educational opportunities, and prestigious occupations.

As examples of mixed personal-adjustment outcomes (a combination of positive and negative consequences), consider this pair of cases:

Case 1: A 10-year-old Vietnamese girl whose family recently immigrated to Western Canada faced difficulty in school because of her poor command of English. However, she fit in well with the school's academic and social-behavior expectations because she brought to her work a cultural tradition of diligent application to school tasks and of strictly abiding by the rules of conduct in the classroom.

Case 2: When an Indonesian college youth from the island of Bali moved to Malaysia, he had the advantage of readily understanding the Malaysian language because the Indonesian and Malaysian dialects are both variants of Malay. However, the youth—as a Balinese Hindu—could be subjected to prejudicial treatment for his religious affiliation, since Malaysia is officially an Islamic nation with special privileges accorded Moslems.

Practical applications: Several implications for understanding and treating children can be inferred from the Thomas and Chess version of dynamic interactionism.

First, wide variations in children's patterns of development should be regarded as natural. Cultures that maintain very narrow, restrictive standards of desirable development can be expected to place an undue burden of stress and guilt on children and youths whose growth patterns do not match those standards.

However, some degree of stress and tension is itself a natural accompaniment of development, for the pursuit of social competence and task mastery is frequently accompanied by emotional pressure. This is not only normal but desirable for advancing development from its present state to a more mature condition.

> To interpret such stress as undesirable . . . is to misinterpret profoundly the dynamic of healthy psychological development. It is only when demands are made for a level and quality of performance that are excessive and inappropriate for the individual that stress and tension become problematic. If demands are not excessive and stress is resolved by mastery, the consequences are positive. Actually, unfavorable consequences may result if caretakers engage in misguided efforts to "protect" the child from stress and tension. (Thomas & Chess, 1980, pp. 51-52)

DEVELOPMENT WITHIN ECOLOGICAL SYSTEMS

Some years ago the concept *ecology* was imported from biology into developmental psychology to reflect the belief that people's psychological development, like the growth of plants and animals, is heavily influenced by the contexts in which persons grow up. Whereas all normal 5-year-old children throughout the world, by virtue of their inherited human nature, share certain characteristics in common, differences among cultures and physical contexts determine that 5-year-olds reared in a Siberian nomadic community will develop somewhat differently than do 5-year-olds raised in a Scottish industrial city or on a Bolivian cattle ranch.

In recent decades, a growing number of psychologists have objected to theories that place heavy emphasis on biological determinants of development. Hence, numbers of these critics have created an expanding variety of proposals focusing attention on the ways different environments fashion the way biological potentialities evolve over the years of childhood and youth. Bronfenbrenner's version has been one of the more popular variations of this ecological-interactionist point of view.

Title: Bioecological Theory, as proposed by Urie Bronfenbrenner, a professor of psychology at Cornell University in Ithaca, New York.

Key tenets: After Bronfenbrenner studied child development in such diverse settings as Nova Scotia, the Soviet Union, China, Eastern and Western Europe, Israel, and the United States, he wrote that

> Seen in different contexts, human nature, which I had previously thought of as a singular noun, became plural and pluralistic; for the different environments were producing discernible differences, not only across but also within societies, in talent, temperament, human relations, and particularly in the ways in which the culture, or subculture, brought up its next generation. (Bronfenbrenner, 1979, p. xiii)

To account for how development occurs in varied cultural contexts, Bronfenbrenner first proposed an *ecological theory*, then later relabeled it a *bioecological theory* in order to recognize the important role of the child's inherited biological equipment in the development process (Bronfenbrenner, 1979, 1994). He depicted the interaction of nature and nurture the following way.

> Especially in its early phases, and to a great extent throughout the life course, human development takes place through processes of progressively more complex reciprocal interaction between an active, evolving biopsychological human organism and the persons, objects, and symbols in its immediate environment. To be effective, the interaction must occur on a fairly regular basis over extended periods of time. Such enduring forms of interaction in the immediate environment are referred to as *proximal processes*. Examples of enduring patterns of proximal process are found in parent-child and child-child activities, group or solitary play, reading, learning new skills, studying, athletic activities, and performing complex tasks. (Bronfenbrenner, 1995, p. 620)

Principal variables: In Bronfenbrenner's model, two categories of variables affecting development are behavior systems and processes that operate within those settings.

Behavior systems. The kaleidoscope of shifting environments with which the growing child or youth continually interacts are referred to as *behavior systems* or *behavior settings*. Bronfenbrenner identified four levels of such systems, each defined in terms of how directly it impinges on the child. The settings that influence the child most intimately are called *microsystems*.

> A microsystem is a pattern of activities, roles, and interpersonal relations experienced by the developing person in a given face-to-face setting with particular physical, social, and symbolic features that invite, permit, or inhibit engagement in sustained, progressively more complex interaction with, and activity in, the immediate environment. (Bronfenbrenner, 1993, p. 15)

Figure 6-1 identifies three microsystems in the life of a 9-year-old English school girl. Each microsystem is a social setting within which the child lives her daily life. This girl's home in St. Albans, a small city north of London, is a two-bedroom brick house she shares with her parents and 15-year-old brother. Her parents occupy one bedroom, the girl occupies another, and her brother sleeps on a couch in the living room. The girl attends a primary school one mile from her home. Her immediate peer group consists of three close-friend neighborhood girls plus her classmates with whom she is less intimate.

At one step away from the girl's immediate microsystem experiences, the three microsystems are encompassed by a *mesosystem* that constitutes the "linkages and processes" that operate between two or more of the developing person's behavior settings. In our example, the girl's actions in the classroom and on the playground on any given day are influenced by her impression of how her parents and peers would regard those actions. Thus, her temptation to copy answers from a classmate's mathematics test is blocked by her assumption that her parents and peers would disapprove.

The next environmental unit beyond the mesosystem is the *exosystem*, consisting of the processes operating between two or more environmental settings, "in which events occur that indirectly influence the processes within the immediate setting in which the developing person lives" (Bronfenbrenner, 1993, p. 22). The three illustrative exosystems in Figure 6-1 are the workplaces of the girl's parents, her brother's rugby team, and the school's governing board that passes regulations affecting the pupils. Because both parents work long hours at distant sites, the girl must arrive home from school to an empty house each day, supervised only by her brother until the parents return. Each time her brother's team practices in the late afternoon, the girl is obliged to supervise herself. When the school board adopts a new dress code for students, the girl's choice of what to wear to school is affected.

Finally, the source of influence most remote from a person's immediate experiences is the array of physical conditions, attitudes, practices, and convictions shared throughout the society. The *macrosystem* is the *cultural milieu*, represented in Figure 6-1 as the large box encompassing the microsystems and mesosystems. For the central purpose of this book, the macrosystem is of special interest, since it is the broad cultural context within which the individual develops. However, microsystems must be of concern as well, for they serve as the immediate transmitters of culture to the individual. The family, school, and companions—along with such mass communication media as books and television—are the functionaries that carry cultural messages directly to the child.

As shown in Figure 6-1, three particularly important features of microsystems are perceived activities, roles, and interpersonal relations. A central conviction in Bronfenbrenner's scheme is that the influence of a behavior setting on an individual's development is not exerted by the "objective" or "true-life" nature of the activities, roles, and interpersonal relations found there. Rather, the influence derives from the individual's interpretation of these factors. Bronfenbrenner has agreed with Kurt Lewin's (1942) early proposal that (a) the phenomenological (internally interpreted or experienced) environment dominates the real environment in guiding behavior; (b) it is folly to try to understand a person's action solely from the objective qualities of an environment without learning what those qualities mean for the person in that setting; (c) it is important to discover how the objects, people, and the events in the situation affect the individual's motivations; and (d) it is essential to recognize the influence on behavior of "unreal" elements that arise from the child's imagination and idiosyncratic interpretations (Bronfenbrenner, 1979, pp. 24-25). Consequently, an observer is best equipped to comprehend the behavior of a person by learning how that person perceives the activities, roles, and interpersonal relations displayed in that context.

The term *activities* refers to what people are doing. *Roles* are the actions expected of people who occupy a given position in the society, such as the positions of parent, infant, sibling, teacher, friend, religious leader, and the like. *Interpersonal relations* are the ways people treat one another, as shown by what they say and do as a result of being together. Bronfenbrenner contended that within each microsystem these three components of a setting form an interacting behavior field in which a change in one component affects the entire configuration and produces a new meaning for the developing child or youth. An obvious methodological problem met in analyzing a microsystem derives from the fact that the components are typically in flux, as determined by shifts in the

Figure 6-1
Embedded Systems of Environments

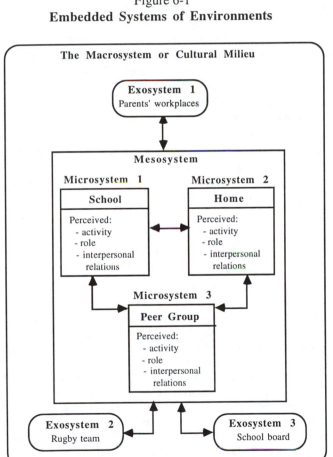

ongoing activities and by readjustments required in the participants' roles and interpersonal relations. Thus, analysts of microsystems are compelled to aim at moving targets.

Environments can initiate transactions with the child or youth that either promote or thwart desirable development. In effect, how individuals grow up is obviously affected by what is said or done to them—or done in their presence— by parents, peers, teachers, and such. Influences on development can also be instigated by such physical conditions of the environment as the place of residence, the food and drink consumed, weather, air quality, noise, threats of danger, and more.

In summary, this bioecological theory interprets human development in relation to (a) four levels of behavior systems and (b) the ways that the biopsychological child or youth interacts with environmental components of those systems.

Differences among cultures: The way the elements of Bronfenbrenner's theory may vary from one culture to another can be demonstrated with examples of how microsystems are influenced by a society's cultural milieu, that is, by the macrosystem's standards. In other words, how are the activities, roles, and interpersonal relations as observed in microsystems affected by people's physical/ cultural settings?

In way of illustration, evidence from life among Eskimos and among fisher-men in various parts of the world demonstrates how different geographical settings influence the linkage (a) between an environment's physical character-istics and the society's cultural patterns and (b) between those patterns and the competencies nurtured in people living in that culture.

Climatic conditions. Eskimos living in Arctic zones are required to live under extreme cold and to struggle with treacherous terrain and weather. To survive under these conditions, Eskimo children must acquire the cultural habits that promote their welfare within such a macrosystem.

> Eskimos rely on keen observation to avoid unnecessary expenditures of energy and unnecessary dangers. Foresight is particularly crucial, as shown by their unwillingness to travel onto sea ice in winter unless they have carefully excluded all potential signs that they might be set adrift on a loose floe. . . . Eskimos seldom act in the Western manner of doing things for the excitement of taking a chance. Instead they carefully avoid percentage risks, even when the risk may be as low as 20%. Alertness is valued, and seldom do they give their full attention to a single activity. Instead, they . . . survey their surroundings. This avoids the danger of being carried away by floating ice, presents opportunities for hunting other animals than the one being stalked, and familiarizes each person with his surroundings. . . . Cooperativeness in hunting also enhances the survival chances of the individual. (Moran, 1981, p. 9)

In contrast to the physical conditions of an Arctic setting, conditions in a seacoast town of West Africa's Guinea Bissau or a Tahitian village of the

Southeast Pacific provide much different macrosystems, offering far different cultural milieus that dictate different attitudes and competencies among members of those societies.

Occupational conditions. The vocation of ocean fishing, viewed from the perspective of Bronfenbrenner's model, includes microsystems (life aboard a fishing vessel, life at home when the fisher is not at sea), mesosystems (linkages between life at sea and on land), exosystems (locations of fish markets, market prices of fish, boat-repair drydocks), and a macrosystem that embraces all of these components. The macrosystem's physical, social, and economic features encourage particular attitudes, personality traits, and competencies among those who ply the trade. Many of the cultural features associated with fishing are devices intended to reduce the uncertainty of success that results from fishermen's lack of control over the weather and the location of fish. Consider, for instance, two such cultural features—(a) the social structure of the fishing boat's crew and (b) ritual and magic.

A variety of studies (Acheson, 1981) suggest that around the world relationships of crew members on fishing boats are remarkably egalitarian. Although there is a captain in charge, the captain's authority is rarely directly exercised. Various reasons have been offered for such an arrangement. An efficient fishing boat requires a well-trained crew. Hence, as crew members' competencies increase, the need for the captain to tell them what to do decreases, so that captain and crew interact more as equals. A further argument is that the egalitarian nature of crews is directly related to the risks. To avoid disaster and increase fishing effectiveness, crew members operate as mutually dependent equals (Acheson, 1981, p. 279).

Acheson notes that despite the development of better fishing and communication technology, "the sea is still a dangerous and risky environment for a terrestrial animal such as man" (1981, p. 287). So, as Malinowski (1922, 1948) suggested decades ago, people cope with irreducible risk through ritual and magic. He reported that in the Trobriand Islands there was no magic associated with lagoon fishing that involved no physical danger. "While in open-sea fishing, full of danger and uncertainty, there is extensive magical ritual to secure safety and good results" (Malinowski, 1948, p. 31).

> Other anthropologists have documented cases in which magic and superstitions in fishing societies are associated with high risk. Johnson (1979) argues that a large number of witches were thought to inhabit the environs of a Portuguese fishing community before the advent of motorized fishing craft. When motors were adopted, which made it much safer to negotiate a dangerous bar at the entrance of the harbor, the witches disappeared almost immediately and the level of religious observance declined as well. (Acheson, 1981, p. 288)

Microsystem/mesosystem interaction. Children living in what ostensibly is the same culture can differ in their development because of the composition of the microsystems that compose their mesosystem. This point was demonstrated in a study by Campos and her associates of the development of 200 street youths, ages 9-18, in a Brazilian metropolis. The mesosystems inhabited by the youths were divided between two categories. For one group, their mesosystem was made up of two microsystems: (a) the street life that the youngsters led as they attempted to eke out a living and (b) a home and family life to which they retired at day's end. But the other group's mesosystem consisted of a single microsystem—the streets, where the youths were obliged to live 24 hours a day, for they had no homes to which they could retire. Each mesosystem pattern led to identifiable developmental outcomes.

> Youngsters who lived at home and worked on the street appeared to be experiencing orderly development despite their impoverished circumstances. Youngsters who lived [solely] on the street showed hallmarks of psychological and physical risk, including parental loss, diminished social support, substance abuse, and early onset of sexual activity. (Campos et al., 1994, p. 319)

The child's developmental history. While recognizing the importance of environments in shaping the culture that affects individuals' lives, Damon (1996) has cautioned against undervaluing the growing child's developmental history in determining present behavior. At every juncture of an individual's life, the past interaction between heredity and environment has fashioned a particular personality—composed of present skills, values, knowledge, attitudes —that strongly influences how the individual performs during each new environmental engagement.

> Fundamental developmental processes, experiential legacies, and behavioral continuities do reside in the individual, no matter how powerful the forces of culture and society may be. A child who has learned to greet others with hostility and suspicion will create a different sort of developmental pathway for himself than a child who has learned more positive and friendly modes of responding. Although not necessarily permanently entrenched—there is always a possibility for change—the child's behavior sustains itself across time and settings, because it has the capacity to at least partly shape the nature of those settings. (In this example, the hostile greeting provokes a hostile response, which further feeds the child's suspicious orientation.) The individual's behavior is affected by the individual's particular history; and in this sense, there are behavioral continuities that reside in the individual and contribute to the direction of the individual's future development. (Damon, 1996, p. 463)

Cross-cultural encounters: From the vantage point of bioecological theory, cultures can vary in ways that influence the outcome of cross-cultural engagements. Consider, for instance, typical differences across cultures at each of the four levels of Bronfenbrenner's hierarchy of systems (micro, meso, exo, macro).

First, any microsystem, such as the family, can differ from one culture to another in its composition, meaning (a) the kinds and numbers of people comprising that kind of microsystem; (b) the functions (roles) those people perform; (c) the values they share; and (d) their interrelationships in terms of power, privilege, and responsibility. Second, the composition of microsystems that make up a mesosystem can vary across cultures. Third, exosystems can be composed of different combinations of mesosystems in different cultures. Fourth, the general milieu is not identical across societies.

The nature of such differences—and problems they may cause—is shown in an encounter across social-class cultures in a large U.S. city. The case involves two 17-year-old high school students, a girl and a boy. The girl represents one version of middle-class American culture, whereas the boy represents one version of lower-class, inner-city American culture. The pair have become close friends, spending increasing amounts of time with each other, a trend that distresses the girl's parents who tell her, "He's a bad influence. He's going to get you in trouble."

When interpreted from the perspective of Bronfenbrenner's theory, the case can be depicted as follows:

Microsystems within mesosystems. The most significant behavior settings (microsystems) in the girl's life are her home, school, and church. The peers who most directly influence her values and actions are agemates she meets at school and at church. In comparison, the most important behavior settings in the boy's life are his home, school, and the street, where he spends much time in a gang whose members are his most significant peers. Interactions among these microsystems within the two youths' mesosystems are pictured in Figure 6-2.

Figure 6-2
Differences in Two 17-Year-Olds' Mesosystems

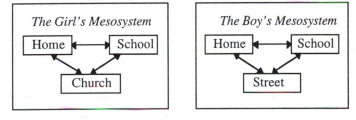

At first glance, the boy and girl may appear to share home and school microsystems in common. But when the composition of these systems is analyzed, their contrasting natures becomes apparent.

The girl's home is a six-room house, owned by her parents and occupied by her father and mother—married for the past 23 years—and a 14-year-old brother and 12-year-old sister. Her father works as an insurance agent and her mother as a part-time nurse. Much of the family's social life involves church activities.

The boy's home is a three-room rented apartment, where he lives with his unmarried mother and four younger siblings, only two of whom are from the same father. The mother occasionally works as a waitress in a nearby bar, but most of the family income is from a welfare agency.

At school, the 17-year-old girl is known to be "a pretty good student," partly because her parents supervise her homework and provide such educational-support materials as an encyclopedia, reference books, television cable service, and computer access to the Internet. She has a record of steady attendance and is well liked by her teachers for being polite and attentive.

The 17-year-old boy misses school more than half the time. Among school personnel he is known as a "very poor student" who rarely completes assignments and often "acts up" in class to amuse his peers. He has engaged in several fights on the school grounds and been expelled from classes for a 3-week period for threatening a member of a rival street gang with a switch blade. Although he earns failing grades on tests, teachers usually award him a "barely passing D-grade" to prevent him from repeating their classes.

At church, the girl sings in the choir and is an active member of the Christian Youth Crusade, a club that sponsors dances, picnics, and sporting events and conducts social-service activities in the community.

Figure 6-3
Differences in Two 17-Year-Olds' Exosystems

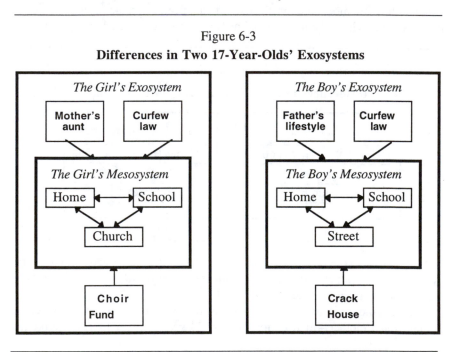

Most of the boy's time outside of school is spent on the streets with his fellow gang members, ingesting alcohol and illicit drugs, holding contests of strength and daring, keeping members of other street gangs "off our turf," and engaging in petty theft for money to buy drugs. He has been arrested on three occasions and been held for brief periods in a juvenile detention facility for his gang activity.

For several reasons, the girl's parents object to their daughter's dating the boy. They fear he will entice her to use alcohol and drugs and will sexually seduce her, so she might become pregnant or contract a venereal diseases or AIDS. They also believe the portrayal of an acceptable relationship between men and women typified by the boy's home life is a model he will adopt, one they fear could destroy their daughter's future.

Exosystems. At the next level of analysis, the two youths' development is affected by components of their exosystems. Consider, for example, three components in the social-psychological ecology of the girl's life and three of the boy's life. First, in the girl's ecological sphere her mother's aunt died, leaving the mother a house that could be sold or used as rental property to bolster the family income, thereby making it easier for the family to finance the girl's college education at a university away from the city and thus away from the influence of the boyfriend. Second, the city's newly instituted curfew law that requires youths under age 18 to be off the streets at night limited the chance that the girl might be out late at night with the boyfriend. Third, a group of church members raised money for the choir to tour the Western United States during the upcoming summer, thus removing the girl from the city for nearly a month and increasing the likelihood that she would meet boys who more closely met her parents' standards than did her current boyfriend.

Three components of her boyfriend's exosystem are his father's lifestyle, the city's curfew law, and the recent appearance in his neighborhood of a house in which crack cocaine was manufactured and sold. First, a man in the community whose apparent occupation is bookmaking and gambling has been identified by the boy's mother as the 17-year-old's father, even though the man never pays attention to either the mother or the boy. But the boy imagines that the bookmaker is indeed his father, and he admires the bookmaker's expensive car, clothes, and women friends. Second, the curfew law increases the risk that the boy will be arrested for staying out on the streets late at night. Third, the boy and other members of his gang are being recruited by the operators of the crack house to sell their product to high school students.

The macrosystem. Both 17-year-olds share the same general milieu that affects their development—the same language, national and city laws, climate, telephone system, television program choices, and the like.

In sum, factors influencing the development and personal-social adjustment of the two youths include ones unique to their personal lives as well as ones seated in components that differ between middle-class and lower-class values and life-styles found in typical American urban cultures.

Practical applications: As demonstrated in the case of the 17-year-olds, bio-ecological theory can be used for identifying likenesses and differences among the variables that influence cross-cultural encounters, thereby suggesting the kinds of differences that lead to disagreements between the individuals or groups involved in the encounters.

ID, EGO, ENVIRONMENT, AND SUPEREGO

Title: Psychoanalytic Theory, as created by Sigmund Freud, a psychiatrist practicing in Vienna, Austria, during the latter years of the 19th century and the early decades of the 20th.

Key tenets: Freud's model is founded on the following series of assumptions.

1. All human behavior is driven by inborn instincts that express themselves through actions in the real world. In other words, people must find ways to fulfill their instinctual needs by interacting with their physical and social environments. However, not just any type of behavior is acceptable to the environment, because each culture imposes rules and customs that dictate which ways of expressing instincts will be permitted and which will not.

2. Agents in the individual's environment monitor the person's methods of fulfilling needs, informing the person about which methods are acceptable and which are not. As a means of influencing the individual's methods of need fulfillment, such cultural agents as parents, teachers, pastors, the police, and others reward approved methods and punish forbidden ones.

3. As children grow up, they gradually incorporate into their own personalities the expectations about behavior that have been imposed on them by significant agents. These expectations are the individual's values. As the values become internalized, it is no longer necessary for outside agents to apply sanctions to control the person's behavior. Instead, the individual's conscience now serves as the monitor, rewarding approved actions with feelings of pride and self-worth, and punishing forbidden acts with feelings of guilt, shame, and fear.

Principal variables. Freud presumed that the adult personality consists of three operatives—*id, ego,* and *superego*—that have evolved over the first two decades of life and function at various levels of consciousness. These three components interact with the external world to determine how the person behaves. In the course of a child's development, the three operatives do not arise simultaneously. The id comes first—already present at birth. The ego begins to develop during infancy and early childhood. The superego appears some time later. In order to explain how the id, ego, and superego evolve in relation Freud's stages of psychosexual development, I first describe the functions of these three psychic operatives, then later describe their relationships to Freud's growth stages.

Instincts and the id.   Freud contended that the energy needed to activate all growth and behavior derived from instincts that reside in the unconscious.   After experimenting with several conceptions of instincts, he finally settled on a fundamental pair of forces—the *life* and *death* instincts—which he said competed for dominance in directing psychic energy throughout the life span. The life instinct (*eros*) expresses itself in constructive acts of love, creation, self-sacrifice, and altruism, and is embedded in the sensual, sexual drive.   The death instinct (*thanatos*) displays its influence in destructive acts, hate, and aggression.

From the perspective of instincts, the process of development consists of a constant struggle between the life and death forces—love against hate, life preservation against self-destruction.

In Freud's system, the id is the psychic agent representing the instincts.   It is the single operating component in the newborn's personality.   The id "contains everything that is inherited, that is present at birth, that is laid down in the constitution—above all, the instincts" (Freud, 1938, p. 2).   Libidinal energy within the id builds up as a form of pressure searching for expression.   The pressure represents needs that demand fulfillment.   Release of the pressure is experienced by the infant as pleasure.   The postponement or blocking of release is felt as pain.   Thus, the id operates on the *pleasure principle* of getting as much enjoyment and avoiding as much pain as possible.

The ego.   Freud explained that "the ego is that part of the id which has been modified by the direct influence of the external world through the medium" of conscious perception (Freud, 1923, p. 15).

> It is to this ego that consciousness is attached; the ego controls the . . . discharge of excitations into the external world; it is the mental agency which supervises all its own constituent processes, and which goes to sleep at night, though even then it exercises the censorship on dreams. (Freud, 1923, p. 7)

Whereas the id resides entirely in the unconscious and displays no awareness of the reality of the world, the ego is conscious and well aware of the opportunities and restrictions of the environment.   The ego thus serves as a go-between or referee that negotiates between the id's demands and the requirements of the physical and social environments, endeavoring to find realistic ways of satisfying the id's needs within the limitations imposed by the society in which the child is reared.

The superego.   In Freudian theory, no attitudes or values are inborn.   Infants arrive in the world *amoral*—with no sense of right or wrong.   Although neonates are devoid of values, what they do bring into the world is the capacity to gradually incorporate into their personalities the convictions imposed on them by significant agents in their environment.   The initial agents are parents and immediate caregivers.   Subsequently, the growing child acquires values from ever-widening circles of acquaintances—age-mates, teachers, religious leaders, counselors, coaches, and mass-communication media.

Stages of development. In Freud's opinion, every individual's personality structure evolves over the first two decades of life through a sequence of psychosexual stages. Each stage is characterized by a special zone of sensual gratification and by attitudes of other people toward such gratification. Each stage represents a distinctive way that the primary driving force behind behavior—the sexual or life instinct—is expressed at a particular time of life. How successfully the growing child masters the developmental task that a stage poses determines whether the child will move on to the next stage unencumbered by a residue of unresolved problems that can cause neurotic symptoms. The body's zone of satisfaction that is associated with a stage, and the activities pursued for achieving that satisfaction, are normal for people who are in the age range suited to that stage. But for people who have passed beyond the stage's usual age range, concentrating on that zone and its related activities is neither normal nor mentally healthy. Thus, psychosexual growth that is arrested at such a stage is deemed abnormal, symptomatic of personality maladjustment. An exaggerated, obsessive fixation on the activities of a given stage, when carried into later periods of life, is indicative of a destructive personality. The stages are summarized in Table 6-1. They start with the oral zone.

[Following birth,] the baby's obstinate persistence in sucking gives evidence in an early stage of a need for satisfaction which, though it originates from and is instigated by the taking of nourishment [from the mother's breast or a nippled bottle], nevertheless strives to obtain pleasure independently of nourishment and for that reason may and should be termed *sexual*. (Freud, 1938, p. 11)

Table 6-1

Freud's Psychosexual Stages of Development

Age Range in Years	*Zone of Principal Gratification*	*Significant Agents of Cultural Transmission*
0-1	oral—lips, mouth	parents, primary caregivers
2-3	anal, urethral	parents, primary caregivers
3-6	genital (infantile type)	parents, primary caregivers, siblings
7-12 or so	sexual interest repressed (latency period)	parents, school mates
12-18 or so	postpuberal genital	parents, peers, TV, videos, movies, books, periodicals
beyond 18	genital (adult type)	peers, mass media

How the infant's caregivers respond to this oral need, and the resulting degree of satisfaction the baby derives, establishes an initial expectation that the child will carry regarding how accommodating the world is likely to be.

In the second and third years of life, much of parents' attention is directed toward getting young ones to establish proper control of their bowels.   In psychoanalytic parlance, this is the *anal period* or, more completely, the *anal-urethral period*, because control of the urinary function is also involved. The dominant zones of gratification or of energy investment become the anal cavity, the sphincter muscles of the lower bowel, and the muscles of the urinary system. During the anal period, much of children's emotionally charged contact with adults is related to toilet training.

The boy's penis and the girl's clitoris and vulva become the focus of erotic pleasure during the third major psychosexual period.

> The object that has been found turns out to be almost identical with the first object of the oral pleasure-instinct, which was reached by attachment (to the nutritional instinct).   Though it is not actually the mother's breast, at least it is the mother. We call the mother the first *love-object.* (Freud, 1917a, p. 329)

At this same time the boy realizes that he cannot have his mother all to himself, for his father has already won her affections. Freud applied the label *Oedipus complex* or *Oedipus conflict* to the resulting dilemma—the boy's wanting to possess his mother but prevented by the powerful father. The girl finds herself in the opposite dilemma, yearning for her father as her love partner but being defeated in this contest by her mother. Freud labeled the girl's plight the *Electra complex.*

The resolution of the Oedipus/Electra complex through the repression of sexual desires inaugurates the latency phase of the infantile-genital stage. Although the dominant zone of gratification is still the genital region, this focus is seldom displayed in children's behavior, since both girls and boys are repressing expressions of sex in order to control their unacceptable yearning for their parental love objects. Because children have adopted both the gratifying and punishing parental roles, they now consider talk and displays of sex to be vile and nasty.

With the advent of puberty, girls begin to menstruate and to display such secondary bodily changes as the rounding of the breasts and the growth of pubic and underarm hair. Boy's maturation involves the growth of the genital organs, the appearance of sperm, nocturnal emissions of semen (often accompanied by erotic dreams), lowering of the voice pitch, and the growth of facial and bodily hair. The principal zone of erotic pleasure is still the clitoral area in the girl and the penis in the boy, but now gratification involves sexual orgasm. Furthermore, the dominant erotic activity becomes copulation with a partner of the opposite sex. This mode of gratification advances to an adult form in the third decade of life as the older youth engages in a mature sexual relationship in marriage.

Freudian theory sees the experience that children have with satisfying instinctual drives at a particular psychosexual stage as forming a model for attitudes or relationships with the world that may be carried over to later life. Freudians suggest that there are two ways children's psychosexual development can be arrested at a given stage. One way is for them to gain too little satisfaction at that stage, thereby leaving unfulfilled remnants of needs to be carried in the unconscious through subsequent periods of life. The other way is for children to gain too much satisfaction at the stage—to so completely relish overindulgence that they are unwilling to face the tasks of the next stage in the sequence.

The resulting message for people engaged in rearing the young is that children (a) should have sufficient trauma-free satisfaction of each stage's mode of need fulfillment to avoid carrying a damaging residue of unmet needs into later periods of life, yet (b) the satisfaction gained at a given period should not be so long extended that children are unwilling to tackle the problems of subsequent stages. Neurotic behavior is a sign that the normal advance from one stage to the next has gone awry. Neuroses can include phobias, obsessive thoughts, compulsive actions, bodily ailments, persistent misconceptions about social relations, unreasonable aggression, deviant sexual practices, and more.

Differences among cultures: From the viewpoint of psychoanalytic theory, cultures can vary in (a) how they foster or frustrate healthy progress through the psychosexual stages, (b) how suitable political and cultural conditions are for the adoption of the theory, and (c) how well they adapt to the original Viennese therapeutic techniques.

Stage progress. Freudian theory contends that development during the oral stage of early infancy will progress satisfactorily only if the newborn receives proper nourishment and sucking opportunities, accompanied by the comforting warmth of being held affectionately during feeding. The word *proper* means "suited to that infant's particular needs," yet the feeding process should not result in such extreme satisfaction that, as the months advance, the child becomes fixated at the oral stage and fails to advance to further stages. Thus, the infant-feeding practices of different cultures can be expected to influence how well this psychoanalytic prescript is applied.

In a similar manner, from a psychoanalytic perspective cultures can either promote or frustrate children's progress at subsequent stages of development. According to Freudian theory, if societies demand early bowel and urinary continence before the young child's sphincter muscles are under the child's conscious control, the resulting personality disorders can pursue the child into adulthood. Likewise, punishing and condemning children's interest in sexual stimulation during genital periods of growth and failing to aid children in conquering the conflicts of the Oedipal period can result in neuroses and mar individuals' ability to fashion a satisfactory sex life in later years.

Political and cultural conditions. Societies can vary in the extent to which changing political conditions affect a theory's acceptance. In Czarist Russia from 1907 until the Communist revolution in 1917, psychoanalysis gradually grew in popularity among the intellectual elite and without opposition from the government. The theory was also tolerated by the Communist regime from its inception in 1917 until Stalin came to power in 1931 and outlawed the Soviet Association of Psychoanalysis that had been formed in 1922. However, beginning with the Khruschchev era in 1958, psychoanalytic theory slowly acquired devotees. Following the mid-1980s, as relations between the Western democracies and the Soviet Union improved, enthusiasm for psychoanalysis grew markedly and the Russian (former Soviet) Association of Psychoanalysis was reestablished. In the 1990s, "the restoration of psychology and syncretic forms of psychoanalysis is taking place against a background of social pathology involving alcoholism, an alarming rate of child mortality, and flagrant criminal activity. Brutal attempts to introduce economic reform are making life difficult for the artistic and scientific intelligentsia" who have led the campaign for individualism as against "the totalitarian model" (Mikihalevich, 1993, p. 39).

Therapeutic techniques. Sudir Kakar (1991), a psychoanalytic practitioner in India, noted that the Western conception of mind on which Freudian theory is founded differs from the traditional conception of mind-body relations in Hindu societies. As a consequence, if psychoanalytic therapy is to succeed with Hindu clients, it must be revised in ways that suit the worldview to which those clients already subscribe.

Cross-cultural encounters: The export of Freudian theory from its birthplace of Vienna, Austria, to other cultural settings has met with mixed success. Its greatest popularity has been in such societies as those of Germany, Great Britain, the United States, Canada, and Argentina. For instance, by the late 1990s Argentina had the second-largest community of practitioners in the world affiliated with the International Psychoanalytic Association. In major Argentine cities, "psychoanalytic terms and language have permeated almost all levels of public discourse" (Plotkin, 1998, p. 271).

When Freud's theory was introduced in the United States during the early years of 20th century, it was generally rejected by the psychiatric and psychological communities as well as by the informed public. But its popu-larity spread rapidly during the 1920s and well into the 1950s, thereafter diminishing in favor of other views of human development, while still retaining a coterie of staunch proponents. Even among many people who prefer other theories, certain of Freud's proposals—such as his concepts of infantile sexuality and ego-defense mechanisms—have become incorporated into their belief systems.

However, the same pattern of popularity has not taken place in Asian cultures. In George DeVos's (1980) attempt to explain why so few Japanese have adopted Freudian theory, he suggested that psychoanalysis is intrinsically connected with Western individualism and is profoundly oriented toward the autonomy of the individual, who creates meaning in his or her own life and becomes free from the family. This contrasts and conflicts fundamentally with basic Japanese cultural values and social patterns, in which persons remain deeply embedded throughout life with family and group relationships, parental figures are greatly respected, and major and even minor life decisions are made through the guidance of the hierarchical superior. If Japanese should become aware of their intense negative feelings toward their mothers or other family members, as they would in psychoanalysis, . . . this would seriously disrupt family cohesion and become highly destructive. . . . [Furthermore,] the Japanese are not oriented toward the analytic discursive reasoning and talk of Westerners. Rather, they express themselves in visual-spatial metaphorical language, and have a cultural ideal toward more verbal restraint than self-expression and the free association of psychoanalysis. (DeVos, 1980, pp. 71-72)

Roland (1988) also identifies cultural constraints on the acceptance of psycho-analytic theory in India, where Freud's model was introduced during the early 1920s but has since attracted only a few members of Westernized elites in such urban centers as Delhi, Bombay, and Calcutta. According to Roland, part of the problem has been the conflict between India's deep-set religious foundation in Hinduism and its derivatives and Freudian theory's antireligious position that places faith in the rational man and explains religious experience as psychopathology. A further cause is the contradiction between (a) the aim in typical Western psychoanalytic practice of arming patients to liberate them-selves from restrictive family ties of their childhood and (b) the aim in Indian culture to maintain strong bonds of kinship throughout the life span "where the sense of self is deeply involved with others, where relationships are governed by reciprocal hierarchical principles [respect for, and obedience to, elders and others in authority], and where there is a constant need for approval to maintain and enhance self-regard" (Roland, 1988, p. 60).

Practical applications: The two most publicized applications of psychoana-lytic theory are efforts to prevent and correct neuroses. Prevention involves child-rearing and educational practices. Correction takes the form of psycho-analytic therapy.

Child-rearing and educational practices. From a psychoanalytic perspective, here are some typical *do's* and *don'ts* for children's caretakers.

Do accept the notion of childhood sexuality, which is expressed throughout childhood and adolescence in the young gaining sensual satisfaction from a succession of erotic zones of the body—mouth/lips, anal/urethral region, and genital apparatus. Do acknowledge that seeking pleasure in the manipulation of these zones is normal. Don't punish children for showing their interest in the erotic zones. Do teach them to display their interest in a manner acceptable within the culture in which they are raised.

Do encourage children to express their fears, doubts, shame, resentment, and anger without censuring them, so long as their modes of expression don't harm others.   Opportunities for such expression help relieve the psychological pressures that cause children to drive their distress into the unconscious where it seethes and rises to the surface in the form of neuroses.

During the oral stage (birth to age 2), do give infants plenty of opportunities to be cuddled and to satisfy their sucking needs, especially at feeding time.

During the anal/urethral stage (age 2 to 3) don't attempt toilet training too early nor enforce it in a punitive fashion. Don't accompany toilet training with distressing emotional outbursts or even by half-disguised expressions of disgust, which the child interprets as threats of the withdrawal of caregivers' love if the child does not perform how, when, and where the caregivers desire.

As an example of basing a school practice on psychoanalytic theory, an experimental class in a New England preparatory school encouraged teenage girls to openly express their innermost feelings and thoughts, on the teacher's belief that "education should be conducted in an atmosphere in which the universal and recurrent emotional disturbances and repressive tendencies of childhood can be resolved as soon as they arise, and before they become chronic" (Kubie, 1960, p. vii).

[In school, children must be encouraged] to talk out loud about love and hate and jealousy and fear, about curiosity over the body, its products and its apertures; about what goes in and what comes out; about what happens inside and what happens outside; about their dim and confused feelings about sex itself; about the strained and stressful relationships within families, which are transplanted into schools. (Kubie, 1960, p. viii)

Measures of the effect of the experimental class on participants' attitudes toward themselves and toward race prejudice, as compared with attitudes of students in regular classes, suggested that

The [class] worked no miracles. There were no neurotics cured, nor was anyone's future happiness assured. A measurably significant increase in attitudes of self-acceptance was observed, which, in the author's opinion, justified the investments made by the students and by the teacher; certainly the results justify such an enterprise as a worthwhile addition to a high school curriculum. . . . As an *indirect* effect, . . . the reduction in race prejudice represents a real bonus. (Jones, 1960, p. 110)

Psychoanalysis. Psychoanalytic therapy is founded on the conviction that the seeds of a patient's neurotic behavior lie in events in the person's childhood, particularly in events involving sexual relationships within the family (Freud, 1946). The assumption is that these events were psychologically so painful that they were repressed. In other words, the distressing incidents were buried in the individual's unconscious where they continued to fester, creating the neurotic symptoms the client now suffers—phobias, obsessions, compulsions, or psychogenic bodily ailments. The goal of therapy is to unearth the hidden conflicts so they can now be psychologically lived through—in the sense of talked through—in a more constructive, acceptable fashion. In effect, psychoanalysis assumes that when the disordered past is recast in a new perspective, the conflicts become resolved and the patient's symptoms will abate, freeing her or him to lead a more bearable or positive way of life henceforth.

In psychoanalysis, the therapist is expected to encourage the patient to speak freely about past and present concerns, letting all feelings and thoughts flow out uncensored. The therapist's task is to select from this stream of free associations those items that seem symbolic of repressed conflicts from the past. The therapist explains to the client the meaning of those utterances, encouraging the individual to view such events in a new light, thereby dispelling the destructive feelings of fear, guilt, and shame that were originally attached to the incidents during childhood.

METEMPSYCHOSIS AND KARMA

Title: Hinduism is a religious tradition and conception of human development that traces its beginnings back perhaps 4,000 years. By the close of the 20th century, there were an estimated 765 million followers of the Hindu faith throughout the world, most of them in India. Hinduism is essentially a theory of moral development, in contrast to theories of physical, cognitive, emotional, or social development.

Key tenets: Hindu theory is constructed on a framework of convictions about the form of human personality, the nature of reality, the goal of moral development, and the influence of the consequences of people's actions.

Personality structure. People are constructed with a body and a soul. Each person's body has been newly created 9 months before birth by the mating of a man and woman. The ultimate demise of the body comes with corporeal death that normally occurs after six to eight decades unless ended sooner by accident or illness. Following death, the body decomposes into the four elements from which all physical matter is constructed—earth, air, fire, and water. The soul, in contrast, was not conceived anew at the time the body was created. Rather, each person's soul was created at some indefinite time in the far distant past. Across the centuries the soul has inhabited numerous other bodies, periodically passing out of one deceased frame to enter another newly conceived one. This process of a soul's vivifying one body after another over eons of time is known as *metempsychosis* or *the transmigration of the soul.*

Reality. All matter in the universe—animate and inanimate—is organized according to a hierarchy of blessedness or nearness to moral perfection. Such inanimate objects as stones and trees are very low in the system—far distant from moral purity. Above the inanimate objects are the earth's animals, with some species higher than others on the scale. Cats are above insects, monkeys above mice. Humans, being morally closer to perfection than animals, reside on the uppermost levels of this edifice of moral goodness. Reality includes not only the visible objects and events of the everyday world but also such invisible forces as spirits and gods.

The goal of moral development.   The aim of moral development can be divided into two parts—the immediate and the ultimate. Hinduism teaches that life on earth is fraught with pain and tribulation. Therefore, the ultimate goal of life is to win release from this burden of pain so as to enter a state of everlasting peace.   That goal is reached through accomplishing the intermediate aim of abiding by the precepts of moral thought and conduct laid down by one or more of the supernatural forces that control the world. These precepts are to be found in such Hindu writings as the *Manu Smriti* (Laws of Manu) and *Grihya-Sutras* (Rules of Vedic Domestic Ceremonies) (Buhler, 1886; Oldenberg, 1886).

The influence of consequences. A core concept of Hinduism is that of *karma* or *karman*, a term that literally means *deeds*. Karma can be viewed as both a process and a product. The process is founded on the following convictions:

1. People's actions can be either morally good (faithful to the revered rules), or morally bad (in violation of the rules), or neutral (unrelated to the rules).

2. Good behavior produces a positive effect or residue in the soul, bad behavior produces a negative effect, and neutral behavior produces no effect.

3. Karma, as a product, consists of the algebraic sum of the positive and negative effects in a person's soul up to the present time. Karma is thus a kind of moral bank balance, with the bad deeds subtracted from the good deeds to yield a total that can be either dominantly negative or dominantly positive.

4. At the time of a person's earthly death, the ratio of good to bad deeds—the karmic algebraic sum—determines two outcomes.

The first outcome concerns the kind of body the soul will next occupy. Karma that has been produced chiefly by sinful acts relegates the soul to a new body that lies low in the moral stratification system—perhaps in the form of an insect or worm. Karma burdened with somewhat fewer sinful acts may assign the soul to a species higher on the scale—an elephant or horse. Karma with a higher ratio of good than bad deeds can result in the soul's entering a human body for its next sojourn on Earth.

The second outcome concerns the advantages and disadvantages (pain and pleasure) that the next inhabited body will experience during its lifetime. Differences among humans in the quality of their lives depend to a great extent on the karma they have inherited. More pain and travail are endured by people whose souls are burdened with a higher ratio of negative effects than by people whose souls carry less negative residue.

As the description of karma illustrates, the keystone of Hindu moral theory and its derivatives is the concept of justice. In people's development, they get what they earned—exactly what they deserve. Whatever they sow, that they will reap, even though the harvest is postponed until the soul's subsequent life on Earth.

Principal variables: In Hindu theory a person's moral development results from the interaction of three sources of cause—karma, free will, and the forces that control the operation of the universe. By dint of the karma process, people produce the material and moral condition to be experienced by the soul's next life on Earth. However, even in people's present state, which they predestined by their behavior in a previous life, they still have the freedom of will to decide how faithfully they will abide by the moral rules and thereby generate karma that will improve their lot during a subsequent life on Earth. Religious instruction is intended to guide people in making wise decisions about how to behave. The third source of cause is the set of forces—spirits, gods—that establish the manner in which the universe functions. These forces determine the rewards and punishments to be expected for different types of behavior. Much of moral development consists of people learning the rules by which the universe is governed and then seeking to guide their lives in accordance with such knowledge.

Differences among cultures: Cultures can vary in the dominant explanations that the populace accepts for such phenomena as (a) personal success and misfortune and (b) the ultimate goal of human development. Consider, for example, how a Hindu perspective toward these two matters can differ from several other popular viewpoints.

Personal success and misfortune. As noted above, Hindu doctrine holds the individual responsible for the pleasure and pain experienced during the person's current life span. The quality of the karma carried by the transmigrated soul from one lifetime into a subsequent lifetime is the result of the individual's behavior during the earlier of these periods on Earth and is the principal cause of the person's fate during the latter of the periods.

In contrast to Hindu theory, the belief system attributed to Confucius and still practiced in China, Japan, Korea, and Taiwan teaches that most people are born with very similar potential ability. Very few are innately superior in intellect, and relatively few are born mentally deficient. Therefore, the degree of success or failure that people experience depends, not on genetic endowment, environmental opportunity, or those individuals' behavior in an earlier existence, but on the strength of the motivation and diligence they dedicate to their daily endeavors. Confucius asserted that

> When the archer misses the centre of the target, he turns round and seeks for the cause of his failure in himself. . . . . He rectifies himself, and seeks nothing from others. . . . . He does not murmur against Heaven, nor grumble against men. (Legge, 1983, P. 396)

Thus, whereas in Hinduism a person's present condition is determined chiefly by that person's behavior during a previous existence, in Confucianism people's present state is a product of how hard they are now working to fulfill their responsibilities.

Studies that compare such East Asian cultures as those of China and Japan with that of North America suggest that Americans, more often than East Asians, attribute personal success or failure to individuals' genetic endowment (a biological cause) or to social context (a sociological cause) than to diligence (a psychological cause) (Stevenson et al., 1986).

Karl Marx, in his theory of how societies evolve, accounted primarily for individuals' success and failure by the nature of the society in which they live. He focused particular attention on the system of producing and apportioning goods and services throughout the population. In Marx's opinion, the elite at the top of a feudal or capitalist society's power structure enjoy great success simply because of their social position, with their condition of privilege far exceeding their contribution to the general good. In contrast, the masses of people at the bottom of the power structure are the main producers of the society's goods and services, but they receive in payment far less than they deserve. Thus, the social context rather than individuals' abilities or diligence is credited with, or blamed for, people's success or failure (Marx, 1898).

The ultimate goal of development. Hinduism depicts life on Earth as a painful, oppressive experience. Thus, the aim of human development is to release people from the succession of lives on Earth by their achieving such purity of thought, feeling, and action that they enter a state of nothingness. Their goal is to become entirely free of sorrow, joy, fear, and anger, thereby worthy of merging into the Cosmic Soul, never to return for another agonizing sojourn on Earth. The sought-after state of sublime oblivion is referred to in Hinduism as *moksha* and in Buddhism as *nirvana.*

Confucianism, as initially conceived, was not a religion, in the sense of a belief system with such supernatural features as unseen spirits and life after death. Instead, Confucianism was a scheme for regulating social relations within a political state. Only later were supernatural elements attached by certain of the system's adherents. Therefore, in Confucianism's original version—and in its dominant practice today—the goal of human development has been to manage the relationships among individuals and groups in a way that enables them live together in an efficient, amicable, and morally proper manner. The focus of development is on immediate existence, not existence in an anticipated hereafter.

In Christian and Islamic traditions, as built on a foundation of Judaism, the final goal of development is to spend eternal life after death in ecstatic communion with God. Life on Earth is simply a term of trial and preparation for life after death. In pursuit of that goal, humans while on Earth are obliged to obey the Lord's commandments.

Cross-cultural encounters: Faithful adherents of Hindu culture can experience a variety of consequences during their engagements with proponents of other cultures. The following examples illustrate encounters relating to child-rearing practices and responses to misfortune.

Child-rearing practices. Although in Hindu theory the principal determinant of people's fate during the present life span is the karma accumulated in a previous existence, a portion of individuals' life condition is the result of their parents' behavior before and after their birth.

> If a man wishes that a son should be born to him who will be a famous scholar, frequenting assemblies and speaking delightful words, a student of all the Vedas [holy scriptures], and an enjoyer of the full term of life, he should have rice cooked with the meat of a young bull or of one more advanced in years, and he and his wife should eat it with clarified butter. Then they should be able to beget such a son. (Nikhilananda, 1956, pp. 374-375)

Child-raising practices in Hindu theory consist of both direct and mediated treatments. A *direct treatment* is something that caregivers do to the child to effect proper development. For instance, after newborns have been beast-fed for 6 months, they should receive their first food consisting of curds, honey, and ghee (butter clarified by boiling and skimming) (Oldenberg, 1886, Vol. 30, p. 216). In contrast, a *mediated treatment* is a rite performed to an intermediary force, such as the Cosmic Soul or a particular god, with the expectation that this force will then effect the desired results in the child's development. An example of a treatment that is primarily mediated but includes a bit of direct application is the care proposed for a child who suffers the "dog demon" malady (epilepsy).

> When the attack assails the boy, the performer of the ceremony arranges his sacrificial cord over his left shoulder, sips water, and fetches water with a cup that has not yet been used. In the middle of the hall he elevates the earth at that place in which they . . . gamble; he besprinkles it with water, casts the dice, spreads them out, makes an opening in the thatched roof of the hall, takes the boy in through that opening, lays him on his back on the dice, and pours a mixture of curds and salt-water upon him, while they beat a gong towards the south. (Oldenberg, 1886, Vol. 30, p. 219)

In cultures other than Hinduism, such child-rearing practices can be regarded as nonsense, viewed with disapproval, and their believers derided. Present-day medical research in Western societies does indeed endorse the notion that what mothers ingest during their term of pregnancy can affect later characteristics of the yet-unborn child. For instance, extensive alcohol use during pregnancy can result in such disorders in the newborn as fetal alcohol syndrome (cleft lip and palate, heart defects, abnormal limb development, and below-average intelligence). However, such research does not support the belief that if expectant parents eat rice cooked with the meat of a bull they can destine the unborn to become a famous scholar.

Furthermore, Western medical theory proposes that epileptic seizures are caused by abnormal electrochemical activity in the brain which can result from a wide variety of diseases or injuries.   Thus, treatment should take either a chemical form—usually anticonvulsant drugs—or, in some cases, surgery. Consequently, traditional Hindus, in the eyes of Western observers, are foolish if they sip water and cast dice to remedy epileptic seizures.

Responses to misfortune.   As explained earlier, in Hindu theory the main cause of one's present condition is the karma (karman) compiled during past existences, so there is little one can do to correct one's own current adversity or that of anyone else.   As explained in the *Adhyatama-Ramayana*, "No one can ever be the cause of fortune or misfortune of another. The *karman* which we ourselves have accumulated in the past, that alone is the cause of fortune and misfortune" (Renou, 1961, p. 197).   Thus, the best a sufferer can do is to (a) accept one's ill fate as deserved punishment and (b) prepare for a better fate during the next time the soul returns to Earth in a different guise. This preparation consists of doing deeds that will yield credit in the form of increased virtuous karma. For a student who is under the tutelage of a Hindu teacher, such deeds include diligently studying the *Vedas* that describe the rules of proper behavior, honoring one's teacher and parents, honoring the elderly, offering daily libations of water to the gods, placing fuel on the sacred fire, and embracing the feet of his teacher's wife upon returning from a journey.   Students are also forbidden to eat honey or meat, to flavor food, to keep the company of women, to use shoes or an umbrella, to sing, to dance, or to feel sensual desires, anger, or covetousness (Buhler, 1886, pp. 62-63, 138-139).

Guided by the foregoing convictions, Hindus who have settled in societies populated chiefly by traditional Jews, Christians, Muslims, or Marxists could be dubbed ridiculous, misguided, and perhaps dangerous by members of those societies. For instance, dedicated Jews, Christians, and Muslims, when assailed with misadventure, would be expected limit their behavior to (a) praying to God for deliverance from the ill fortune and, at the same time, (b) taking steps to solve the problem by whatever mundane means seem reasonable on the belief that "The Lord helps those who help themselves."

Doctrinaire Marxists, who confront adversity from the perspective of an atheist, place their faith in empirical science and dialectical materialism. They would directly attack the apparent worldly causes of their suffering. Those causes would be seen as either physical (diseases resulting from bacteria, earthquakes resulting from the slippage of geological plates, floods resulting from the denuding of forests) or social (allowing entrepreneurs to amass fortunes at the expense of the proletariat).   From a Marxist standpoint, Hindu reactions to adversity could be labeled superstitious nonsense that inevitably fails to better the sufferer's lot. In Marx's words, "Religion . . . is the opium of the people" (1843).

Practical applications: An educational approach that is intended to encourage greater tolerance of traditional Hindu belief on the part of people who subscribe to other views of development consists of teaching a course, or a unit within a course, on comparative theories of human development.   Both secular and religious theories can be included.   One activity designed to foster tolerance of the Hindu perspective involves comparing theories in terms of the evidence adduced in support of their proposed answers to significant questions.   The discussion questions can include ones focusing on concepts central to Hindu doctrine.   The aim of this activity is to have students consider whether the evidence they use to support their convictions is either better or worse than that on which Hindus base their beliefs.   Here is an example:

> Do you think the world operates on the basis of justice, in the sense that people get what they deserve?   In other words, do people get the consequences that their actions warrant—good consequences for good actions, bad consequences for bad actions—whether or not those consequences come sooner or later?

> If you believe that life probably does operate on the basis of justice, do you think Hindu theory offers a reasonable account of how justice results—that the karma earned in one lifetime determines a person's fate in a next lifetime?   Or do you have a different   explanation of how justice comes about?

> On what evidence do you base your belief?   In effect, how do you know your belief is correct?   Is the evidence supporting your belief more reasonable or trustworthy than the evidence on which Hindus ground their belief?   Can you prove that a belief in karma and transmigration of souls is incorrect?   If so, how do you prove it?

> Christians perceive their belief system as being correct, as do Hindus.   How could the two groups discuss their differing beliefs in a way that is mutually respectful?

SUMMARY

The scheme introduced at the beginning of the chapter for analyzing forms of interaction provides a framework for comparing the chapter's four theories.   In the following summary, the interaction forms that figure prominently in each theory are illustrated with examples from the chapter's description of the theories.

The analysis of interactions within the four theories employs the concepts introduced at the beginning of the chapter: (a) *altering* and *generative*, (b) *unidirectional* and *reciprocal*, (c) *singular, periodic,* and *continuous*, and (d) *substitutive* and *cumulative*.

A Dynamic Interactionist Theory: The model proposed by Thomas and Chess implied two forms of altering interactions. The first is unidirectional and appears immediately after birth as the culture's agents (careproviders) begin imposing cultural expectations on the child, who acquire the contents of those expectations as adequately as the child's inherited learning capacity permits.

With the passing of time, the interaction between the child and the culture's agents becomes increasingly reciprocal (Figure 6-4). The agents not only affect the child's development, but the child's temperament or behavior style also influences the agents' development. An important element of behavioral style is the children's motivations, as reflected in both their interests and their strength of drive. As the years advance, new careproviders contribute to new variations of interaction with the individual's temperament or behavioral style.

Figure 6-4

Two Forms of Dynamic Interaction

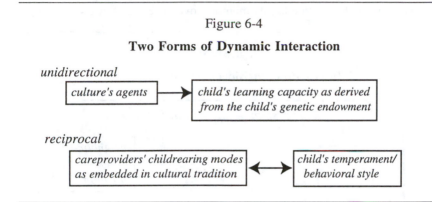

The frequency of the influence of cultural agents that the child encounters varies with the nature of the agents and with the period of the individual's development. Parents' influence is usually continuous over the first two decades of life and is periodic thereafter. A teacher's influence is continuous during the current school year, then comes to an end or is henceforth only singular or periodic.

The influence of cultural agents can either be cumulative, with one agent's influence building on another's, or else substitutive, with one agent's effect replacing another's. An instance of replacement would be a youth's abandoning one religion for another, such as giving up Protestant Christian beliefs for those of Buddhism.

Bronfenbrenner's Bioecological Model: One rendition of interactions in Bronfenbrenner's scheme was depicted earlier in the chapter. As another option, Figure 6-5 pictures the relationships among Bronfenbrenner's four systems in a slightly different form.

In the diagram, the four microsystems with which the person immediately interacts are the family, peers, school, and the Internet. The mesosystem consists of the network of interconnections among the four microsystems. The exosystem includes the four components located in rectangles (parents' work, neighborhood location, tax money for schools, type of browser the person uses to search the Internet). Exosystem elements indirectly affect the person's development through the medium of the mesosystem and microsystems. All three systems are embedded in the macrosystem—the cultural environment of the general society in which the person is obliged to live.

As in the Thomas-Chess theory, Bronfenbrenner's proposal implies that interactions with some aspects of cultures can be singular, involving a lone experience with a rarely encountered microsystem that affects development. An example could be a 4-year-old's becoming lost for hours at Disneyland. Other interactions can be periodic, as when the daughter of a divorced couple visits her father only occasionally. Still others are continuous, as when a person lives in the same home with the same family members over a period of years.

Figure 6-5

Interactions in Bioecological Theory

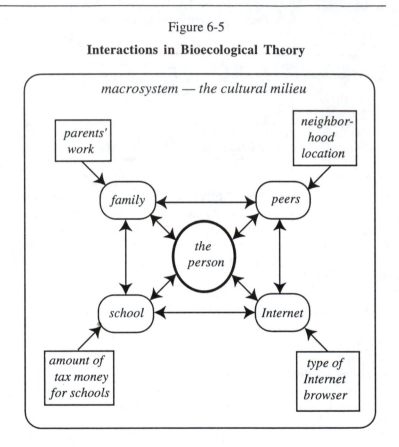

Psychoanalytic Theory: Freud's conception of how the components of the personality evolve during childhood is an example of *generative interaction* (Figure 6-6). Following birth, the infant's instinct-driven *id* demands immediate and complete need gratification but is prevented by the culture's rules and expectations. From this id/culture confrontation, the *ego* is gradually generated out of the id as the personality's negotiator between id and culture. In later childhood, the *superego* is generated out of the ego as an internal representative of the culture.

Figure 6-6

Generative Interaction in Freudian Theory

from infancy to later childhood and adolescence

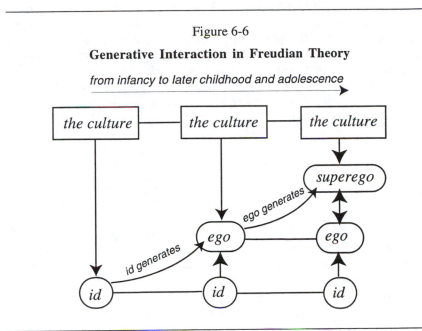

Reciprocal interactions: As shown in Figure 6-7, by the time of late childhood and early adolescence the person's current behavior and future development are products of interactions among the four components that evolved during the early

Figure 6-7

Reciprocal Interactions in Freudian Theory

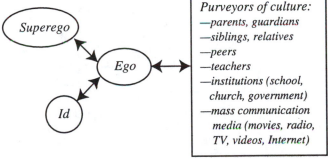

Purveyors of culture:
—*parents, guardians*
—*siblings, relatives*
—*peers*
—*teachers*
—*institutions (school, church, government)*
—*mass communication media (movies, radio, TV, videos, Internet)*

years—culture, id, ego, and superego. Each component may be altered in some degree during the multiplicity of events that comprise daily living. The id continually urges its demands on the ego, but in the id must yield some of its energy to fuel the ego and superego. The ego forces the id to postpone gratification while it seeks ways of need fulfillment that are acceptable to the culture and to the superego (the conscience). The superego, while pressuring the ego to live up to cultural expectations, is obliged to accept the ego's compromises that are intended to pacify both the id and the culture. The culture is constantly in a state of transition, partly as a result of pressures from the id— via the ego—to modify cultural expectations. As suggested by Figure 6-7, all of a person's negotiations with the culture are mediated by the ego. Furthermore, as the child grows up, different purveyors of culture (people, institutions, media) are influential at different periods of development.

Hindu Religious Tradition: Our Hindu model illustrates a combination of unidirectional and reciprocal interactions. According to the model, an individual's development is determined by four components. The first is supernatural, consisting of gods or spirits that control the universe and can dictate the fate of individuals and cultures. The developing person seeks to influence the gods in at least a modest measure by means of rituals, offerings, and abiding by the dictates of the sacred scriptures. The basic destiny of individuals during their current sojourn on Earth is set by karma that was accumulated in past existences. However, through their free will, people can still wield some control over their present behavior and thereby have hopes of accumulating positive karma for future lives on Earth. In day-to-day existence, individuals' development is also affected by reciprocal interactions with their culture, that is, with the people and institutions that share their environment.

Figure 6-8

Interactions in a Hindu Model

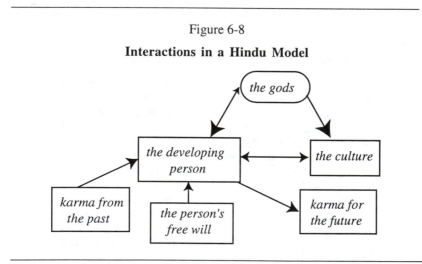

Part III
Final Words

The single brief chapter that comprises Part III offers an estimate of trends in theories of human development and in cultures that might be expected during the 21st century.

7

The Future of Theories and Cultures

This final chapter opens with a brief recounting of the main purposes of previous chapters, then continues with estimates of the likely nature of theories of development and of cultures in the years ahead.   As those estimates propose, trends in theorizing over recent decades suggest that models of human development will increase in number, diversity, and specificity over the coming years. Trends in cultures portend fewer varieties of culture across the world but more diversity within any given society.

THE BOOK'S CONTENTS IN RETROSPECT

The following have been the aims of the preceding six chapters:

Chapter 1: Visions of Culture, Visions of Development, and
　　　　　Careproviders' Interventions
- Introduce the book's principal theme, which is the proposition that different theories of human development contribute to an understanding of the influence of different cultures on young people growing up during the first quarter century of their lives.
- Define the meanings assigned to *culture* and to *theories of human development* throughout the book.
- Indicate how viewing cultures through the windows of 25 theories may suggest ways careproviders can foster the development of young people who are engaged in cross-cultural encounters.

Chapter 2: Cognition
- Illustrate differences in cultures that can be revealed by viewing them through the lenses of six theories of cognition.

Chapter 3: Learning
- Demonstrate what can be discovered about different cultures from the perspectives of four theories that focus on successive steps in the learning process.
- Illustrate various cultural explanations of behaviors which, in present-day Western societies, are interpreted as symptomatic of a learning disorder called *autism.*
- Distinguish between cultural and noncultural (idiosyncratic) features of the environment that affect what people learn.

Chapter 4: Attitudes, Emotions, and Values
- Identify aspects of culture that can be revealed through four representative theories about attitudes, emotions, and values.
- Show how theories focusing on the same general phenomenon can be on different levels of specificity.

Chapter 5: Development Configurations
- Direct attention to how components can be patterned differently in five illustrative theories and suggest how such patterning may vary across cultures.

Chapter 6: Forms of Interaction
- Propose a scheme for analyzing forms of interaction among components of development theories.
- Identify patterns of interaction in four models that reflect differences among cultures in those aspects of development on which those models focus.
- Compare the four models in terms of the scheme for analyzing interactions.

TRENDS IN THEORIES

Throughout the first half of the 20th century, many theorists in the field of human development sought to create universal models referred to as *macrotheories*—ones whose principles were intended to explain a broad spectrum of development in any and all cultural settings. By *broad spectrum* I mean theories designed to explain a wide range of human thought and behavior. Examples of macrotheories have been Skinner's behaviorism, Bandura's social cognition, Piaget's genetic epistemology in the realm of cognition, Vygotsky's sociohistorical proposal, and Havighurst's developmental tasks. However, a growing number of critics have charged that the explanatory and predictive power of such models is often weak and off target when applied to specific aspects of people's lives. For example, some observers have charged that Skinner's behaviorism does not adequately account for such things as people's dreams or emotions.   Others have pointed out that Piaget's proposals about mental development fail to explain children's sex life, physical growth, and friendship patterns.

Such putative shortcomings of macrotheories have led to greater emphasis in recent times on the creation of *minitheories* or *microtheories*—models limited to explaining only a restricted facet of human thought, appearance, or behavior. The advantage of the most general macromodels is that they embrace many facets of development, but their very abstractness causes them to neglect the multitude of variables that differentiate one facet from another. As a consequence, they are relatively useless for explaining or predicting specific aspects of development with any precision.   Consider, for example, the key elements of Kurt Lewin's all-encompassing macrotheory.   He posited five principles that govern the way humans grow up in all aspects of their development.   In his opinion, with the passing of time the characteristics of the growing child become more *differentiated*, the boundaries between regions of the child's life become more *rigid*, the aspects of life that the child's personality encompasses *expand*, those aspects increase in their *complexity of organization*, and the child's behavior becomes more *realistic* in terms of what the world requires (Barker, Dembo, & Lewin, 1943, pp. 441-442).   However true these generalizations may be, they are of little or no help to someone who wishes to understand precisely the thought processes, emotions, values, and overt behavior of children of different ages as those children solve math problems, face the death of a parent, interact with peers, make moral judgments, or acquire their gender characteristics.   In effect, proponents of the minitheory movement assert that minitheories produce more accurate analyses and predictions than do macrotheories for those aspects of development on which the minitheories focus. Among the minitheories included in this book are Ambert's conception of peer abuse, Jung's dream analysis, Eve's social-exchange proposal, Baron-Cohen's explanation of autism, and Sanders' portrayal of grief and bereavement.   In keeping with recent trends, I believe minitheories will continue to expand in number and popularity in the future.

A further challenge to macrotheories of the past has come from postpositivists and postmodernists who have accused traditional European and American theorists of egocentrism and ethnocentrism that causes them to ignore two considerations:

- That theories and the data on which they are founded do not reflect the "objective truth" about reality.   Rather, they represent an individual's or group's estimation of reality and are thus either individual or social creations (constructions) of what development is all about.
- That the explanations of development found within a culture are heavily laden with assumptions that derive from the dominant worldview to which members of that culture subscribe.   Therefore, understanding a conception

of development requires that we recognize the ontological (the nature of reality) and espistemological (the nature of knowledge and how it is acquired) assumptions that undergird the model. Such recognition comes from a sympathetic attempt to adopt, at least temporarily, the worldview of the culture from which the model derives. This attempt may require what the English poet Coleridge described as the "willing suspension of disbelief."

In summary, it's my guess that the years ahead will produce an expanding collection of minimodels and a greater recognition of, and tolerance for, theories that derive from a wider range of cultures than generally has been true in the past.

I also believe that theorists will be attempting to discover better answers for the following perennial questions:

- What is the exact relationship between the *mind* and the *brain*? More precisely, when a change occurs in the mind, what happens in the brain and why? What is happening in the brain when a person's encounter with the environment affects the mind, such as when the person learns a new concept or skill or experiences an emotion?

- How can we best create overarching metatheories that identify the logical linkages among—and the commonly held characteristics of—two or more minitheories? In other words, what sorts of macrotheories can reasonably embrace seemingly disparate minitheories?

- For a given minitheory, what are the main variables that interact to produce a developmental outcome? How can the power or degree of influence of each variable's contribution to the outcome be best assessed?

- How can the relationship between the concepts (a) stage-wise development and (b) imperceptibly incremental development be convincingly rationalized?

TRENDS IN CULTURES

I believe that predictions about the future of cultures can usefully be founded on at least three sets of rather obvious generalizations.

First set: Barriers to communication among peoples promote the development of separate cultures. The more impervious the barriers and the longer the barriers remain, the greater the differences become among cultures. On the other hand, increases in communication among peoples expand individuals' knowledge of other cultures and decrease intercultural differences.

The rationale. Over past eons of time, thousands of individual cultures developed when societies were separated from each other by distances—mountains, deserts, seas—and by habits and antagonisms that discouraged social interaction. What might once have been a people's single language and set of beliefs became a polyglot of mutually unintelligible dialects and convictions as members of a society traveled in diverse directions, settled in separate territories, and grew their own disparate versions of their original tongue and their original beliefs during succeeding generations of separation from their original homeland. However, recent centuries—and particularly the 20th century—have clearly changed all that. The postal service, telephone, radio, television, and the Internet with its e-mail now provide peoples all over the earth with instant insight into other cultures, no matter how far away each is located. Ships, automobiles, and airplanes have produced an increasingly mobile world community in which both tourism and migration advance at a growing pace. Consequently, people of one culture not only know more about other cultures than ever before, but this knowledge is increasingly gained from face-to-face contact as societies rapidly become multicultural, composed of members of markedly diverse origins.

This increase in ease of communication and transportation that produces more interaction among peoples from different cultures has led not only to an increase in intercultural understanding, but also to a higher incidence of intercultural frustration and conflict as more individuals are obliged to adjust to others' unfamiliar, peculiar modes of thought and action.

Second set: It requires less energy and less risk of failure for people to continue with their traditional cultural habits than to adopt new beliefs and practices. Older people find it more difficult to acquire new ways of life than do younger people.

The rationale. There is considerable evidence to support the assertion that people's sense of identity and their confidence that their understanding of the world is correct derive to a great extent from holding fast to the worldview of the culture within which they grew up. Therefore, a crisis of personal adjustment can occur when they encounter cultural beliefs and practices contrary to their own. Their tendency is to seek security in retaining their original convictions and avoiding or actively rejecting the strange language, values, and customs of the new culture they now face. Consequently, migrants (from homeland to foreign land, from rural to urban) tend to cope with their cross-cultural engagements by (a) settling in neighborhoods populated by people from their home culture, (b) as far as possible, interacting socially with people from their own culture, (c) speaking their native language in as many situations as possible, and (d) maintaining traditional lifestyles—rituals, ceremonies, occupations, modes of dress, foods, religious beliefs, and the like. Adopting the odd practices of the new culture into which immigrants have moved requires energy, dedication, and risk of error that can lead to frustration, ridicule, and being regarded as inferior by members of the new culture. As a result, immigrants often consider it easier to maintain their traditions than to try acquiring the beliefs and practices of a foreign society. Furthermore, a host of evidence suggests that the older people are, the more difficult it is for them to replace their traditional beliefs with ones from another culture. Thus, children generally can be expected to more readily acquire the language and habits of the new society than will their parents and grandparents.

Consequently, as migration continues to accelerate, societies can expect an increase in cross-cultural problems—more conflicts between ethnic and religious groups and more individuals suffering personal adjustment disorders.

Third set: Multiple forces operate to alter cultural patterns. Prominent among such forces are ones in the realms of technology, politics, economics, and education. In modern times, the speed at which such forces exert their influence has been increasing.

Technological change. Not only will technological advances continue to enhance people's communication and mobility, but they can be expected to continue changing societies' occupational structures, job opportunities, and the skills and knowledge that workers require. Technological progress forces workers to shift to new jobs several times during their vocational career or at least to upgrade their work skills as new technology changes the culture of their occupation. These developments not only strain people's ability to adjust to change but can also produce intergenerational tensions as the gap increases between (a) the work skills and attitudes required of youths and (b) the ones already held by their parents and grandparents.

Recreational pursuits are also affected by technological modernization. Television viewing, computer games, and the Internet divert individuals' attention from books and from actively engaging in sports.

In effect, the prospect for the future is that more rapid cultural change will occur as a result of an accelerating pace of technological innovation that alters the nature of the hardware of daily living and of ways the hardware is utilized. National cultures will become increasingly alike and homogenized as the same technologies are adopted by societies worldwide—highrise hotels and office buildings, mechanized modes of transportation, television and radio, and computer-controlled communication, transportation, and industrial production.

Political conditions. The word *political,* as intended here, refers to the exercise of power and control over people's opportunities, welfare, and behavior. Politics affect culture when those who advocate a given set of beliefs and practices try to impose their convictions on people who have subscribed to a different set. The aspects of culture that may be the object of political action can include social structure (type of government, how power is distributed, how government is financed), religious convictions and rituals, architecture, foods, methods of warfare, ways of producing and distributing goods and services, modes of education, the arts, recreational activities, and more. Methods of imposing cultural elements can range from intimidation and brute force to gentle persuasion and the advertising of cultural objects and practices.

Several of the commonly recognized political processes that can operate in confrontations between cultures are those of elimination, assimilation, parallel accommodation, marginalization, and integration.

Elimination occurs when one culture gains domination by destroying competing cultures. The most drastic form of elimination consists of one group slaughtering another group. A slightly less drastic means consists of enslaving people from the dominated group and thereby imposing by force the customs of the conquerors. Or, instead of attempting physical slavery, a dominant culture can be imposed through legal orders that proscribe and punish cultural practices other than those of the group in political control. Least radical, but often equally effective, is *assimilation,* by which a submissive culture accedes to a dominant culture through subtle pressures and appeals rather than by drastic action. Assimilation is often accomplished through enticement that lures members of other cultures into abandoning their traditional ways in favor of the apparent advantages of the dominant group.

Parallel accommodation involves two or more cultures living side by side in a sometime uneasy acceptance of each others' right to exist. The multiculturalism found today in so many societies is of this sort. The analogies "tossed salad" and "mosaic" have been coined as labels for parallel accommodation. Parallel accommodation can involve the *marginalization* of a culture that clings to the edges of a dominant culture, often resulting in the demoralization of the members of marginalized group (Berry, 1994, p. 126). When viewed in the long term, parallel accommodation may be merely a transitional state of a culture on its way to a more permanent condition of elimination, assimilation, or integration.

Integration or *reciprocal bicultural integration* involves the amalgamation of components of different cultures to comprise a unified hybrid form. The term "melting pot" is the traditional figure of speech applied to cultural integration.

It should be apparent that encounters between cultures can involve different political processes for one set of cultural components than for another. The methods of governance of Culture A may be eliminated by Culture B at the same time that the architectural styles and culinary practices of Culture A are widely adopted within Culture B. Such technological innovations as computers and television from Culture C may be welcomed in Culture D (and thereafter parallel and gradually replace traditional Culture D modes of communication) while the religious persuasions of Culture C are rejected in Culture D.

In speculating about likely political affects on cultural change over the coming decades, I would guess that:

- Parallel accommodation as a process will become increasingly prominent throughout the world as migration accelerates, particularly in societies in which minority groups become better organized and skilled in concerted mass action.
- The attempted elimination of ethnic, religious, and regional cultures by both violent and legal-order means will continue in societies in which (a) political differences have not traditionally been resolved by peaceful

negotiation and/or (b) a strong central government that kept ethnic, religious, and regional conflicts under control has dissolved or been defeated. Several sub-Saharan African nations and such Eastern European countries as the former Yugoslavia have been examples of those societies during the 1990s.

Economic conditions. A society's economic circumstances can affect culture by how the monetary health of the society influences which goods and services are available and which of those goods and services different individuals can acquire.

The rationale. Typically, the world's advanced industrial societies display a well-stocked, richly varied cafeteria of objects to buy and services to purchase. In contrast, less developed societies offer a restricted variety of goods and services. Thus, the lived cultures of the two types of societies are markedly different.

Furthermore, societies can vary in how the distribution of wealth among the citizens affects which goods and services individuals can acquire. For example, in a predominantly socialistic political/economic system, such as that of Sweden, taxes on individual wealth are high so that the available money can be pooled and distributed rather evenly throughout the populace in the form of government-financed goods and services. In contrast, in the dominantly capitalistic economy of the United States, taxes on wealth are lower and market forces are freer to operate, thereby allowing individuals to accumulate substantial wealth but also requiring those without wealth to exist on a low income. In such a society, the culture of the well-to-do can differ markedly from that of the poor because of the two groups' contrasting levels of purchasing power.

Which goods and services people acquire is also influenced by cultural customs. Among the Japanese, the habit of accumulating personal savings is widespread. In the United States, the habit of accumulating personal savings has become dwarfed by the custom of deficit spending through the use of credit cards, easily acquired loans, long-term charge accounts, and no-down-payment plans. Consequently, more Americans than Japanese acquire goods and services that are paid for only at a later date and at an ultimately higher cost because of the interest charged on the borrowed funds.

As for the future interaction between economics and culture, I would estimate that:

- In keeping with current tends, the economic systems of all nations will continue to become increasingly intertwined, producing an ever-tightening worldwide financial network within which the fate of each society can be significantly affected by economic and political events in every other society.
- The vitality of the world's economies will, as in the past, periodically rise and fall, producing changes in the "lived culture" (in the sense of "the style

of life") that individuals are obliged to experience at any given period of their lifespan.

Educational practices. The word *education* is used here to mean any intentional effort to improve people's knowledge, skills, values, self-perceptions, and social adjustment. Therefore, not only does formal schooling qualify as education, but so also do parents' intentional childrearing practices, counselors' methods of aiding their clients, television's news and information programs, artistic performances and products, libraries' book-distribution services, and the like.

Education, as a cultural force, can sustain and propagate an existing feature of culture or can serve to alter or replace that feature. First, consider these examples of efforts to propagate culture in the sense of passing cultural elements along to succeeding generations.

Education via artistic performances. For centuries Javanese villagers have witnessed shadow-puppet shows designed to teach religious lore, models of morality, etiquette, and cultural attitudes. During the 1930s in Germany, Wagnerian operas were performed to convey to the populace the Hitlerian ideal of a master race (Flood, 1989, p. 12).

Correcting breaches of custom. Administrators at Thailand's Chulalongkorn University in 1998 threatened to reduce the grades of women students who persisted in wearing miniskirts on campus. Authorities asserted that short skirts violated the Thai cultural expectation that women behave in a modest fashion so as not to entice sexual predators. To illustrate their concerns, officials displayed posters around the campus showing a crocodile salivating at the sight of a woman in a miniskirt (Dispatch case, 1998).

Historical accounts. The teaching of history in a nation's schools is usually intended to foster patriotism in the young, particularly by glorifying the country's past and disregarding or excusing shameful acts. In Japan throughout the 1990s, struggles between Japanese conservatives and liberals intensified over issues of teaching patriotism. In particular, conflicts arose over how the nation's wartime military participation should be described in history textbooks. For example, after three decades of legal delays engineered by Japan's Ministry of Education, the nation's Supreme Court in a 3-2 decision found the Ministry guilty of having eliminated from a high school history book an account of World War II atrocities committed by Japan's military forces in Northern China. The ruling brought to a successful close the efforts of the textbook author, 83-year-old historian Saburo Ienaga, to have ministry officials censured for illegally deleting portions of his work that they found politically unsavory. The disputed passages were then restored to Ienaga's textbook. In 1998 Tokorozawa High School students refused to participate in graduation ceremonies that involved the nation's flag and the national anthem, thereby reflecting the national teachers' union policy of resisting the use of the flag and anthem in schools. At the same time the Ministry of Education directed all schools to fly the flag and sing the anthem. Furthermore, the new film *Pride* was lauded by conservatives for portraying General Hideki Tojo, the architect of Japan's military conquests in World War II, as a gentle family man who was the victim of American bigotry (Gutek & Thomas, 1998; Japan rethinks its role, 1998).

Reinstituting indigenous culture. Curriculum reforms in India during the 1990s took a more nationalistic turn as a growing number of foundation-sponsored private schools supplemented the government syllabus of subjects from British colonial times with studies of Indian culture, music, philosophy, and the Sanskrit language. In addition, uniforms in many convent schools were replaced by Indian traditional garb. Hindu nationalists of the Bharatiya Janata Party sought to replace Western science in schools by introducing Vedic mathematics and the ancient science of *vastu shastra*. Party spokesmen charged that Western science was a source of imperialism and rationalism that conflicted with Hindu tradition (Gutek & Thomas, 1998).

Next, consider four educational measures intended to alter existing aspects of culture.

Academic specializations. The social turmoil that accompanied the political and economic collapse of the Soviet Union and its Eastern European satellites encouraged university students to depart from the favorite fields of study in Soviet times in order to learn skills that might equip them to succeed in the new political-economic culture that they saw on the horizon. In 1978 more than two thirds of Russian college students had been in departments of engineering, medicine, agriculture, and pure and applied sciences. By 1998 less 25% of students were in engineering, whereas more than 25% were enrolled in economics, up from 10% in the 1980s. In addition, increased numbers were enrolled in language courses and such new fields as environmental studies ("Different Subjects Popular," 1998).

Computer literacy. In 1997, Ireland's education minister announced his government's intention to establish Ireland as the "information services hub" for Europe by ensuring that all Irish children would be computer literate by the end of their school career. In pursuit of this goal, the government planned to increase annual spending on education from $3.3 billion to $4.6 billion by 2002. Of that amount, $71 million would be used to acquire information and communications equipment, training, curriculum manuals, and Internet connections for 4,000 schools (Burns, 1997).

A new national education policy in Botswana aimed to prepare students for an industrial economy driven by information technology. A key feature of the plan would be a computer awareness program in all secondary and tertiary institutions. The program, organized in a 10-year basic computer education curriculum, was designed to develop students' skills in word processing and the use of spreadsheets and databases.

Changed teacher-student relations. In the United States, the failure of educators' efforts to persuade teachers to enrich their lessons with advanced technology motivated officials of the Olympia, Washington, school district to create an 18-week course for training secondary-school students in computer technology so those students could help teachers improve classroom instruction. The course taught participants how to use the World Wide Web, e-mail, digital photography, network conferencing, and newly created web pages to enhance instruction. Then each student acquired a teacher as a partner, with the teacher serving as the learning expert and the student as the technical expert in cooperatively developing technology-enhanced lessons for the teacher's class. The success of the Olympia program prompted the federal government, the Washington state government, and corporate sponsors to fund a multimillon-dollar expansion of the plan to other school systems. By 1999 more than 175 school districts in 17 states were implementing the program, with several hundred additional districts waiting to be included (Thomas, 1999).

School-choice options. The school-voucher movement in the United States gained momentum during the 1990s. Typical voucher programs conducted by selected states and cities furnished parents a stipend ranging from $1,500 to $5,000 per year to help pay the cost of sending a child to a school of the parents' choice. Whereas in 1994 only 45% of respondents in a nationwide Gallup poll endorsed voucher plans, in a 1998 survey 51% favored full or partial government subsidies to pay tuition costs at any public, private, or church-related school. Support for vouchers was also expressed in legal decisions and monetary contributions from nongovernmental sources (Byrne, 1998).

Finally, what may the future hold for trends in education as a cultural force? I believe the years ahead will witness an increase in:

- Similarities among cultures in their educational goals, curricula, administrative systems, teaching methods, and evaluation procedures as developing societies continue to model their schooling practices on those of advanced industrial societies. Changes in educational procedures in the dominant industrial nations will be copied in the developing regions.

- Further attempts on the part of cultural groups (ethnic, religious, regional, feminist) to promote their special interests by influencing curriculum contents, teaching methods, the appointment of educational personnel, and the financing of education. However, most efforts of ethnic and religious minorities to maintain or revive traditional curriculum content and teaching methods will probably be defeated by the spread of advanced technology and the international homogenization of culture that has occurred at an accelerating rate. Vestiges of indigenous cultures will become curiosities barely kept alive through history books and the arts—music, dance, film, painting, weaving, and sculpture.

CONCLUSION

If the estimates of trends proposed in this chapter are accurate, or nearly so, then the future should provide a greater variety of theories of human development and a changed patterning of the world's cultures. As a consequence, there will be more diverse theoretical windows than currently exist through which to view the newly evolving—but less diverse—styles of culture.

References

Abu-Lughod, L. (1996). Honor and shame. In M. Jackson, *Things as they are: New directions in phenomenological psychology* (pp. 51-69). Bloomington: Indiana University Press.

Acheson, J. M. (1981). Anthropology of fishing. In B. J. Siegel, A. R. Beals, & S. A. Tyler (Eds.), *Annual review of anthropology* (pp. 275-316). Palo Alto, CA: Annual Reviews.

Adler, L. L. (Ed.). (1993). *International handbook on gender roles*. Westport, CT: Greenwood.

Adler, M. A., & Brayfield, A. (1996). East-west differences in attitudes about employment and family in Germany. *Sociological Quarterly, 37* (2), 245-260.

Alger, A. (1996). The new American way of death. *Forbes, 158* (10), 324-326.

Almagor, U. (1978). *Pastoral partners*. Manchester, England: Manchester University Press.

Almunzri, A. (1977). *Saheeh Muslim* (The Sunnah), (Vols. 1 & 2). Damascus: Al Makteb Elislami.

Amato, P. R. (1995). Single-parent households as settings for children's development, well-being, and attainment. In N. Mandell & A. M. Ambert (Eds.), *Sociological studies of children* (Vol. 7, pp. 19-47). Greenwich, CT: JAI.

Ambert, A. M. (1995). Toward a theory of peer abuse. In N. Mandell & A. M. Ambert (Eds.), *Sociological studies of children* (Vol. 7, pp. 177-205). Greenwich, CT: JAI.

Averill, J. R., & Nunley, E. P. (1993). Grief as an emotion and as a disease: A social-constructionist perspective. In M. S. Stroebe, W. Stroebe, & R. O. Hansson (Eds.), *Handbook of bereavement* (pp. 77-90). Cambridge, UK: Cambridge University Press.

Azoulay, K. G. (1997). *Black, Jewish, and interracial*. Durham, SC: Duke University Press.

Bandura, A. (1969). *Principles of behavior modification.* New York: Holt, Rinehart & Winston.

Bandura, A. (1977). *Social learning theory.* Englewood Cliffs, NJ: Prentice Hall.

Bandura, A. (1986). *Social foundations of thought and action: A social cognitive theory.* Englewood Cliffs, NJ: Prentice Hall.

Barker, R. G., Dembo, T., & Lewin, K. (1943). Frustration and regression. In R. G. Barker, J. S. Kounin, & H. F. Wright (Eds.), *Child behavior and development.* New York: McGraw-Hill.

Baron-Cohen, S. (1995). *Mindblindness.* Cambridge, MA: MIT Press.

Battan, M. J. (1994). Scientific weather modification. *Encyclopaedia Britannica* (Vol. 16, pp. 518-521). Chicago: Encyclopaedia Britannica.

Beaglehole, E., & Beaglehole, P. (1941). *Pangai: A village in Tonga.* Wellington, New Zealand: The Polynesian Society.

Belser, A., & Clark, J. (1992). Rights, privileges, and gay lovers. *Advocate* (597), pp. 56-58.

Berry, J. W. (1971). Ecological and cultural factors in spatial perceptual development. *Canadian Journal of Behavioral Science, 3*, 324-336.

Berry, J. W. (1994). An ecological perspective on cultural and ethnic psychology. In E. J. Trickett, R. J. Watts, & D. Birman (Eds.), *Human diversity* (pp. 115-141). San Francisco: Jossey-Bass.

Bettleheim, B. (1967). *The empty fortress.* New York: Free Press.

Biddle, B. J. (1979). *Role theory.* New York: Academic Press.

Biggs, J. B. (1976). Schooling and moral development. In V. P. Varma & P. Williams (Eds.), *Piaget, psychology, and education.* Itasca, IL: F. E. Peacock.

Birman, D. (1994). Acculturation and human diversity in a multicultural society. In E. J. Trickett, R. J. Watts, & Dina Birman (Eds.), *Human diversity* (pp. 261-284). San Francisco: Jossey-Bass.

Block, J. H. (1983). Differential premises arising from differential socialization of the sexes: Some conjectures. *Child Development, 54*, pp. 1335-1354.

Booth, N. S. (1936). *Teaching a Bantu community.* Unpublished doctoral dissertation, Hartford Seminary Foundation, Hartford, CT.

Bronfenbrenner, U. (1979). *The ecology of human development.* Cambridge, MA: Harvard University Press.

Bronfenbrenner, U. (1993). The ecology of cognitive development: Research models and fugitive findings. In R. H. Wozniak & K. W. Fischer (Eds.), *Development in context: Acting and thinking in specific environments.* Hillsdale, NJ: Lawrence Erlbaum.

Bronfenbrenner, U. (1995) Developmental ecology: A future perspective. In P. Moen, G. H. Elder, Jr., & K. Lüscher (Eds.), *Examining lives in context.* Washington, DC: American Psychological Association.

Bronfenbrenner, U., & Ceci, S. J. (1994). Nature-nurture reconceptualized in developmental perspective: A bioecological model. *Psychological Review, 101* (4), 568-586.

Buhler, G. (1886). *The laws of Manu: Manu smriti.* London: Oxford University Press (Volume 25 of F. M. Muller (Ed.) *The sacred books of the east*).

Burdin, J. L., & Thomas, R. M. (1995, 1996). Education. In *Encyclopaedia Britannica book of the year.* Chicago: Encyclopaedia Britannica.

Burns, M. (1997). Teaching high-tech (Ireland), *Europe.* No. 369, pp. 26-27.

Burrell, B. (1996). Nine night: Death and dying in Jamaica. *American Visions, 11* (5), 25-27.

Burton, L. M., Obeidallah, D. A, & Allison, K. (1996). Ethnographic insights on social context and adolescent development among inner-city African-American teens. In R. Jessor, A. Colby, & R. A. Shweder (Eds.), *Ethnography and human development.* Chicago: University of Chicago Press.

Byrne, H. J. (1998, December 12). Growing support for school vouchers. *America,* p. 7.

Calhoun, D. R. (Ed.). (1998). *Britannica book of the year.* Chicago: Encyclopaedia Britannica.

Calligan, M. E. (1992). *Penal code, abridged California edition.* San Clemente, CA: Qwik-Code Publications.

Campbell, J. (Ed.). (1971). *The portable Jung.* New York: Viking.

Campos, R., et al. (1994). Social networks and daily activities of street youth in Belo Horizonte, Brazil. *Child Development, 65,* 319-330.

Chen, X., Rubin, K. H., & Li, Z. Y. (1995). Social functioning and adjustment in Chinese children: A longitudinal study. *Developmental Psychology, 312* (4), 531-539.

Ciaccio, N. V., & El Shakry, O. S. (1993). Egypt. In L. L. Adler (Ed.), *International handbook on gender roles* (pp. 46-58). Westport, CT: Greenwood.

Colby, A., Kohlberg, L., Gibbs, J., & Lieberman, M. (1983). A longitudinal study of moral development. *Monographs of the Society for Research in Child Development,* Serial No. 200, Vol. 48, Nos. 1-2. Chicago: Society for Research in Child Development.

Cole, M., Gay, J., Glick, J. A., & Sharp, D. W. (1971). *The cultural context of learning and thinking.* New York: Basic Books.

Copper, J. (1990). Taiwan: A nation in transition. In Y. M. Shaw (Ed.), *The Republic of China on Taiwan today* (pp. 37-47). Taipei: Kwang Hwa Publishing Company.

Copper, J. (1996). *Taiwan: Nation-state or province?* Boulder, CO: Westview.

Cosmides, L., Tooby, J., & Barkow, J. (1992). Introduction: Evolutionary psychology and conceptual integration . In J. Barkow et al. (Eds.) *The adaptive mind.* Oxford: Oxford University Press.

Damon, W. (1996). Nature, second nature, and individual development: An ethnographic opportunity. In J. Jessor, A. Colby, & R. A. Shweder (Eds.), *Ethnography and human development.* Chicago: University of Chicago Press.

D'Andrade, R. (1990). Some propositions about the relations between culture and human cognition. In J. W. Stigler, R. A. Shweder, & G. Herdt (Eds.),

Cultural psychology: Essays on comparative human development (pp. 65-129). Cambridge, UK: Cambridge University Press.

Davido, R. D., & O'Donoghue, M. A. (1993). France. In L. L. Adler (Ed.), *International handbook on gender roles* (pp. 77-84). Westport, CT: Greenwood.

Davidov, V. V. (1990). Soviet theories of human development. In R. M. Thomas (Ed.), *The encyclopedia of human development and education.* Oxford, UK: Pergamon.

Davis, E. E. (1993). Canada. In L. L. Adler (Ed.), *International handbook on gender roles* (pp. 28-45). Westport, CT: Greenwood.

deLacey, P. R. (1973). Classificatory ability. In G. E. Kearnery, P. R. deLacey, & G. R. Davidson (Eds.), *The psychology of aboriginal Australians* (pp. 59-70). Sydney: Wiley.

deLaslo, V. S. (Ed.). (1959). *The basic writings of C. G. Jung.* New York: Random House.

DeLong, G. R., Teague, L. A., & Kamran, M. M. (1998). Effects of fluoxetine treatment in young children with idiopathic autism. *Developmental Medicine & Child Neurology, 40* (8), 551-562.

Denzin, N. K. (1997). *Interpretive ethnography.* Thousand Oaks, CA: Sage.

Desjarlais, R. (1996). Struggling along. In M. Jackson (Ed.), *Things as they are: New directions in phenomenological psychology* (pp. 70-93). Bloomington: Indiana University Press.

Devisch, R. (1996). The cosmology of life transmission. In M. Jackson (Ed.), *Things as they are: New directions in phenomenological psychology* (pp. 94-114). Bloomington: Indiana University Press.

DeVos, G. A. (1980). Afterword. In D. K. Reynolds, *The quiet therapies.* Honolulu: University Press of Hawaii.

Diaz-Guerrero, R., & Rodriguez de Diaz, M. L. (1993). Mexico. In L. L. Adler (Ed.), *International handbook on gender roles* (pp. 199-217). Westport, CT: Greenwood.

Different subjects popular in Soviet days. (1998, May 7). *Los Angeles Times,* p. A22.

Dispatch case. (1988, February 13). *Chronicle of Higher Education,* p. A55.

Dorsky, S., & Stevenson, T. B. (1995). Childhood and education in highland north Yemen. In E. W. Fernea (Ed.), *Children in the Muslim Middle East* (pp. 309-324). Austin: University of Texas Press.

Douyon, C., Philippe, J., & Frazier, C. (1993). Haiti. In L. L. Adler (Ed.), *International handbook on gender roles* (pp. 98-107). Westport, CT: Greenwood.

Downey, W. E. (1998). Secular rites: With the number of Christians declining, a new kind of funeral speaker has emerged. *Christian Century, 115* (11), 358-359.

Duran, E., & Duran, B. (1995). *Native American postcolonial psychology.* Albany: State University of New York Press.

Dying in the countryside. (1998). *Moscow News, 23,* p. 10.

Eagle's embrace. (1995). *Economist, 336*, pp. 21-23.

Eckensberger, L. H., & Zimba, R. F. (1997). The development of moral judgment. In J. W. Berry, P. R. Dasen, & T. S. Saraswathi (Eds.), *Cross-cultural psychology : Vol. 2. Basic processes and human development* (2nd ed.; pp. 299-338). Boston: Allyn & Bacon.

Education. (1998). In D. R. Calhoun (Ed.), *Britannica book of the year* (pp. 880-885). Chicago: Encyclopaedia Britannica.

Elder, G. H., Jr. (1996). Human lives in changing societies: Life course and developmental insights. In R. B. Cairns, G. H. Elder, Jr., & E. J. Costello (Eds.), *Developmental science.* Cambridge, UK: Cambridge University Press.

Elder, G. H., Jr., Modell, J., & Parke, R. D. (1993). Studying children in a changing world. In G. H. Elder, Jr., J. Modell, & R. D. Parke (Eds.), *Children in time and place.* Cambridge, UK: Cambridge University Press.

Eliade, M. (1964). *Shamanism.* Princeton, NJ: Princeton University Press.

Elkind, D. (1976). *Child development and education.* New York: Oxford University Press.

Ellenberger, H. F. (1968). Psychiatric impressions from a trip to Dakar. *Canadian Psychiatric Association Journal, 13* (6), 539-545.

Ellis, A. (1985). Rational-emotive therapy. In T. Husén & T. N. Postlethwaite (Eds.), *International encyclopedia of education* (Vol. 5, pp. 3139-3140). Oxford, UK: Pergamon.

Epstein, A. L. (1998). Strange encounters: Dreams and nightmares of high school students in Papua New Guinea. *Oceania, 68* (3), 200-212.

Epstein, S. (1993). Bereavement from the perspective of cognitive-experiential self-theory. In M. S. Stroebe, W. Stroebe, & R. O. Hansson (Eds.), *Handbook of bereavement* (pp. 112-125). Cambridge, UK: Cambridge University Press.

Erikson, E. H. (1959). *Identity and the life cycle.* In *Psychological Issues* (monograph), Vol. 1, No. 1. New York: International Universities Press.

Erikson, E. H. (1987). *A way of looking at things: Selected papers from 1930 to 1980.* New York: Norton.

Eve, R. A. (1986). Children's interpersonal tactics in effecting cooperation by peers and adults. In P. A. Adler & P. Adler (Eds.), *Sociological studies of child development* (Vol. 1, pp. 187-208). Greenwich, CT: JAI.

Famighetti, R. (Ed.). (1996). *World almanac.* New York: Funk & Wagnalls.

Farb, P. (1978). *Humankind.* Boston: Houghton Mifflin.

Farver, J. A. M., Kim, Y. K., & Lee, Y. (1995). Cultural differences in Korean- and Anglo-American preschoolers' social interaction and play behaviors. *Child Development, 66*, 1088-1099.

Ferdows, A. K. (1995). Gender roles in Iranian public school textbooks. In E. W. Fernea (Ed.), *Children in the Muslim Middle East* (pp. 325-336). Austin: University of Texas Press.

Ferster, C. B. (1961). Positive reinforcement and behavior deficits of autistic children. *Child Development, 32*, 437-456.

Field, T., Lasko, D., Mundy, P., & Henteleff, T. (1997). Brief report: Autistic children's attentiveness and responsivity improve after touch therapy. *Journal of Autism & Developmental Disorders, 27* (3), 333-338.

Finn, C. E., Jr. (1998). Giving it away: An open letter to Bill Gates. *Commentary, 105* (1), 19-23.

Flood, C. B. (1989). *Hitler, the path to power.* Boston: Houghton Mifflin.

Friedman, J. (1992). Cross-cultural perspectives on sexuality education. *SIECUS Report, 20* (6), 5-11.

Freud, S. (1917). Introductory lectures on psychoanalysis, part III. In J. Strachey (Ed.), *The standard edition of the complete psychological works of Sigmund Freud* (Vol. 16, pp. 243-482). London: Hogarth, 1957.

Freud, S. (1923). *The ego and the id.* London: Hogarth, 1974.

Freud, S. (1938). *An outline of psychoanalysis.* London: Hogarth.

Freud, S. (1946). *The ego and the mechanisms of defense.* New York: International Universities Press.

Furth, H. G., & Wachs, W. (1975). *Thinking goes to school.* New York: Oxford University Press.

Garcia Coll, C. , Lamberty, G., Jenkins, R., McAdoo, H. P., Crnic, K., Wasik, B. H., & Garcia, H. V. (1996). An integrative model for the study of developmental competencies in minority children. *Child Development, 67,* pp. 1891-1914.

Gardner, H. (1983). *Frames of mind.* New York: Basic Books.

Gardner, H. (1991). *The unschooled mind.* New York: Basic Books.

Gardner, H. (1995). The development of competence in culturally defined domains: A preliminary framework. In N. R. Goldberger & J. B. Veroff (Eds.), *The culture and psychology reader* (pp. 222-244). New York: New York University Press.

Gaskins, S. (1996). How Mayan parental theories come into play. In S. Harkness & C. M. Super (Eds.), *Parents' cultural belief systems* (pp. 345-363). New York: Guilford.

Geertz, C. (1976). *The religion of Java.* Chicago: University of Chicago Press.

Geertz, C. (1973). *The interpretation of cultures.* New York: Basic Books.

Gerber, E. R. (1985). Rage and obligation: Samoan emotion in conflict. In G. M. White & J. Kirkpatrick (Eds.), *Person, self, and experience: Exploring Pacific ethnopsychologies* (pp. 121-167). Berkeley: University of California Press.

Gesell, A., & Ilg, F. L. (1949). *Child development: An introduction to the study of human growth.* New York: Harper & Row.

Gesell, A., Ilg, F. L., Ames, L. B., & Bullis, G. E. (1977). *The child from five to ten.* New York: Harper & Row.

Gibson, E. (1997). An ecological psychologist's prolegomena for perceptual development: A functional approach. In C. Dent-Read & P. Zukow-Goldring (Eds.), *Evolving explanations of development.* Washington, DC: American Psychological Association.

Gibson, E., & Rader, N. (1990). Attention, the perceiver as performer. In G. A. Hale & M. Lewis (Eds.), *Attention and cognitive development* (pp. 1-21). New York: Plenum.

Gibson, J. J. (1979). *The ecological approach to visual perception.* Boston: Houghton Mifflin.

Gilligan, C. (1982). *In a different voice.* Cambridge, MA: Harvard University Press.

Goodale, J. C. (1995). *To sing with pigs is human.* Seattle: University of Washington Press.

Goodwin, G. (1969). *The social organization of the Western Apache.* Tucson: University of Arizona Press. (Original work published 1942)

Gress-Wright, J. (1993). The contraception paradox. *Public Interest, 113,* pp. 15-25.

Grzymala-Moszczynska, H. (1993). Poland. In L. L. Adler (Ed.), *International handbook on gender roles* (pp. 269-280). Westport, CT: Greenwood.

Gutek, G. L., & Thomas, R. M. (1997, 1998). Education. In *Encyclopaedia Britannica book of the year.* Chicago: Encyclopaedia Britannica.

Hadwin, J., Baron-Cohen, S., Howlin, P., & Hill, K. (1997). Does teaching theory of mind have an effect on the ability to develop conservation in children with autism? *Journal of Autism & Developmental Disorders, 27* (5), 519-537.

Hall, C. S., & Nordby, V. J. (1973). *A primer of Jungian psychology.* New York: Taplinger.

Hallpike, C. R. (1977). *Bloodshed and vengeance in the Papua mountains.* Oxford, UK: Oxford University Press.

Hammersley, M. (1992). *What's wrong with ethnography?* London: Routledge & Kegan Paul.

Harkness, S., & Super, C. M. (1995). Child-environments' interactions in the socialization of affect. In M. Lewis & C. Saarni (Eds.), *The socialization of emotions* (pp. 21-36). New York: Plenum.

Harris, P. L. (1989). *Children and emotion.* Oxford, UK: Basil Blackwell.

Havighurst, R. J. (1953). *Human development and education.* New York: Longmans, Green.

Heider, F. (1958). *The psychology of human relations.* New York: John Wiley.

Hernstein, R. J., & Murray, C. (1994). *The bell curve: Intelligence and class structure in American life.* New York: Free Press.

Hersh, R. H., Miller, J. P., & Fielding, G. D. (1980). *Models of moral education.* New York: Longman.

Herzfeld, M. (1993). In defiance of destiny: The management of time and gender at a Cretan funeral. *American Ethnologist, 20* (2), 241-255.

Herzfeld, M. (1996). In defiance of destiny. In M. Jackson (Ed.), *Things as they are: New directions in phenomenological psychology* (pp. 149-168). Bloomington: Indiana University Press.

Hertzig, M. E., Birch, H. G., Thomas, A., & Mendez, O. A. (1968). Class and ethnic differences in the responsiveness of preschool children to cognitive demands. *Monographs of the Society for Research in Child Development,* *33* (1).

Hilgard, E. R., & Bower, G. H. (1975). *Theories of learning* (4th ed.). Englewood Cliffs, NJ: Prentice Hall.

Hilger, M. I. (1971). *Together with the Ainu: A vanishing people.* Norman: University of Oklahoma Press.

Hoffman, M. L. (1987). The contribution of empathy to justice and moral judgment. In N. Eisenberg & J. Strayer (Eds.), *Empathy and its development* (pp. 47-80). New York: Cambridge University Press.

Hofstede, G. (1980). *Culture's consequences: International differences in work-related values.* Beverly Hills, CA: Sage.

Hofstede, G. (1996). Gender stereotypes and partner preferences of Asian women in masculine and feminine cultures. *Journal of Cross-Cultural Psychology, 27* (5), 533-546.

Holy Bible. (1611). (King James authorized version). Philadelphia: John C. Winston, 1930.

Honda, H., Shimizu, Y., Misumi, K., & Niimi, M. (1996). Cumulative incidence and prevalence of childhood autism in children in Japan. *British Journal of Psychiatry, 169* (2), 228-235.

Howard, A. (1970). *Learning to be Rotuman.* New York: Teachers College Press.

Howard, H. C., & McKim, P. C. (1983). *Contemporary cultural anthropology.* Boston: Little, Brown.

Husu, L., & Niemelä, P. (1993). Finland. In Adler (Ed.), *International handbook on gender roles* (pp. 59-76). Westport, CT: Greenwood.

Jackson, M. (1996). *Things as they are: New directions in phenomenological psychology.* Bloomington: Indiana University Press.

Japan rethinks its role. (1998, June 22). *Christian Science Monitor,* p. 6.

Jensen, A. R. (1972). *Genetics and education.* New York: Harper & Row.

Jensen, A. R. (1973). *Educability and group differences.* New York: Harper & Row.

Johnson, O. (Ed.). (1997). *Information please almanac.* Boston: Houghton Mifflin.

Johnson, W. I. (1979). Work together, eat together: Conflict and conflict management in a Portuguese fishing village. In R. Andersen (Ed.), *North Atlantic maritime cultures* (pp. 241-252). The Hague: Mouton.

Jones, R. M. (1960). *An application of psychoanalysis to education.* Springfield, IL: Charles C Thomas.

Joshi, M. S., & MacLean, M. (1994). Indian and English children's understanding of the distinction between real and apparent emotion. *Child Development, 65,* 1372-1384.

Kakar, S. (1991). Western science, eastern minds. *Wilson Quarterly, 15* (1), 109-116).

Kanner, L. (1943). Autistic disturbance of affective contact. *Nervous Child, 2,* 217-250.

Kapavalu, H. (1993). Dealing with the dark side in the ethnography of childhood: Child punishment in Tonga. *Oceania, 63* (4), 313-329.

Katz, I (1981). *Stigma: A social psychological analysis.* Hillsdale, NJ: Lawrence Erlbaum.

Katz, I., & Hass, R. G. (1988). Racial ambivalence and American value conflict: Correlational and priming studies of dual cognitive structures. *Journal of Personality and Social Psychology, 55*(6), 893-905.

Keats, D. M. (1982). Cultural bases of concepts of intelligence: A Chinese versus Australian comparison. In P. Sukontasarp, N. Youngsiri, P. Intasuwan, N. Jotiban, & C. Suvannathat (Eds.), *Proceedings of the Second Asian Workshop on Child and Adolescent Development (pp. 67-75).* Bangkok: Burapasilpa Press.

Kegan, R. (1982). *The evolving self: Problem and process in human development.* Cambridge, MA: Harvard University Press.

Kelley, H. H. (1967). Attribution theory in social psychology. In D. Levine (Ed.), *Nebraska Symposium on Motivation* (Vol. 15, pp. 192-240). Lincoln: University of Nebraska Press.

Kelley, H. H. (1971). *Attribution in social interaction.* Morristown, NJ: General Learning Press.

Kelley, H. H. (1992). Common-sense psychology and scientific psychology. In M. R. Rosenzweig & L. W. Porter (Eds.), *Annual review of psychology* (Vol. 43, pp. 1-23). Palo Alto, CA: Annual Reviews.

Keppler, A. L. (1993). Poetics and politics in Tongan laments and eulogies. *American Ethnologist, 20* (3), 474-501.

Kim, T. L. (1993). Korea. In L. L. Adler (Ed.), *International handbook on gender roles* (pp. 187-198). Westport, CT: Greenwood.

Kirkpatrick, J. (1985). Some Marquesan understandings of action and identity. In G. M. White & J. Kirkpatrick (Eds.), *Person, self, and experience: Exploring Pacific ethnopsychologies* (pp. 80-120). Berkeley: University of California Press.

Kohlberg, L. (1967). Moral and religious education in the public schools: A developmental view. In T. R. Sizer (Ed.), *Religion and public education.* Boston: Houghton Mifflin.

Kohlberg, L. (1971). From is to ought. In T. Michel (Ed.), *Cognitive development and epistemology.* New York: Academic Press.

Kohlberg, L. (1984). *The psychology of moral development.* San Francisco: Harper & Row.

Kohlberg, L., & Kramer, R. (1969). Continuities in childhood and adult moral development, *Human Development, 12,* (2), pp. 93-120.

Kroeber, A. L., & Kluckhohn, C. (1952). Culture: A critical review of concepts and definitions. *Papers of the Peabody Museum of American Archeology and Ethnology, Harvard University, 47* (1).

Kubie, L. S. (1960). *Introduction*. In R. M. Jones, *An application of psychoanalysis to education*. Springfield, IL: Charles C Thomas.

Landrine, H., Klonoff, E. A., Alcaraz, R., Scott, J., & Wilkens, P. (1995). Multiple variables in discrimination. In B. Lott & D. Moluso (Eds.), *The social psychology of interpersonal discrimination* (pp. 183-224). New York: Guilford.

Legge, J. (1893). *Confucius: Confucian analects, the great learning, and the doctrine of the mean*. New York: Dover, 1971 reprint.

Lestheaeghe, R. (1998). On theory development: Applications to the study of family formation. *Population and Development Review, 24* (1), 1-14.

LeVine, R. A., & LeVine, B. B. (1963). Nyansongo: A Gusii community in Kenya. In B. B. Whiting (Ed.), *Six cultures: Studies of child rearing* (pp. 15-202). New York: John Wiley.

Levy, R. I. (1996). Essential contrasts: Differences in parental ideas about learners and teaching in Tahiti and Nepal. In S. Harkness & C. M. Super (Eds.), *Parents' cultural belief systems* (pp. 123-142). New York: Guilford.

Lewin, K. (1942). Field theory and learning. In *Forty-first yearbook, National Society for the Study of Education* (Part II). Bloomington, IL: Public School Publishing Company.

Lewis, M., & Michalson, L. (1982). The socialization of emotions. In T. Field & A. Fogel (Eds.), *Emotion and early interaction* (pp. 189-212). Hillsdale, NJ: Lawrence Erlbaum.

Lewis, M., & Saarni, C. (1985). Culture and emotions. In M. Lewis & C. Saarni (Eds.), *The socialization of emotions* (pp. 1-17). New York: Plenum.

Lotter, V. (1978). Childhood autism in Africa. *Journal of Child Psychology & Psychiatry & Allied Disciplines, 19* (3), 231-244.

Lutz, C. (1985). Cultural patterns and individual differences in the child's emotional meaning system. In M. Lewis & C. Saarni (Eds.), *The socialization of emotions* (pp. 37-53). New York: Plenum.

Lynch, M. W. (1998). Enforcing "statutory rape." *Public Interest,* (132), pp. 3-16.

Ma, K. H., & Cheung, C. K. (1996). A cross-cultural study of moral stage structure in Hong Kong Chinese, English, and Americans. *Journal of Cross-Cultural Psychology, 27* (6), 700-713.

Maimonides, M. (1967). *Sefer Ha-Mitzoth of Maimonides* (Vol. 2). London: Socino Press.

Malinowski, B. (1922). *Argonauts of the Western Pacific*. London: Routledge & Kegan Paul.

Malinowski, B. (1948). *Magic, science, and religion and other essays*. Garden City, NY: Doubleday.

Marek, J. C. (1988). A Buddhist theory of human development. In R. M. Thomas (Ed.), *Oriental theories of human development* (pp. 75-115). New York: Peter Lang.

Maretzki, T. W., & Maretzki, H. (1963). Taira: An Okinawan village. In B. B. Whiting (Ed.), *Six cultures: Studies of child rearing* (pp. 363-539). New York: John Wiley.

Martini, M. (1994). Peer interactions in Polynesia: A view from the Marquesas. In J. L. Rooparie, J. E. Johnson, & F. H. Hooper (Eds.), *Children's play in diverse cultures* (pp. 73-103). Albany: State University of New York Press.

Marx, K. (1843). *Critique of Hegel's "philosophy of right."* J. O'Malley (Ed.), Cambridge, UK: Cambridge University Press, 1970.

Marx, K. (1959). Wages, price, and profit. In *Marx & Engels: Basic writings on politics and philosophy.* New York: Doubleday. (Original work published 1998)

Mattoon, M. A. (1981). *Jungian psychology in perspective.* New York: Free Press.

McDonald, H. (1994). Born in chains: Untouchables still struggle to break bonds of caste, *Far Eastern Economic Review, 157* (44), 32.

Mead, M. (1928/1937). *Coming of age in Samoa.* New York: American Museum of Natural History.

Meador, B. D., & Rogers, C. R. (1979). Client-centered therapy. In R. J. Corsini (Ed.), *Current psychotherapies* (2nd ed.). Itasca, IL: F. E. Peacock.

Mikihalevich, A. (1993, March). Russia: The revenge of subjectivity. *UNESCO Courier,* March, pp. 36-39.

Minturn, L., & Hitchcock, J. T. (1963). The Rajputs of Khalapur, India. In B. B. Whiting (Ed.), *Six cultures: Studies of child rearing* (pp. 203-361). New York: John Wiley.

Mishra, R. C. (1997). Cognition and cognitive development. In J. W. Berry, P. R. Dasen, & T. S. Saraswathi (Eds.), *Cross-cultural* psychology: Vol. 2. *Basic processes and human development* (2nd ed., pp. 143-175). Boston: Allyn & Bacon.

Mongolia. (1994). *Encyclopaedia Britannica* (Vol. 24, pp. 330-342). Chicago: Encyclopaedia Britannica.

Moran, E. F. (1981). Human adaptation to arctic zones. In B. J. Siegel, A. R. Beals, & S. A. Tyler (Eds.), *Annual review of anthropology* (pp. 1-25). Palo Alto: Annual Reviews.

Morren, G. E. B. ,Jr. (1986). *The Miyanmin: Human ecology of a Papua New Guinea society.* Ann Arbor: UMI Research Press.

Morrison, A. D. (1998). Teen prostitution in Japan: Regulation of telephone clubs. *Vanderbilt Journal of Transnational Law, 31* (2), 457-497.

M'Timkulu, D. (1977). Some aspects of Zulu religion. In N. S. Booth, Jr. (Ed.), *African religions: A symposium* (pp. 13-30). New York: NOK.

Munn, N. D. (1986). *The fame of Gawa.* Cambridge, UK: Cambridge University Press.

Newell, P. (Ed.). (1972). *A last resort? Corporal punishment in schools.* Middlesex, UK; Penguin.

Nikhilananda, S. (1956). *The Upanishads: Aitareaya and Brihadaranyaka* (Vol. 3). New York: Harper.

No crime for love. (1991, April 29). *Time, 137* (17), 33.

Nurcombe, B. (1973). Precausal and paracausal thinking. In G. E. Kearney, P. R. deLacey, & G. R. Davidson (Eds.), *The psychology of aboriginal Australians* (pp. 105-126). Sydney: Wiley.

Ogbu, J. I. (1994). Racial stratification and education in the United States: Why inequality persists. *Teachers College Record, 96* (2), 264-288.

Oldenberg, H. H. (1886). *The grihya-sutras: Rules of vedic domestic ceremonies.* (Volumes 29 and 30 (*The Sacred Books of the East*, Vols. 29 & 30). Oxford, UK: Clarenden

O'Neill, M. (1993). Australia. In L. L. Adler (Ed.), *International handbook on gender roles* (pp. 1-14). Westport, CT: Greenwood.

Ousted official details beatings. (1998, September 30). *San Luis Obispo County Telegram-Tribune,* p. A-4.

Patel, N., Power, T. G., & Bhavnagri, N. P. (1996). Socialization values and practices of Indian immigrant parents: Correlates of modernity and acculturation. *Child Development, 67,* 302-313.

Peel, E. A. (1976). The thinking and education of the adolescent. In V. P. Varma & P. Williams (Eds.), *Piaget, psychology, and education.* Itasca, IL: F. E. Peacock.

Pelissier, C. (1991). The anthropology of teaching and learning. In B. J. Siegel, A. R. Beals, & S. A. Tyler (Eds.), *Annual review of anthropology.* Palo Alto, CA: Annual Reviews.

Phillips, J. L., Jr. (1975). *The origins of intellect: Piaget's theory.* San Francisco, CA: Freeman.

Piaget, J. (1950). *The psychology of intelligence.* London: Routledge & Kegan Paul.

Piaget, J., & Inhelder, B. (1969). *The psychology of the child.* New York: Basic Books.

Plotkin, M. (1998). The diffusion of psychoanalysis in Argentina. *Latin American Research Review, 33* (2), 271-276.

Pollard, M. S., & Zheng, W. (1998). Divergence of marriage patterns in Quebec and elsewhere in Canada. *Population and Development Review, 24* (2), 329-357.

Ponterotto, J. G., & Pedersen, P. B. (1993). *Preventing prejudice.* Newbury Park, CA: Sage.

Popova, V. J. (1996). Sexuality education moves forward in Russia. *SIECUS Report, 24* (3), 14-15.

Potlatch. (1994). In *Encyclpaedia Britannica* (Vol. 9. p. 643). Chicago: Encyclopaedia Britannica.

Prothro, E. T. (1967). *Child rearing in the Lebanon.* Cambridge, MA: Harvard University Press.

Ragúz, M. M., & Pinzás, J. R. (1993). Peru. In L. L. Adler (Ed.), *International handbook on gender roles* (pp. 244-257). Westport, CT: Greenwood.

Ranis, G. (1992). From developing to mature economy: An overview. In G. Ranis (Ed.), *Taiwan: From developing to mature economy* (pp. 1-14). Boulder, CO: Westview.

Rapin, I., & Katzman, R. (1998). Neurobiology of autism. *Annals of Neurology, 43* (1), 7-14.

Raths, L. E., Harmin, M., & Simon, S. B. (1964). *Values and teaching.* Columbus, OH: Merrill.

Redfield, R. (1941). *The folk culture of Yucatan.* Chicago: University of Chicago Press.

Reforming funeral and interment methods. (1997). *Beijing Review, 40* (23), 24-25.

Renou, L. (1961). *Hinduism.* New York: George Braziller.

Rogers, C. (1951). *Client-centered therapy.* Boston: Houghton Mifflin.

Rogers, M. (1997). Gates launches library foundation with 43 grants. *Library Journal, 122*(18), 14-15.

Rogoff, B., & Chavajay, P. (1995). What's become of research on the cultural basis of cognitive development? *American Psychologist, 50* (10), 859-877.

Roland, A. (1988). *In search of self in India and Japan.* Princeton, NJ: Princeton University Press.

Romney, K., & Romney, R. (1963). The Mixtecans of Juxtlahuaca, Mexico. In B. B. Whiting (Ed.), *Six cultures: Studies of child rearing* (pp. 543-691). New York: John Wiley.

Ryan, P. (1972). *Encyclopedia of Papua and New Guinea*, Vol. 1. Melbourne, Australia: Melbourne University Press.

Sallot, J. (1996). Service industry, Japanese style. *World Press Review, 43* (4), p. 35.

Sanders, C. M. (1989). *The mourning after.* New York: Wiley.

Sanua, V. D. (1984). Is infantile autism a universal phenomenon? An open question. *International Journal of Social Psychiatry, 30* (3), 163-177.

Scheff, T. J. (1983). Toward integration in the social psychology of emotions. In R. H. Turner & J. F. Short, Jr. (Eds.), *Annual review of sociology* (Vol. 9, pp. 133-154). Palo Alto, CA: Annual Reviews.

Schieffelin, E. L. (1985). Anger, grief, and shame: Toward a Kaluli ethnopsychology. In G. M. White & J. Kirkpatrick (Eds.), *Person, self, and experience: Exploring Pacific ethnopsychologies* (pp. 168-182). Berkeley: University of California Press.

Schopler, E., & Mesibov, G. B. (1986). Introduction to social behavior in autism. In E. Schopler & G. B. Mesibov (Eds.), *Social behavior in autism* (pp. 1-11). New York: Plenum.

Scribner, S., & Cole, M. (1981). *The psychology of literacy.* Cambridge, MA: Harvard University Press.

Segall, M. H., Dasen, P. R., Berry, J. W., & Poortinga, Y. H. (1990). *Human behavior in global perspective.* Oxford, UK: Pergamon.

Semin, G. R., & Zwier, S. M. (1997). Social cognition. In J. W. Berry, M. H. Segall, & C. Kagitçibasi (Eds.), *Handbook of cross-cultural psychology* (Vol. 3, 2nd ed., pp. 51-75). Boston: Allyn & Bacon.

Shakir, M. H. (Trans.). (1975). *Qur'an.* Elmhurst, NY: Tahrike Tarsele Qur'an.

Shaver, K. G. (1975). *An introduction to attribution processes.* Cambridge, MA: Winthrop.

Six lashes in Singapore. (1994, March 14). *Newsweek*, p. 29.

Skinner, B. F. (1974). *About behaviorism.* New York: Knopf.

Snarey, J. (1985). Cross-cultural universality of socio-moral development: A critical review of Kohlbergian research. *Psychological Bulletin, 97*, pp. 202-232.

Snyder, M., & Miene, P. (1994) On the functions of stereotypes and prejudice. In M. P. Zanna & J. M. Olson, (Eds.). *The psychology of prejudice.* Hillsdale, NJ: Lawrence Erlbaum.

Song, L. H. (1996). Change in funeral customs in contemporary Korea. *Korea Journal, 36* (2), pp. 49-60.

Spae, J. J. (1972). *Shinto man.* Tokyo: Oriens Institute for Religious Research.

Sponheim, E., & Skjeldal, O. (1998). Autism and related disorders: Epidemiological findings in a Norwegian study using ICD-19 diagnostic criteria. *Journal of Autism & Developmental Disorders, 28* (3), 217-227.

Status of women in Iran. (1998). *WIN News, 24* (2), 67.

Stevenson, H., Azuma, H., & Hakuta, K. (Eds.). (1986). *Child development and education in Japan.* New York: Freeman.

Stolz, L. M. (1968). *Father relations of war-born children.* Westport, CT: Greenwood.

Sukemune, S, Shiraishi, T., Shirakawa, Y., & Matsumi, J. T. (1993). Japan. In L. L. Adler (Ed.), *International handbook on gender roles* (pp. 174-186). Westport, CT: Greenwood.

Szatmari, P., & Mahoney, W. (1993). The genetics of autism and pervasive developmental disorders: A review of the evidence. *Journal of Developmental Disabilities, 2* (1), 39-55.

Terrell, J. U. (1971). *American Indian almanac.* New York: World Publishing.

Thailand: Sense about sex. (1992). *Economist, 322* (7745), 32-33.

Thailand: Women and the law. (1997). *WIN News, 23* (4), pp. 48-49.

Thomas, A., & Chess, S. (1980). *The dynamics of psychological development.* New York: Brunner/Mazel.

Thomas, R. M. (1962) Reinspecting a structural position on occupational prestige, *American Journal of Sociology, 67*, 561-656.

Thomas, R. M. (1967). Personal encounter for social understanding, *Educational Leadership, 24* (6), pp. 497-500.

Thomas, R. M. (1987). *From talking chiefs to videotapes—Education in American Samoa, 1700s-1980.* (ERIC Document Reproduction Service No. Ed 273 544).

Thomas, R. M. (1988). A Hindu theory of human development. In R. M. Thomas (Ed.), *Oriental theories of human development* (pp. 29-73). New York: Peter Lang.

Thomas, R. M. (1996). *Comparing theories of child development* (4th ed.). Pacific Grove, CA: Brooks/Cole.

Thomas, R. M. (1997). *Moral development theories—Secular and religious.* Westport, CT: Greenwood.

Thomas, R. M. (1999). Education. In D. Calhoun (Ed.), *Britannica book of the year.* Chicago: Encyclopaedia Britannica.

Thomas, R. M., Hanafiah, R. S., Sumantri, D., Sudiadi, D., & Shiflett, J. (1975). *Social strata in Indonesia: A study of West Java villagers.* Jakarta: Antarkarya.

Tryon, C., & Lilienthal, J. (1950). Developmental tasks: The concept and its importance. In *Fostering mental health in our schools.* Washington, DC: Association for Supervision and Curriculum Development.

Tudge, J., Gray, J. T., & Hogan, D. M. (1997). Ecological perspectives in human development: A comparison of Gibson and Bronfenbrenner. In J. Tudge, M. J. Shanahan, & J. Valsiner, (Eds.), *Comparisons in human development* (pp. 72-105). Cambridge, UK: Cambridge University Press.

Tylor, E. B. (1958). *The origins of culture.* New York: Harper. (Part I of *Primitive culture*, originally published in 1871).

Valsiner, J. (1987). *Culture and the development of children's actions.* Chicester, UK: John Wiley.

Verhoef, H., & Michel, C. (1997). Studying morality within the African context: model of moral analysis and construction. *Journal of Moral Education, 26* (4), 389-407.

Vonéche, J. J. (1987). The difficulty of being a child in French-speaking countries. In J. M. Broughton (Ed.), *Critical theories of psychological development.* New York: Plenum.

Walker, L. J. (1984). Sex differences in the development of moral reasoning: A critical review. *Child Development, 55,* 677-691.

Webb, E. V. J., Lobo, S., Hervas, A., & Scourfield, J. (1997). The changing prevalence of autistic disorder in a Welsh health district. *Developmental Medicine, & Child Neurology, 39* (3), 150-157.

Weightman, G. (1997). Was it British? *History Today, 47* (11), 6-7.

Weiner, B. (1986). *An attributional theory of motivation and emotion.* New York: Springer.

Weiner, J. F. (1991). *The empty place.* Bloomington: Indiana University Press.

White, L. A. (1994). The concept of culture. In *Encyclopaedia Britannica,* Vol. 16. Chicago: Encyclpaedia Britannica.

Winckler, E. A. (1988). Taiwan politics in the 1990s. In H. Feldman & I. J. Kim (Eds.), *Taiwan in a time of transition* (pp. 233-274). New York: Paragon House.

Wing, L. (1983). Social and interpersonal needs. In E. Schopler & G. B. Mesibov (Eds.), *Autism in adolescents and adults* (pp. 337-354). New York: Plenum.

Woodward, K. L. (1997). The ritual solution. *Newsweek, 130* (12), 62.

Wright, S. C., Taylor, D. M., & Ruggiero, K. M. (1996). Examining the potential for academic achievement among Inuit children. *Journal of Cross-Cultural Psychology, 27* (6), 733-753.

Yu, A. Y. (1993). Hong Kong. In L. L. Adler (Ed.), *International handbook on gender roles* (pp. 108-121). Westport, CT: Greenwood.

Name Index

257

Subject Index

About the Author

R. Murray Thomas (PhD, Stanford University) is an emeritus professor at the University of California, Santa Barbara, where for three decades he taught educational psychology and directed the program in international education. He began his 50-year career in education as a high school teacher at Kamehemeha Schools and Mid-Pacific Institute in Honolulu, then continued on the college level at San Francisco State University, the State University of New York (Brockport), and Pajajaran University in Indonesia before moving to Santa Barbara.

His professional publications exceed 300, including 40 books for which he served as author, coauthor, or editor. His field work on culture was conducted primarily in Southeast Asia (Indonesia and Malaysia, 1958-1983) and the Samoan Islands (1968-1975). His earlier books that relate to the contents of *Human Development Theories—Windows on Culture* include:

Social Strata in West Java
A Chronicle of Indonesian Higher Education
From Talking Chiefs to Videotapes—A History of Education in American Samoa
Schooling in East Asia (coeditor)
Schooling in the Pacific Islands (coeditor)
Comparing Theories of Child Development
Oriental Theories of Human Development (editor)
Moral Development Theories—Secular and Religious
The Encyclopedia of Human Development and Education (editor)
Counseling and Life-Span Development